SONY SLT-A77

THE EX

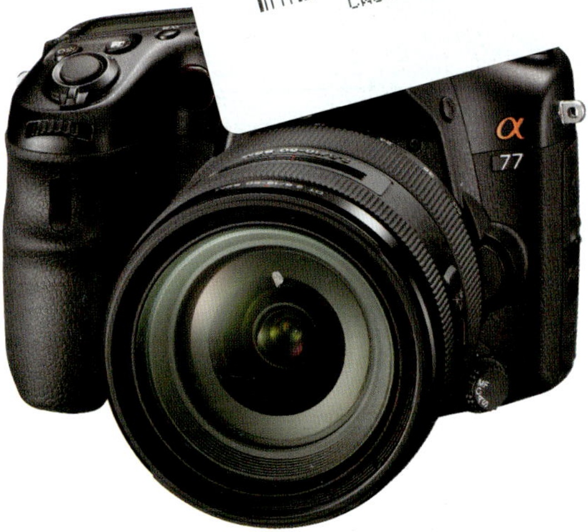

David Taylor

AMMONITE
PRESS

First published 2012 by
Ammonite Press
an imprint of AE Publications Ltd
166 High Street, Lewes, East Sussex, BN7 1XU, UK

ISBN 978-1-90770-885-5

British Library Cataloging in Publication Data: A catalog record of this book is available from the British Library.

Editor: Chris Gatcum
Series Editor: Richard Wiles
Design: Richard Dewing Associates

Typeface: Giacomo
Color reproduction by GMC Reprographics
Printed and bound by in China by Leo Paper Group

PAGE 2 «
The Sony SLT-A77 is capable of producing great results, regardless of what it is you are photographing.

Chapter 1

OVERVIEW

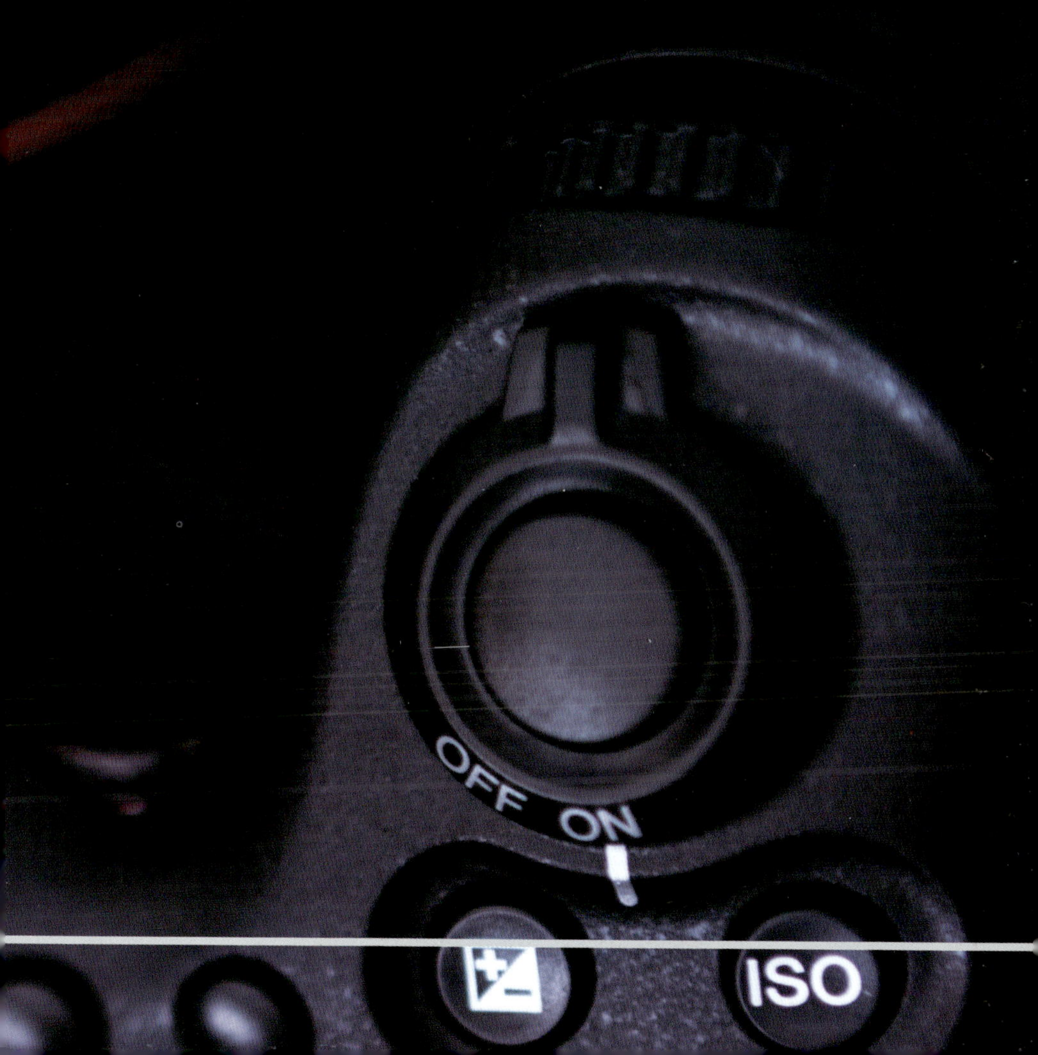

1 OVERVIEW

The SLT-A77 is part of the rapidly evolving range of professional-standard digital cameras produced by the Japanese electronics giant, Sony.

› Beginnings

Sony started life in 1946 when Masaru Ibuka and Akio Morita founded the Tokyo Tsushin Kogyo (Tokyo Telecommunications Engineering Company). Initially, the two entrepreneurs made a living repairing radio sets and manufacturing voltmeters, and in 1958 the company's name changed to Sony Corporation to make it more internationally appealing. Since then, the Sony Corporation has gained a reputation for its impressive range of innovative and successful electronic products, such as the Walkman music player and Playstation games console.

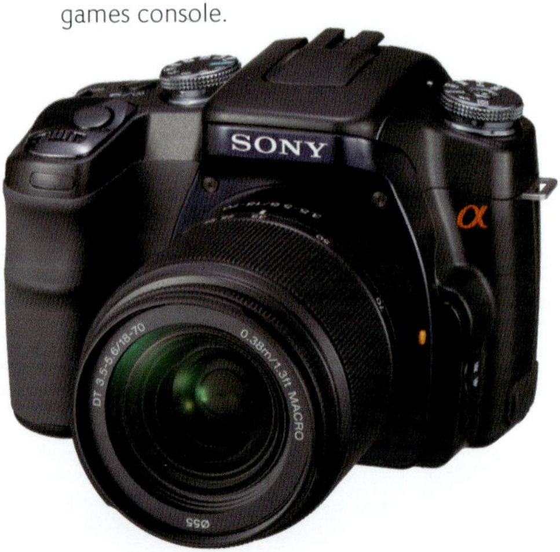

However, despite launching its first digital still camera in 1997 (the Digital Mavica MVC-FD5), Sony did not produce an interchangeable lens camera until July 2006, when it introduced the A100 digital SLR, an APS-C ("cropped") sensor camera. This camera was produced as a result of the acquisition of the photography arm of Konica Minolta earlier that year, using technology developed by Konica Minolta for their range of film and digital SLRs. By using Konica Minolta's technology, Sony was able to enter the interchangeable-lens camera market with a camera that was already part of a mature camera system that had its beginnings in 1985.

Since the A100 was released, Sony has gone on to produce cameras for all types of photographer, with the well received A900 and A850 full-frame cameras sitting at the top of the range. To match the needs of such demanding cameras and their users, the German lens manufacturer Carl Zeiss now produces a small, but growing number of prime and zoom lenses for Sony's cameras. These lenses and cameras

SONY A100 «
Building on the camera heritage of Konica Minolta, the A100 marked Sony's entry into the digital SLR market.

all use the A-mount bayonet fitting, which has been derived from Konica Minolta's original specifications.

› Divergence

In May 2010, Sony took the radical step of launching a new, proprietary lens mount—the E-mount—with the release of its NEX-3 and NEX-5 cameras (although with an optional adapter they can also use A-mount lenses). At the time of release, the NEX-3 and the NEX-5 were the smallest interchangeable-lens cameras on the market, despite using relatively large Sony APS-C sized sensors.

The NEX cameras are mirrorless, relying on a live feed from the sensor to the rear LCD for all camera operations. One of the drawbacks of the traditional digital SLR is that the mechanism to direct light from the lens to the viewfinder is necessarily complex and weighty. Because of their lightweight, but well specified nature, NEX cameras have proven popular since their release. The current top-of-the-range NEX-7 has won many awards and is highly regarded by many photographers.

This desire to reduce size and weight bore fruit with Sony's next innovation, established by the A33 and A55 of August 2010: the SLT (Single-Lens Translucent) series of cameras.

A conventional digital SLR relies on a mirror to bounce light from the lens up to a pentaprism. The pentaprism then folds the light around internally before directing it out to the viewfinder. A drawback to this approach (apart from the weight) is that the mirror has to rapidly move out of the way to allow light to pass to the sensor to make an exposure. The mechanical nature of a digital SLR therefore places a limit on the maximum frame rate that the camera is capable of, and the mirror movement can cause vibration, increasing the risk of camera shake.

Sony's SLT cameras still have a mirror, but the difference is that it does not move. Instead, the mirror is semi-silvered, allowing approximately 70% of the light from the lens to reach the sensor.

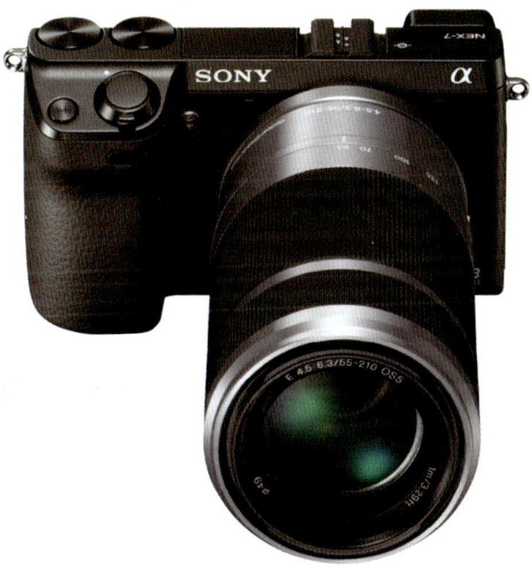

SONY NEX-7 »
A highly regarded E-mount camera.

The remaining 30% of the light is directed upward to the autofocus (AF) sensors to allow fast and accurate phase-detection AF, even when shooting video. As it doesn't have an optical viewfinder, an SLT camera has to rely on a high-resolution electronic viewfinder (EVF) and LCD for all camera functions.

› SLT-A77

The SLT-A77 was announced on August 24, 2011. It uses the same size sensor as the A33, as well as SLT technology, but that is where the comparison ends. The sensor in the A77 is a 24.3-megapixel unit, which was an unprecedented number of pixels for an APS-C sized sensor at the time of its launch. There is always concern at the seemingly unstoppable increase of pixels on each new generation of digital sensors: more pixels mean smaller photosites, with the potential for a decrease in dynamic range and a drop in image quality. However, Sony has pulled off the neat trick of producing a sensor with a high pixel density, which also has a very usable ISO range and image quality to rival many full-frame cameras.

The A77 uses a newly-developed OLED (Organic Light Emitting Diode) screen for its EVF, and while no electronic screen can match the clarity of an optical viewfinder, the A77's EVF comes close. With a resolution of 2.4 megapixels the screen is bright, has a rapid refresh rate (avoiding issues of "tearing" caused when the display changes rapidly), and is capable of displaying a wide color palette. Unlike an optical viewfinder, the EVF allows you to preview image effects before exposure and can display tools such as a spirit level and live histogram.

Another benefit (which derives from the use of an SLT system) is the frame rate of the A77. With a maximum rate of 12 frames per second, the A77 is class leading, and coupled with a fast phase-detection AF system, it means that this camera excels at action photography.

SONY SLT-A77
An SLT camera packed with state-of-the-art technology.

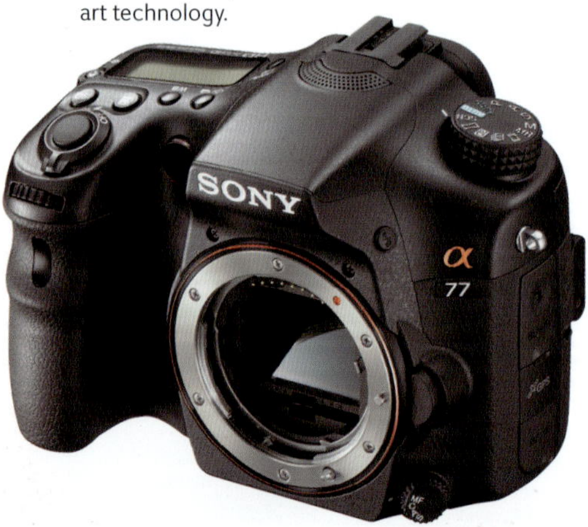

SYSTEMATIC *(opposite)*
A good technique is vital if you want to get the most out of your SLT-A77.

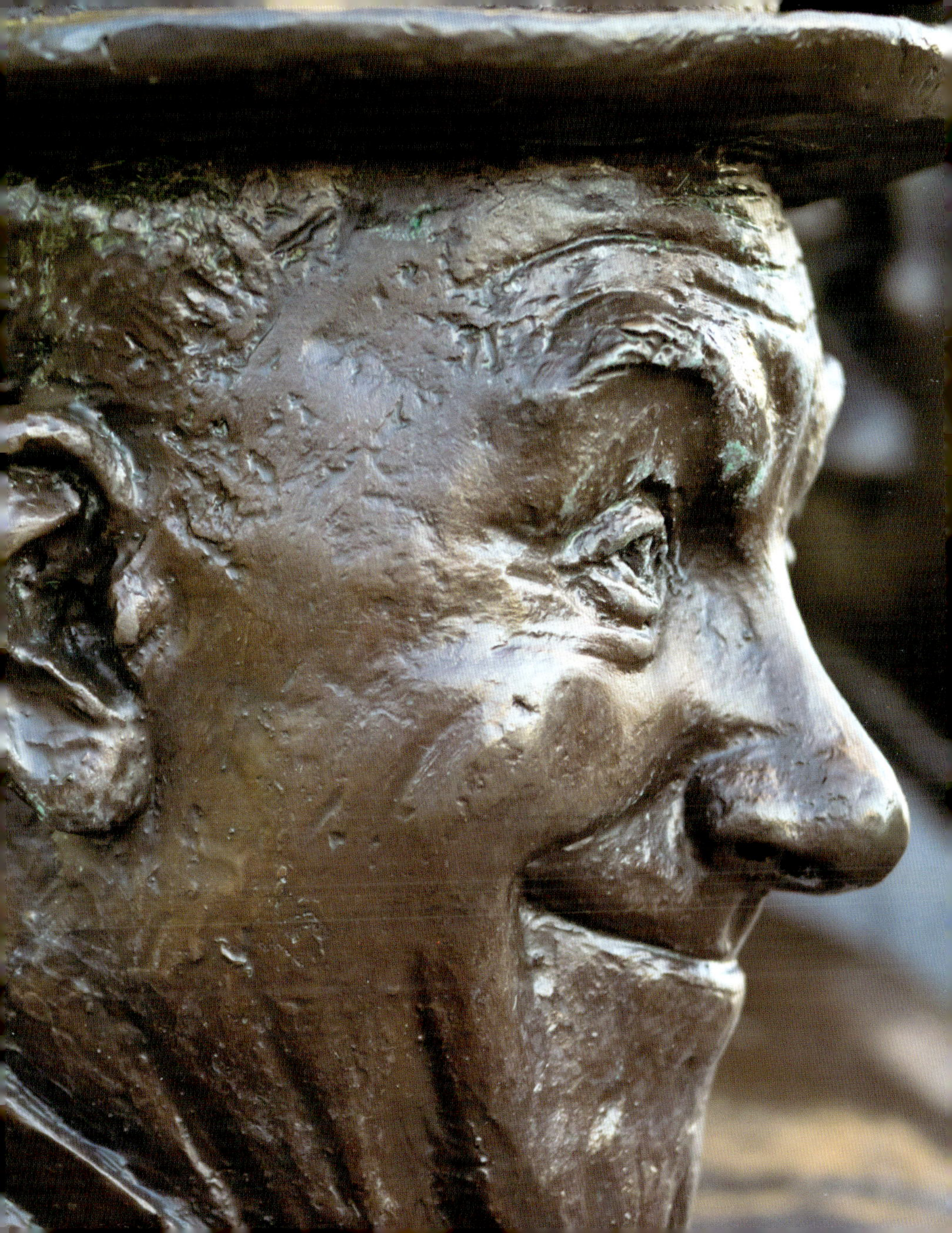

1 » MAIN FEATURES

Body

Dimensions: 5.75 x 4.12 x 3.25 inches (142.6 x 104 x 80.9mm)
Weight: 23.03 ounces (653 grams) without battery
25.8 ounces (732 grams) with battery
Body materials: Magnesium alloy chassis with high-grade plastic exterior
Lens mount: Konica Minolta Maxxum/ Dynax/Alpha/Sony A mount
Operating environment: 32–104°F (0–40°C) at 85% humidity maximum

Sensor and processor

Sensor: 0.92 x 0.61 inch (23.5 x 15.6mm) CMOS type sensor
Aspect ratio: 3:2
Resolution: Approximately 24.3 megapixels (effective)
Dust deletion: Image sensor-shift
Image processor: Bionz

Still image file types and sizes

JPEG resolution:
3:2 aspect ratio 6000 x 4000 (L), 4240 x 2832 (M), or 3008 x 2000 (S)
16:9 aspect ratio 6000 x 3376 (L), 4240 x 2400 (M), or 3008 x 1688 (S)
JPEG compression: Extra fine, Fine, or Standard
Raw file resolution: 6000 x 4000 pixels
Raw format: .ARW
Other: Raw+JPEG simultaneously
JPEG used when shooting Sweep Panorama images. Can also shoot MPO-compliant 3D images

Shutter

Type: Electronically controlled, focal-plane shutter
Shutter speeds: 1/8000 to 30 seconds, plus bulb
Drive modes: Single shot, Continuous shooting at 8 frames per second (fps) or 12 fps (using Continuous Priority AE)
Self-timer: 2 or 10 seconds

LCD monitor

Size: 3.0 inches (7.5cm) diagonal
Resolution: 921,600 pixels
Brightness: 7 user-selectable levels
Other: Grid lines can be overlaid on the display to aid composition

Electronic viewfinder (EVF)

Type: OLED (Organic Light Emitting Diode) screen
Size: 0.5 inches (1.3cm) diagonal
Resolution: 2.4 megapixels
Coverage: 100%
Magnification: 1.09 x with 50mm lens focused at infinity
Diopter adjustment: $-4.0m^{-1}$ to $+3.0m^{-1}$
Eyepoint: Approximately 27mm

Focusing

Type: TTL phase-detection system
AF points: 19 AF points (11 with cross-hair sensors)
AF sensitivity: EV -1 to 18 at ISO 100
AF modes: Single-shot, Automatic, Continuous
AF lock: Always available in Single-shot mode; Subject dependent in Automatic mode
AF assist beam: Yes
Other: Micro AF adjustment can be applied to 30 lenses; Manual focus (MF) is set either on the body or attached lens

Movies

Recording formats:
AVHCD format (MPEG-4 AVC/H.264) with Dolby Digital two channel sound
MP4 format (MPEG-4 AVC/H.264) with MPEG-4 AAC-LC two channel sound
Resolution: 1920 x 1080 pixels (AVHCD), 1440 x 1080 pixels (MP4), VGA
Frame rate: 60/50 or 24/25 frames per second

Exposure

Zones: 1200 zone exposure meter
Metering modes: Multi-segment, Center-weighted, Spot
Metering range: -2–+17EV at ISO 100 (with f/1.4 lens)
Exposure compensation: ±3 stops in ½- or ⅓-stop increments
Exposure bracketing: 3 or 5 frames, up to ±5 stops
ISO: Auto/Manual
ISO 50–16,000 (still images)
ISO 100–1600 (movies)

Flash

Built-in flash: GN 39.3ft (12m) at ISO 100
Coverage: 16mm focal length
Hotshoe: Proprietary Sony hotshoe
Flash control: Mode dependant. Includes wireless flash, flash compensation (±3 stops in ⅓ stop increments), front and rear curtain sync
Flash sync speed: 1/250 sec.
PC flash sync socket: Yes

Memory Card

Type: SD (2Gb max.), SDHC (32Gb max.), SDXC (32Gb+)
Memory Stick Pro Duo Media
Other: Eye-Fi compatible SD media

Software

Windows: Image Data Converter, Picture Motion Browser
Mac OS: Image Data Converter

FRONT OF CAMERA

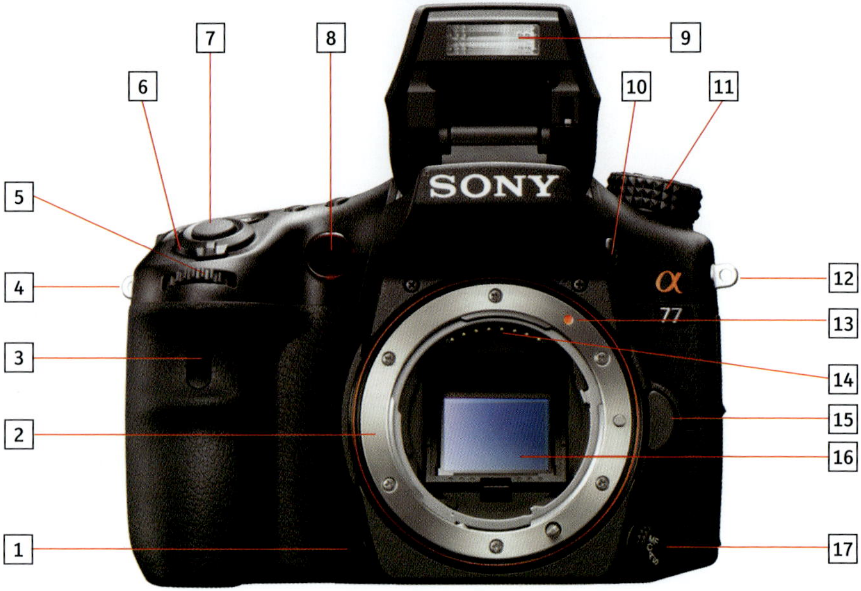

FRONT OF CAMERA

1 Preview button
2 Lens mount
3 Remote sensor
4 Shoulder strap hook
5 Front control dial
6 Power switch
7 Shutter-release button
8 AF illuminator/Self-timer lamp
9 Built-in flash
10 Flash release button
11 Mode dial
12 Shoulder strap hook
13 Lens mount index
14 Lens contacts
15 Lens release button
16 Mirror (and sensor)
17 Focus mode dial

BACK OF CAMERA

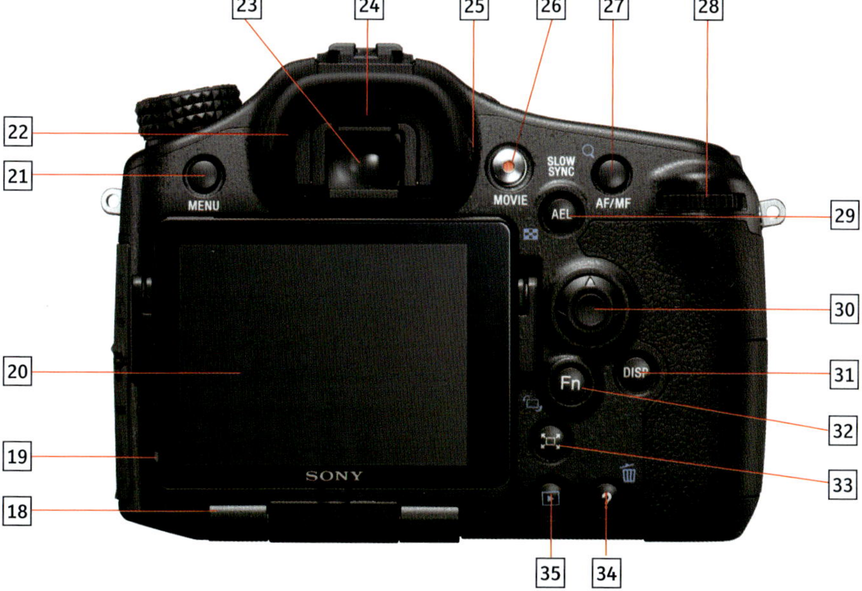

BACK OF CAMERA

18 LCD monitor hinge
19 Light sensor
20 LCD Monitor
21 MENU button
22 Eyecup
23 Viewfinder
24 Eyepiece sensors
25 Diopter adjustment dial
26 MOVIE button
27 AF/MF/View enlarge button
28 Rear control dial
29 AEL/SLOW SYNC/Image index button
30 Multi-selector
31 DISP button
32 Fn/Image rotate button
33 Smart teleconvertor/Focus magnifier button
34 In-camera guide button
35 Playback button

1 » FULL FEATURES AND CAMERA LAYOUT

TOP OF CAMERA

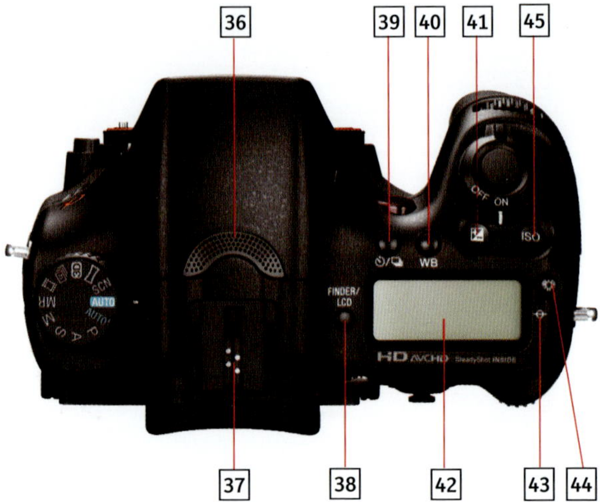

LEFT SIDE OF CAMERA

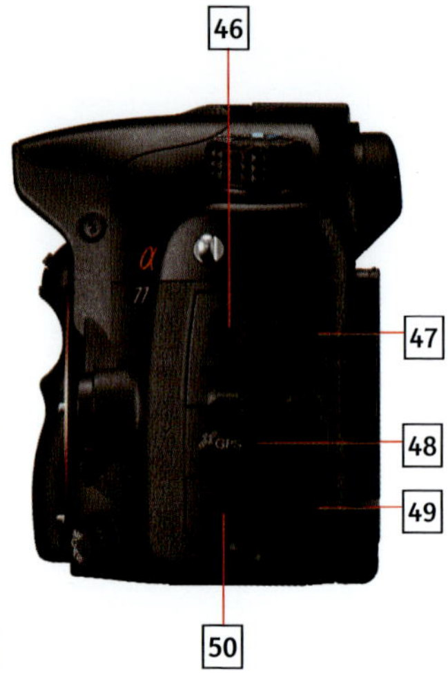

TOP OF CAMERA

- 36 Microphone
- 37 Accessory shoe
- 38 Finder/LCD button
- 39 Drive mode button
- 40 White balance button
- 41 Exposure compensation button
- 42 Display panel
- 43 Focal plane mark
- 44 Display panel light button
- 45 ISO button

LEFT SIDE OF CAMERA

- 46 Flash sync/Remote release terminals
- 47 External microphone jack
- 48 Speaker
- 49 HDMI/USB terminals
- 50 DC power in

RIGHT SIDE OF CAMERA

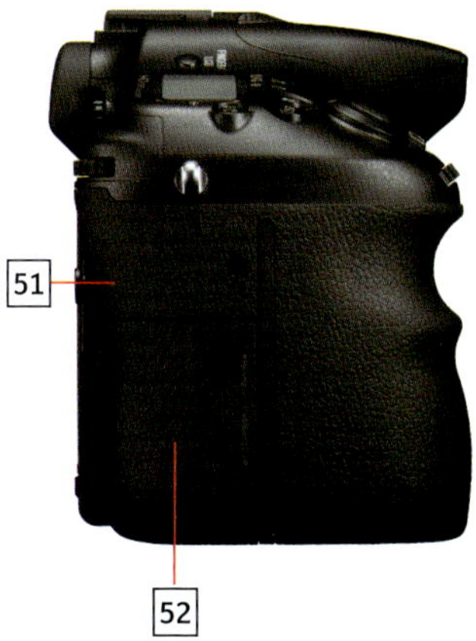

BOTTOM OF CAMERA

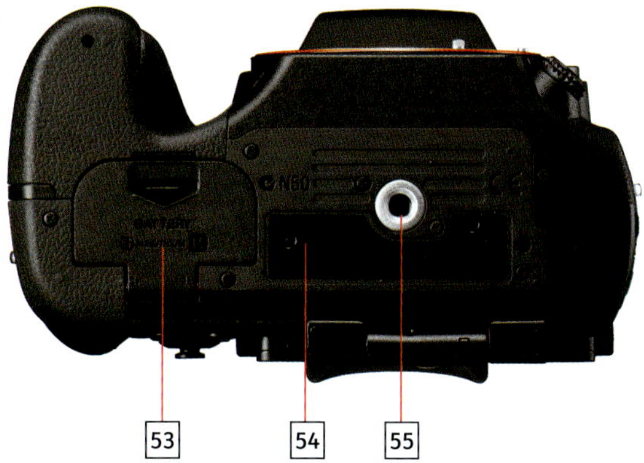

RIGHT SIDE OF CAMERA

51 Access lamp

52 Memory card cover

BOTTOM OF CAMERA

53 Battery compartment cover

54 Serial number panel

55 Tripod mount

» SHOOTING SCREEN

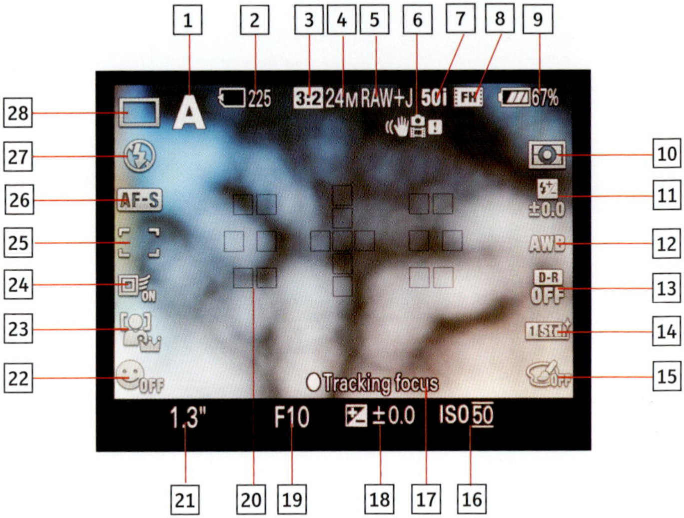

1	Shooting mode	11	Flash compensation	21	Shutter speed setting
2	Memory card/ Remaining images	12	White balance setting	22	Smile shutter
3	Aspect ratio	13	D-Range Optimizer	23	Face detection
4	Image resolution	14	Creative Style	24	Object tracking
5	Image quality	15	Picture Effect	25	Focus area
6	SteadyShot warning	16	ISO setting	26	AF mode
7	Movie frame rate	17	Tracking focus guide	27	Flash
8	Movie size	18	Exposure compensation	28	Drive mode
9	Battery Charge	19	Aperture setting		
10	Metering mode	20	Focus points		

» PLAYBACK SCREEN

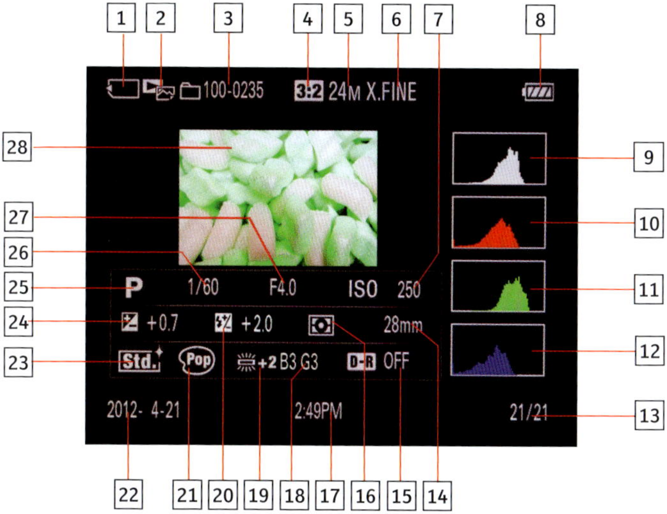

- 1 Memory card
- 2 View mode
- 3 Folder/Image file name
- 4 Aspect ratio
- 5 Image resolution
- 6 Image quality
- 7 ISO speed
- 8 Battery charge
- 9 Luminance histogram
- 10 Red channel histogram
- 11 Green channel histogram
- 12 Blue channel histogram
- 13 Image number/ Viewable images
- 14 Focal length
- 15 D-Range Optimizer
- 16 Metering mode
- 17 Shooting time
- 18 White balance fine adjustments
- 19 White balance preset
- 20 Flash exposure Compensation
- 21 Picture Effect
- 22 Shooting date
- 23 Creative Style
- 24 Exposure compensation
- 25 Exposure mode
- 26 Shutter speed
- 27 Aperture
- 28 Image thumbnail

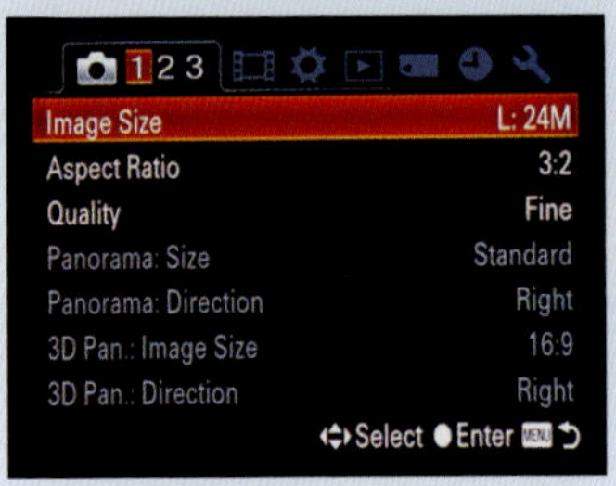

Still Shooting menu 1

- Image Size
- Aspect Ratio
- Quality
- Panorama: Size
- Panorama: Direction
- 3D Pan.: Image Size
- 3D Pan.: Direction

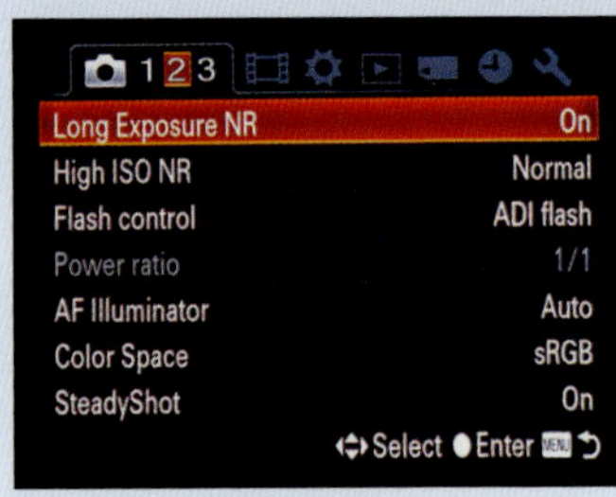

Still Shooting menu 2

- Long exposure NR
- High ISO NR
- Flash control
- Power ratio
- AF Illuminator
- Color Space
- SteadyShot

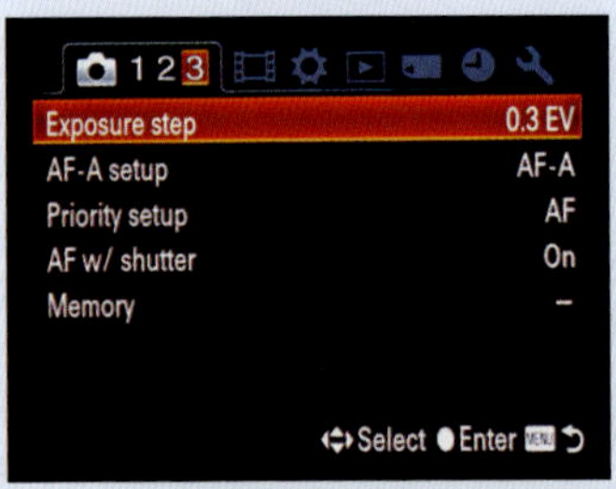

Still Shooting menu 3

- Exposure step
- AF-A setup
- Priority setup
- AF w/ shutter
- Memory

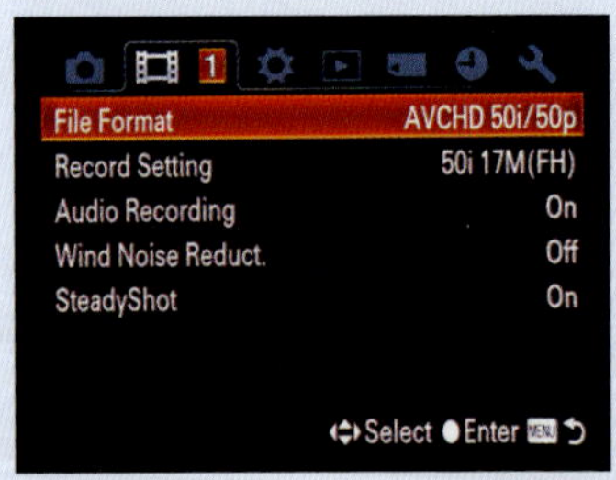

Movie Shooting menu 1

- File Format
- Record Setting
- Audio Recording
- Wind Noise Reduct.
- SteadyShot

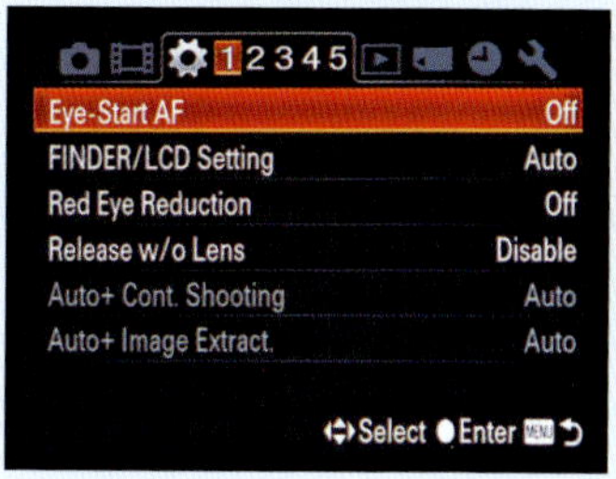

Custom menu 1

- Eye-Start AF
- FINDER/LCD Setting
- Red Eye Reduction
- Release w/o Lens
- Auto+ Cont. Shooting
- Auto+ Image Extract.

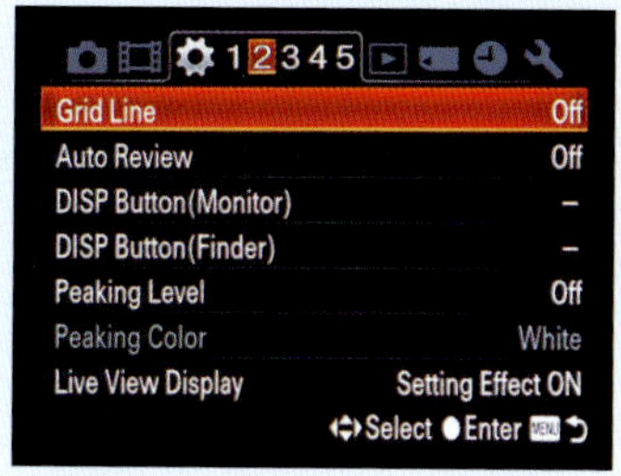

Custom menu 2

- Grid Line
- Auto Review
- DISP Button (Monitor)
- DISP Button (Finder)
- Peaking Level
- Peaking Color
- Live View Display

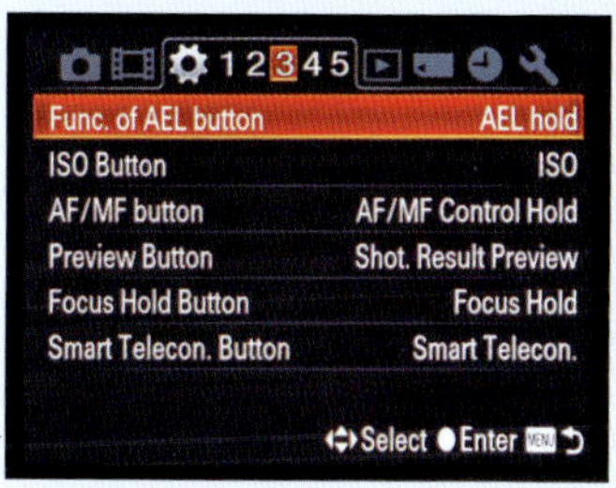

Custom menu 3

- Func. of AEL button
- ISO Button
- AF/MF button
- Preview Button
- Focus Hold Button
- Smart Telecon. Button

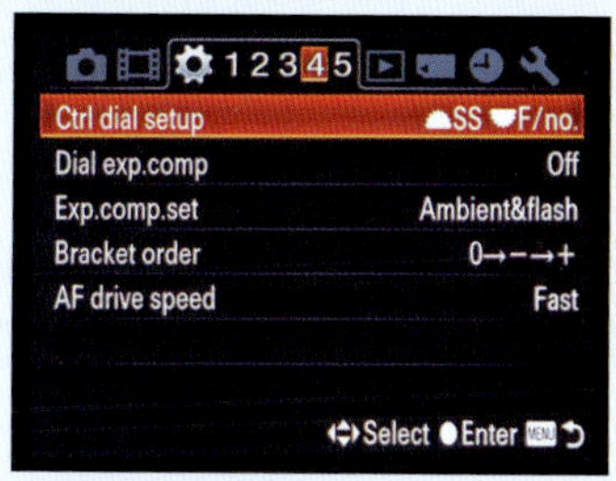

Custom menu 4

- Ctrl dial setup
- Dial exp. comp
- Exp.comp.set
- Bracket order
- AF drive speed

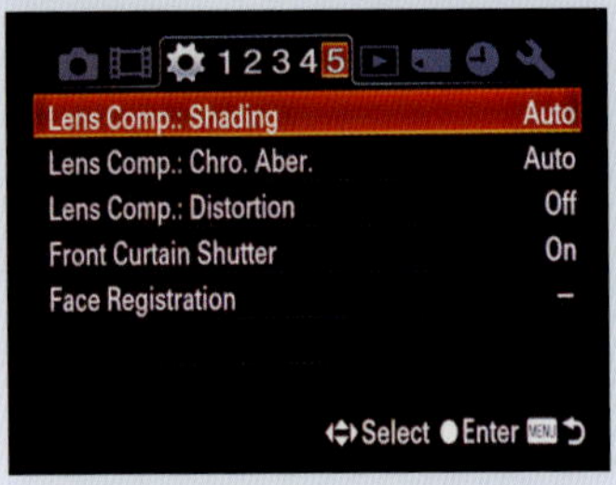

Custom menu 5

- Lens Comp.: Shading
- Lens Comp.: Chro. Aber.
- Lens Comp.: Distortion
- Front Curtain Shutter
- Face Registration

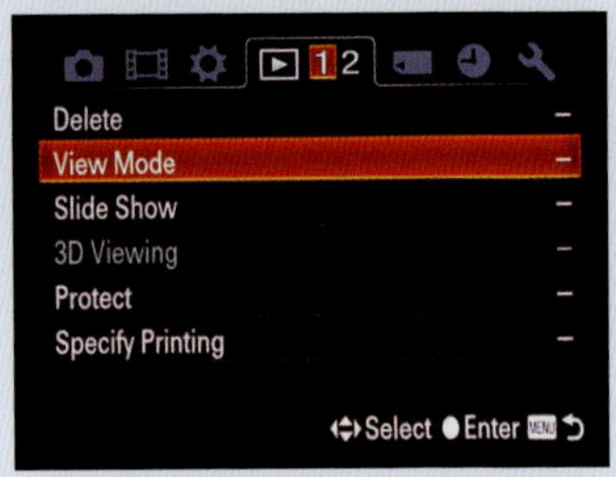

Playback menu 1

- Delete
- View Mode
- Slide Show
- 3D Viewing
- Protect
- Specify Printing

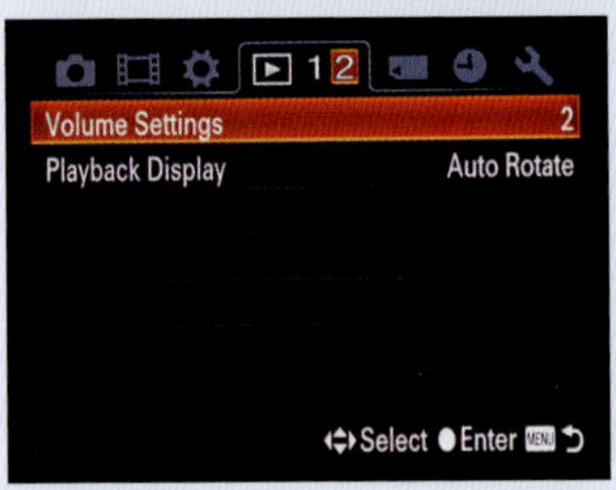

Playback menu 2

- Volume Settings
- Playback Display

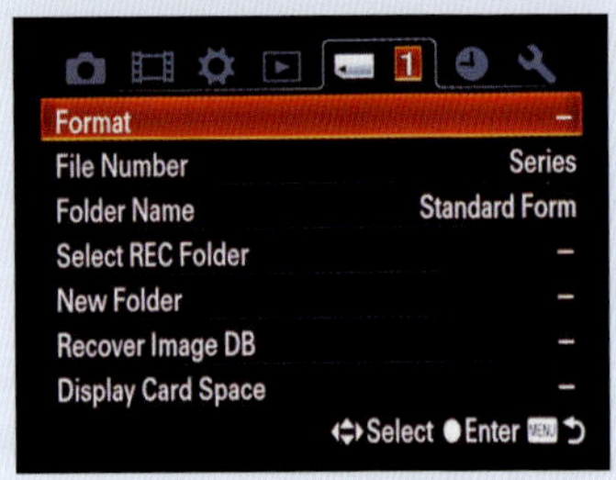

Memory Card menu 1

- Format
- File Number
- Folder Name
- Select REC Folder
- New Folder
- Recover Image DB
- Display Card Space

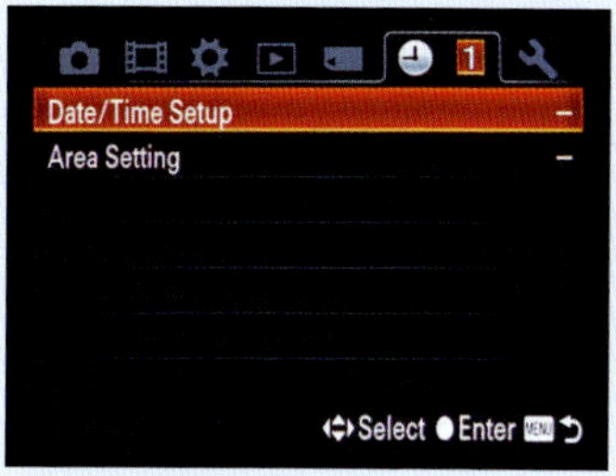

Clock menu 1

› Date/Time Setup
› Area Setting

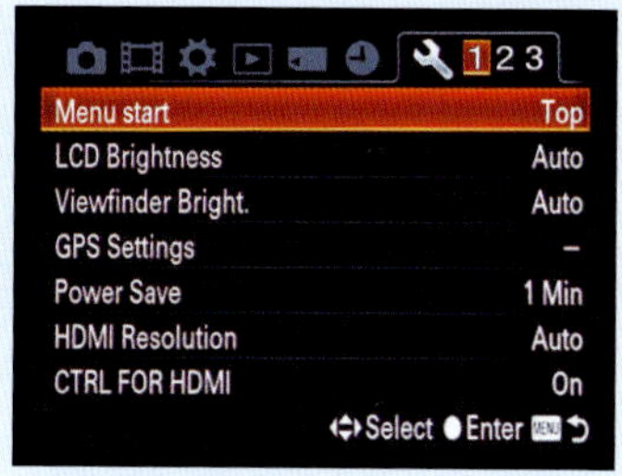

Setup menu 1

› Menu start
› LCD Brightness
› Viewfinder Bright.
› GPS Settings
› Power Save
› HDMI Resolution
› CTRL FOR HDMI

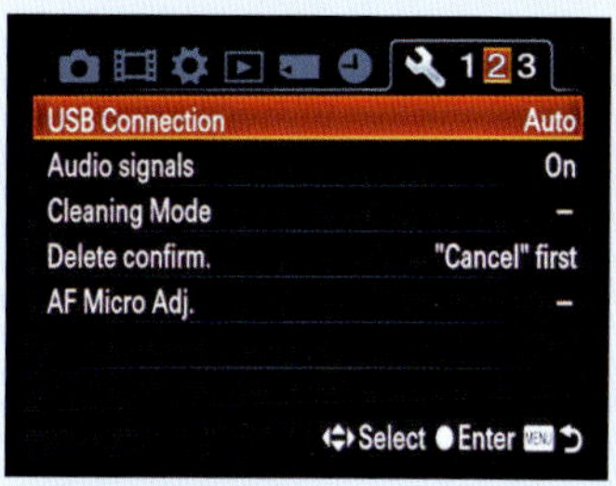

Setup menu 2

› USB Connection
› Audio signals
› Cleaning Mode
› Delete confirm.
› AF Micro Adj.

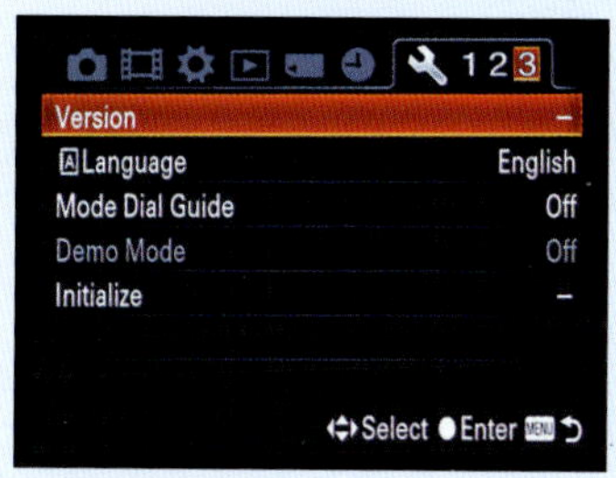

Setup menu 3

› Version
› Language
› Mode Dial Guide
› Demo Mode
› Initialize

Chapter 2
FUNCTIONS

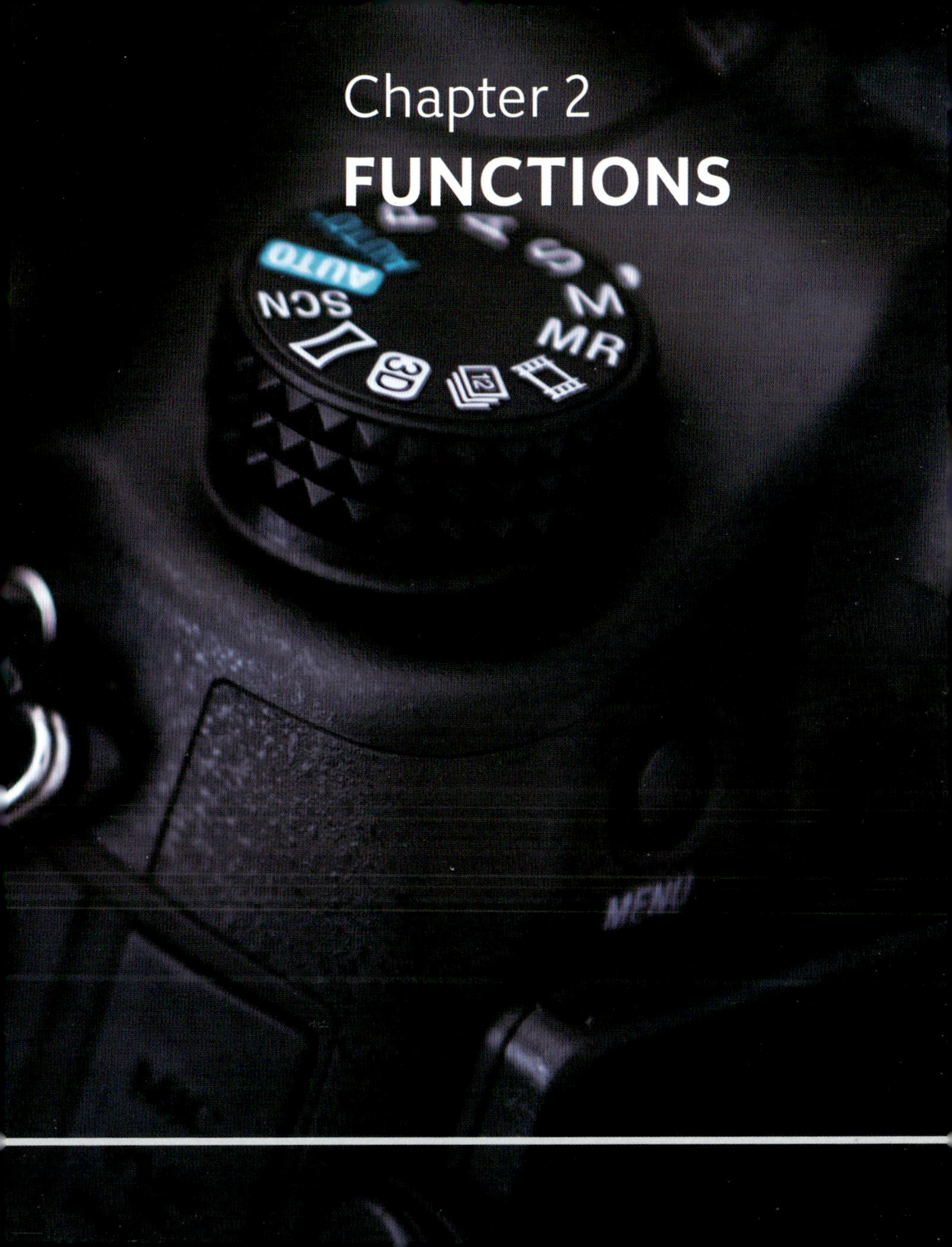

2 FUNCTIONS

Getting the most out of a camera involves becoming familiar with its various controls and options. Ideally, using a camera should become second nature, so you are able to use it without needing to pause and think about how to operate it.

There's no getting around the fact that the A77 is initially a daunting proposition to get to grips with. It is bristling with shooting options that are accessible by pressing buttons on the body or by delving into the comprehensive menu system viewed on the rear LCD or via the EVF. This chapter is a guide to getting your A77 under control, starting with the basics and then moving on to explore the camera's deeper secrets.

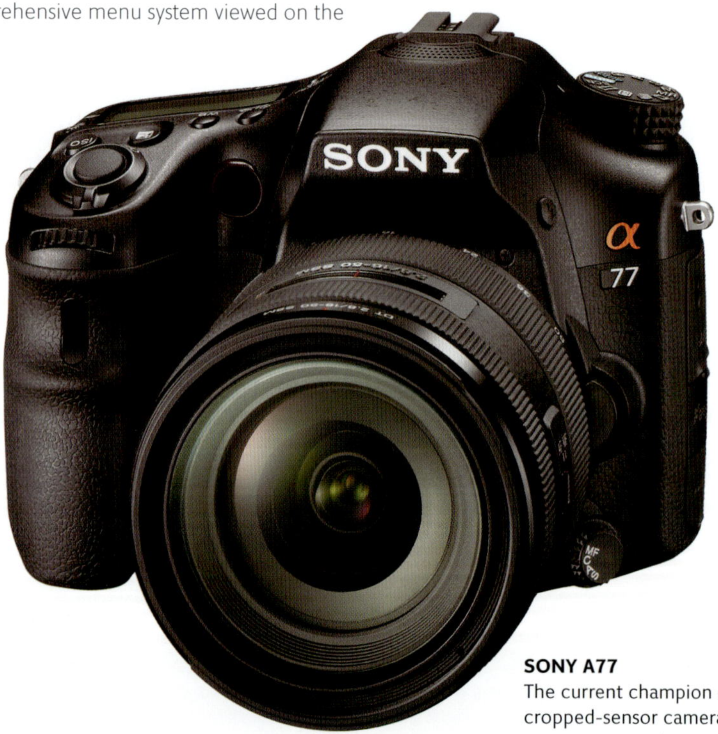

SONY A77 «
The current champion of Sony's cropped-sensor camera range.

» CAMERA PREPARATION

› Attaching the strap

Your A77 is supplied with a neck strap and it's highly recommended that you attach it. Although the camera is comfortable to hold using the handgrip when shooting, it Is not advisable to carry it this way for extended periods of time: maintaining a tight grip can become tiring, so dropping your camera accidentally can become a real possibility.

To attach the strap, feed one end through either the right or left eyelet on the top of the camera. Then, feed the end of the strap under the length of strap that has already passed through the buckle. Allow at least 2in (5cm) of strap to extend beyond the buckle to avoid it being pulled back through. Repeat this for the opposite side of the camera. Adjust the length of the strap as required and pull firmly on the end of the strap to fix it within the buckle.

ADJUSTING THE DIOPTER »
Use the numbers at the bottom of the EVF as a guide to adjusting the diopter.

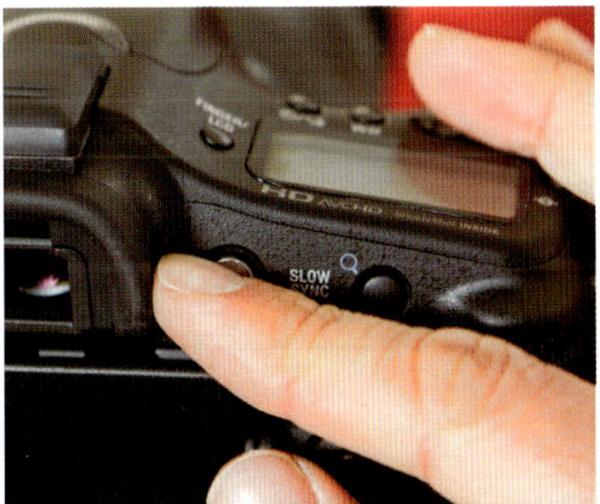

› Adjusting the diopter

Looking through the EVF, with the A77 held to your eye, is the most stable way of handholding the camera when shooting, but you should adjust the viewfinder of the camera to suit your eyesight before you begin. To adjust the diopter, turn your A77 on and then, looking though the EVF, turn the diopter-adjustment dial. Turning the dial clockwise adjusts for long sightedness, while turning it counter-clockwise compensates for short sightedness. Use the numbers at the bottom of the display to judge whether the EVF is focused correctly, rather than the main image, as the lens itself may not be focused correctly!

> ***Note:***
> The eyecup around the A77's EVF can be removed, allowing you to replace it if it gets damaged or to attach the optional FDA-A1AM Angle Finder in place. To remove the eyecup, place your thumbs at the bottom of the eyecup and push gently upward.

› Fitting and removing a lens

The A77 uses Sony's proprietary bayonet lens-mount system known as the A-mount. This means that lenses developed for other camera systems, such as Canon and Nikon, are not compatible with the A77. Naturally Sony sells A-mount lenses, as do a number of third-party manufacturers. A guide to the lenses available for the A77 appears in chapter four.

To mount a lens, first make sure that the camera is switched off. Then, remove the body cap (or lens, if one is already mounted on the camera) by pressing the lens release button (pictured) and turning the cap counter-clockwise (with the front of the camera facing toward you). To attach a lens, align the orange index mark on the lens with the index mark on the camera body and insert the lens carefully into the camera. Turn the lens clockwise until it firmly clicks into place. Do not force the lens if it is not turning correctly—if it is correctly aligned it should turn smoothly. Before using the camera, check that the AF/MF switch on the lens is set to the desired position. Reverse the process when you want to swap lenses or re-attach the body cap.

Warning!

Every time the body cap or a lens is removed, dust will inevitably get inside the camera. Although this should rarely reach the sensor, it will make the mirror dusty. To minimize this, avoid removing a lens on windy days (if possible), or shelter the camera with your body if this is unavoidable. See chapter seven for advice about cleaning the mirror and sensor.

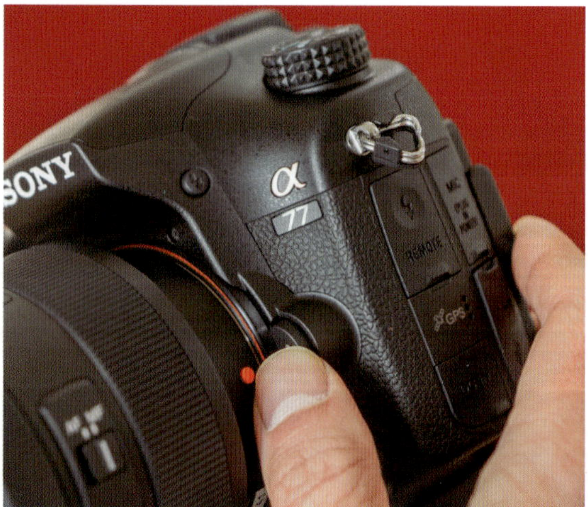

REMOVING A LENS «
Make sure you keep hold of the lens when you press the lens release button.

» POWERING YOUR A77

› Battery life

The A77 uses a Lithium Ion (Li-Ion) NP-FM500H battery. The NP-FM500H is an "infoLITHIUM" battery, which means that it can supply accurate information to your A77 about its charge status. The NP-FM500H battery is rated for approximately 500 charge cycles: a charge cycle is when 100% of the battery's power is used and then recharged. This does not mean that the battery needs to be discharged completely before recharging it though. If you use 25% of the charge in the battery, recharge it, and repeat this process four times, you will have completed one charge cycle.

If you find your battery does not hold its power for long, this probably means that it is coming to the end of its useful life and should be replaced. When fully charged, the battery should be able to power your A77 for approximately 530 shots when you are using the rear LCD screen to compose your images, or last for 470 shots when you are using the EVF.

› Battery charging

Before use, a new battery needs to be fully charged using the supplied BC-VM10A charger. Slide the battery onto the charger with the terminals facing the contacts on the charger until the battery clicks into place. Plug the charger into the wall socket (US and Canada) or connect the battery charger to an AC power cord and insert the plug into the wall socket. The charge lamp will glow until the battery is fully charged. The average time to recharge a fully depleted battery is approximately 175 minutes, but should the charge lamp start to flash, the battery charger has detected an error. Remove the battery and try inserting it into the charger again, or use a different battery.

> ***Note:***
> The BC-VM10A battery charger can be used internationally (100–240v AC 50/60hz) with a suitable plug adapter and so it does not require a separate voltage transformer.

BATTERY INDICATOR	BATTERY LEVEL
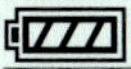	Fully charged
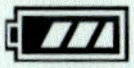	Approximately 75% charged
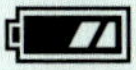	Approximately 50% charged
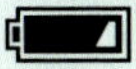	Approximately 25% charged
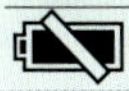	Battery almost depleted—recharge immediately

2

› Inserting the battery

To insert the battery, make sure the A77's power switch is set to Off. Turn the camera upside down and locate the battery cover at the base of the handgrip. Slide the battery cover lever toward the rear of the camera to release the catch and gently open the battery cover door. With the three electronic contacts of the battery facing into the battery compartment, push the battery down with the tip of the battery pressing the blue lock lever as you do so. Once the battery has clicked into place close the battery cover.

To remove the battery, make sure the A77's power switch is set to Off and open the battery cover as described previously. Push the blue lock lever toward the end of the camera and the battery should then spring out slightly. Pull the battery out completely and close the cover.

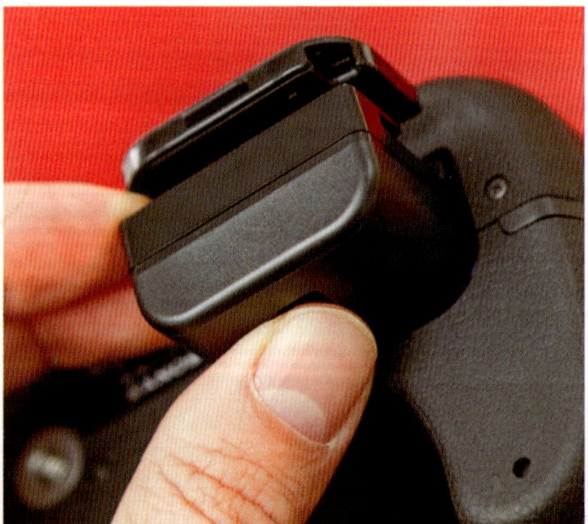

› Internal rechargeable battery

The A77 has an internal battery that maintains the date, time, and other settings, even when the camera is not on and the main battery is not inserted. This internal battery is recharged automatically by the main NP-FM500H battery when it is inserted into your camera.

If your A77 is not used for a while, the internal battery will gradually discharge. If the battery is entirely depleted, the camera can still be used but will not record the date and the time. To recharge the internal battery, insert a freshly charged NP-FM500H and leave it in the camera for 24 hours with the camera switched off. If your camera consistently reverts back to the default date and time settings, the internal battery may need to be replaced by a Sony dealer.

Note:
The A77 can be powered by the optional AC-PW10AM AC adapter. To use the adapter, turn the camera off and plug the adapter into the DC IN terminal on the side of the A77.

INSERTING A BATTERY «
Don't force the battery if it doesn't slot into the compartment smoothly.

COMPOSITION *(opposite)*
As the A77 is taking care of the technical side of photography in AUTO, take the opportunity to think about the artistic side, such has how your images are composed.

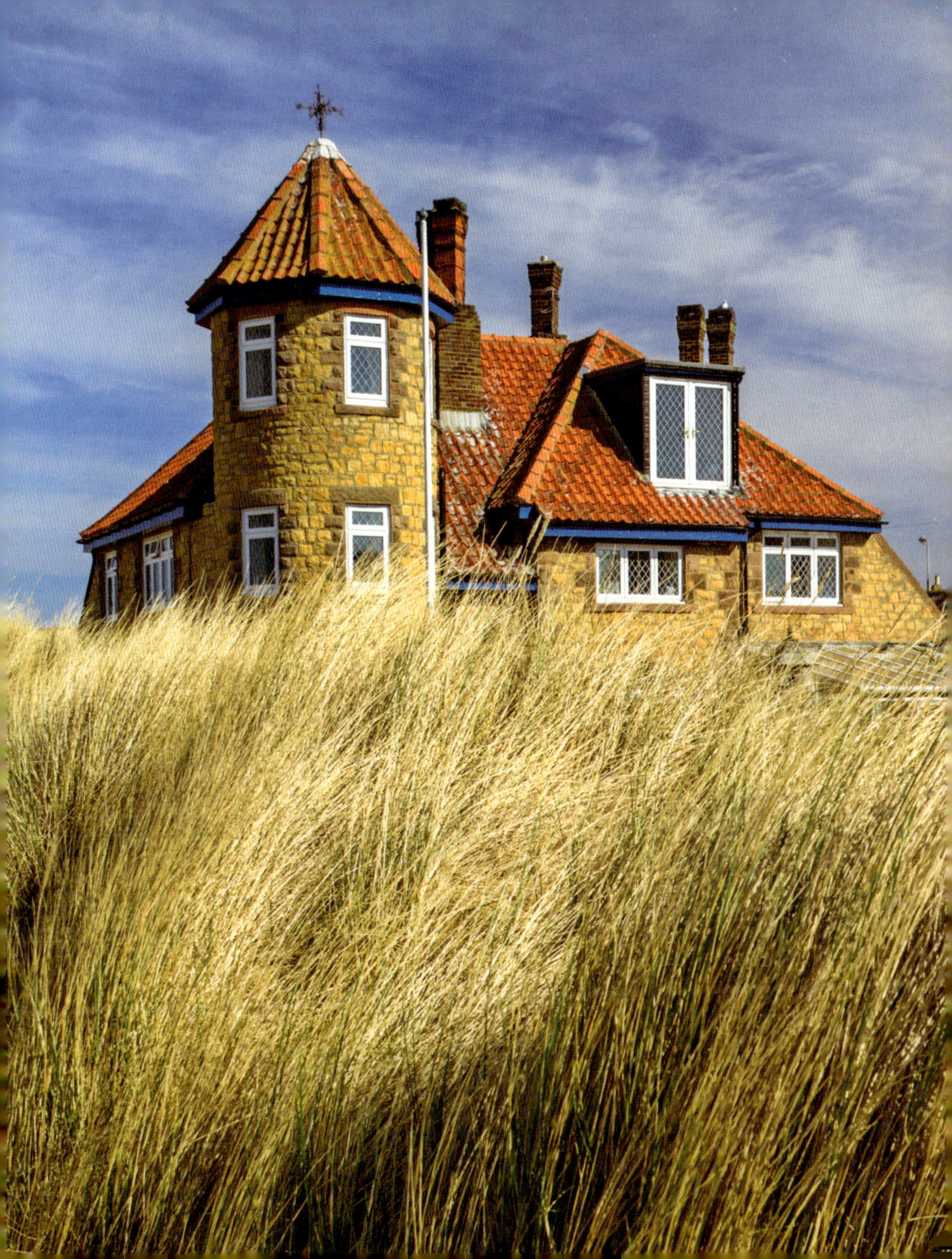

2 » BASIC CAMERA FUNCTIONS

› Controlling your camera

Your A77 can be used entirely automatically, so that all of the shooting functions are set by the camera, or it can be used almost entirely manually so that you are in charge of setting all of the functions such as exposure, focus, and white balance.

Whichever way you choose to use your camera it is important to practice using it so the position of its various buttons, dials, and other controls becomes familiar—there's nothing more frustrating than missing a shot because you were trying to find and set a particular function.

By far the most important switch on your A77 is the On/Off switch surrounding the shutter button. When you switch the camera On, it runs through a variety of checks that take approximately a second before it can be used.

To set the various shooting and playback options, the A77 uses a combination of buttons, a four-way controller "joypad," and front and rear control wheels. There is also a mode dial to set the shooting mode, as well as buttons that access specific shooting, movie, and playback functions.

Throughout the rest of this book the main menu button, to the left of the EVF, will be referred to as **MENU** and the secondary button, below the four-way controller, as **Fn**. The direction that the four-way controller needs to be pushed will be represented as ◀/▲/▶/▼ and when you need to press down on the center of the four-way controller to confirm a setting, ● will be used. The front control dial, below the On/Off switch is shown as [front dial symbol], and the rear control dial as [rear dial symbol]: other control buttons will be shown by the relevant symbol.

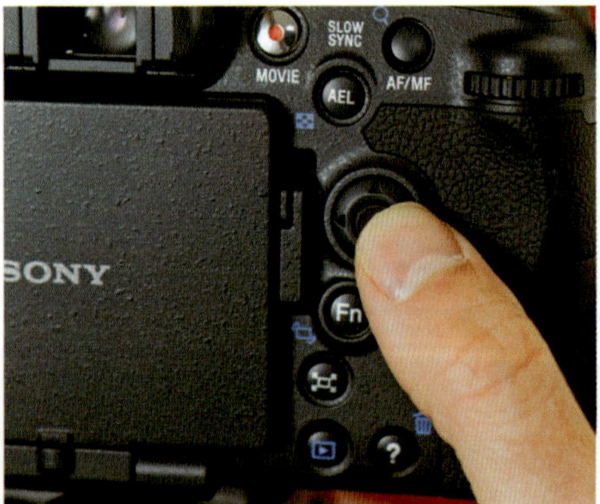

› Buttons

The exterior of the A77 is festooned with buttons that control various functions of the camera. Many of these functions can also be set via the **Fn** menu.

FOUR-WAY CONTROLLER «
The "joystick" is used extensively when navigating the A77's menus. It also acts as the setting confirmation button.

BUTTON	FUNCTION
Front	
Preview	Closes the aperture to the current aperture setting to show depth of field. Note that the smaller the aperture setting, the darker the image on the EVF and LCD will be, unless Preview Button on CUSTOM MENU 3 is set to Aperture Preview.
Flash release	Flash is raised and charged, ready for use.
Top	
FINDER/LCD	Switches the display between the EVF and the LCD.
/	Sets the drive (frame advance) mode.
WB	Lets you set the image white balance.
	Allows you to set exposure compensation in Program Auto, Aperture Priority, and Shutter Priority modes.
ISO	Sets the ISO sensitivity. The function of this button can be reassigned.
Display panel light	Toggles the display panel illumination.
Rear	
MENU	Displays the main camera menus.
Movie	Begins movie recording.
/AF/MF	Magnifies an image during playback or temporarily switches between AF and MF when shooting, allowing you to fine-tune focus. The function of this button can be reassigned.
/AEL/ Slow Sync	Switches to index view mode in playback or locks exposure when shooting. Also used to apply Slow Sync flash to ambient light exposures. The function of this button can also be reassigned.
DISP	Switches between different viewing modes on the EVF and LCD in both shooting and playback.
Fn /	Displays the shooting function menu screen, or rotates an image in playback.
/Focus Check	Activates the Smart Teleconverter. The button can also be reassigned to activate Focus Check.
	Playback button.
?/	Displays a help guide when choosing functions on the main and function menu screens. Also used to delete a single image in playback.

There is a comprehensive array of camera functions that can be altered using the A77's menu system. The various menu screens are divided into categories that are differentiated by a symbol shown on a tab at the top of the menu screen. Four of the categories are subdivided still further into numbered screens, with the number appearing to the right of the category symbol. If a particular function is not available, it is ghosted out and cannot be selected.

Using the menu system

1) Press **MENU**.

2) 📷 1 is automatically highlighted. Use ◀/▶ to highlight the required menu tab.

3) Use ▲/▼ to move the highlight bar up and down the options for the selected menu screen.

4) With the desired option highlighted, press ●.

5) The option sub-menu is displayed. Use ▲/▼ to move the highlight bar up and down the sub-menu options. Press ● to select the highlighted option, or press **MENU** to cancel and return to the main menu screen.

6) Press **MENU** to return to either shooting or playback mode, depending on which of the two was selected when **MENU** was pressed at step 1. Alternatively, press lightly down on the shutter-release button to go straight to shooting mode.

MENU TYPES

📷	Still image shooting. Sets camera functions for still image shooting.
🎞	Movie shooting. Sets camera functions for shooting movies.
⚙	Custom. Allows you to fine tune how your camera operates when shooting.
▶	Playback. Controls playback functions such as delete, protect, and slide show.
▬	Memory card tool. Options for optimizing the memory card, such as format.
🕘	Clock. Sets date and time functions.
🔧	Setup. Controls non-shooting camera functions.

› Setting the time

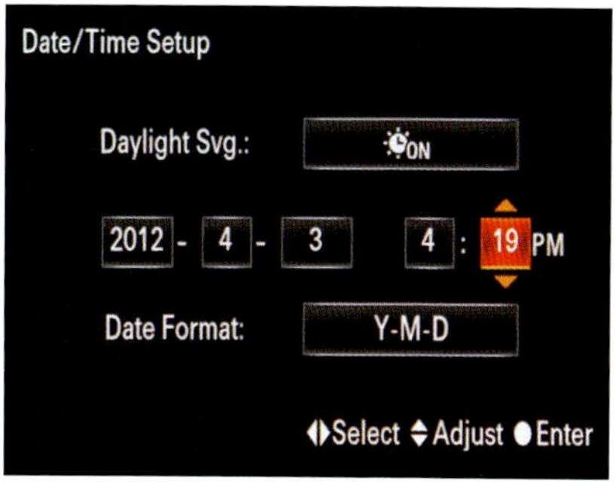

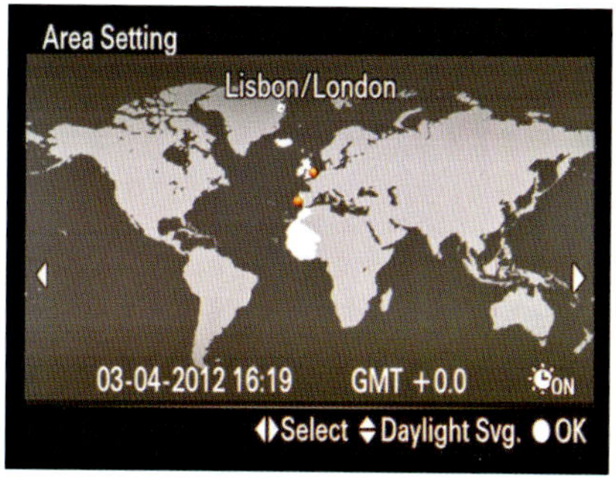

When you first switch on your new A77 you will be prompted to set both the time and date. If you press **MENU** you can skip this stage and begin shooting immediately, but it's a good idea to set the time and date immediately, as this is embedded into the metadata of every image that you shoot. Once images have been copied to your computer you can use the time and date to sort or search for particular images.

Setting the time and date

1) With Enter highlighted, press ●.

2) Highlight the area of the world where you live by using ◀ / ▶ and then press ●.

3) On the Date/Time Setup screen use ◀/▶ to jump between the different options, use ▲ / ▼. to set the highlighted option. Once you're done, press ● to continue.

> **Tips**
>
> *Setting* ***Daylight Svg.*** *to* ***On*** *will advance the clock one hour ahead.*
>
> ***Time/Date Setup*** *and* ***Area Setting*** *can be found on the* 🕘 *Clock menu, and changed at any time.*

2 › Fn button

The A77's **Fn** button is used to quickly set commonly used shooting functions such as the drive mode and ISO settings. The range of options that is available is dependant on the shooting mode selected, with the more automated shooting modes (such as the **SCN** modes) restricting the number of options that can be altered. The detailed shooting information LCD display shows the currently selected custom functions down the sides of the screen.

Using the Fn button

1) In Shooting mode, press **Fn**.

2) Use ◀/▲/▶/▼, to highlight the required function icon. The various icons will be displayed on the left and right of the screen.

3) Press ● when the desired shooting function is highlighted.

4) Highlight the required sub-option and press ● to choose it.

5) The camera will return to shooting mode automatically.

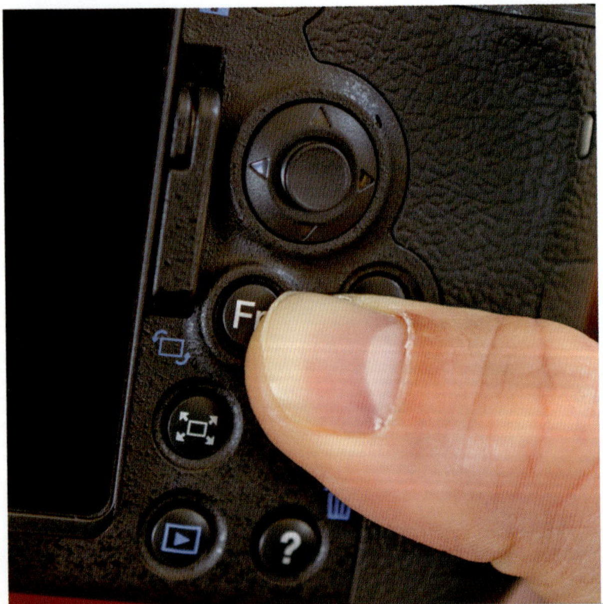

Note:
There are different ways to select the required sub-option, as described on the following pages.

Turn [dial icon] to select a sub-option when a shooting function is highlighted.

› Shutter-release button

The shutter-release button has two stages of operation. Pressing it lightly down, halfway, will activate the AF system and exposure metering. Playback mode will also be canceled automatically. Fully depressing the shutter-release button will then take the shot unless the focus is not locked. (When the camera is set to MF the shutter will fire regardless of whether the image is in focus.)

In Single-shot AF mode, the camera will focus, and both the exposure and the focus point will be locked until either the shutter-release button is released or a photograph is taken.

In Continuous AF mode, neither the exposure nor focus is locked until the shutter-release button is depressed fully and the photograph taken.

When Single Shot drive mode is selected, only one photograph will be taken when the shutter-release button is fully depressed, whereas the camera will continue to shoot at the maximum frame rate (for the mode) in Continuous Shooting and 12 drive modes, until the shutter-release button is released.

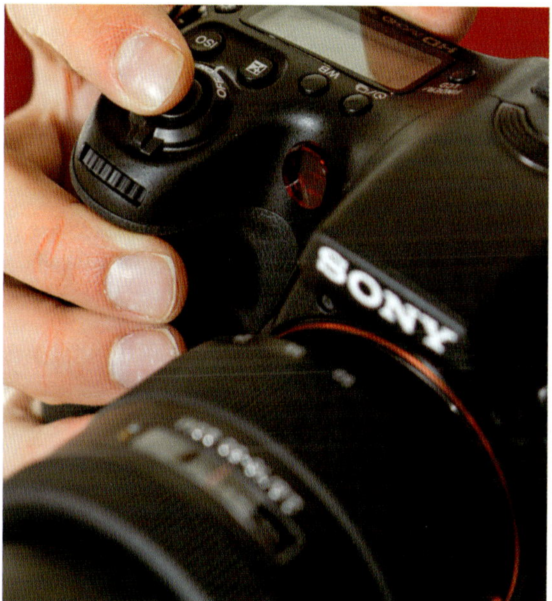

> **Tip**
>
> *Gently and smoothly push the shutter-release button, rather than stabbing it down. This will help avoid camera shake and help the focus to lock.*

The A77 uses both Sony's proprietary Memory Stick PRO Duo/PRO-HG Duo media and the more universally available SD/SDHC/SDXC memory cards. Memory Stick Micro cards can also be used when fitted into an appropriate adapter.

Inserting a memory card

1) Make sure that the camera is switched off and the small red access lamp below is unlit.

2) If your memory card has a write-protect tab, slide the tab to the unlocked position. If the card is locked, **[Memory card locked]** will appear on the LCD and you will not be able to take any pictures.

3) With the front of the A77 facing away from you, slide the memory card cover toward you until it springs open.

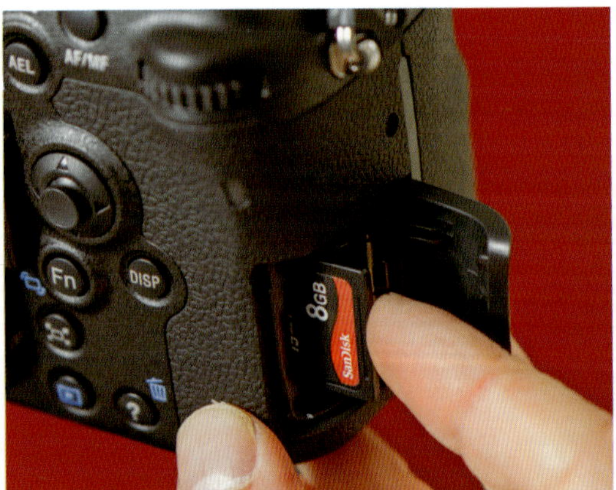

4) To insert the memory card, make sure that the label side is facing toward you with the notch upward. Push the card gently into the slot until there is a slight resistance. Push more firmly (but not excessively) until the card clicks into place. Never force a memory card if there is undue resistance, as it may not be aligned in the slot correctly. Close the memory card cover.

5) To remove a memory card, push it gently further into the memory card slot until there is a click. You should now be able to pull it free from the slot.

> **Warning!**
>
> When the red access lamp is lit the camera is either reading, writing, or erasing image data from the memory card. Do not remove the card or the battery when the lamp is lit as this will corrupt the image data or even potentially damage the camera.

INSERTING A MEMORY CARD «
Never force a memory card if it doesn't slot in smoothly.

› Formatting a memory card

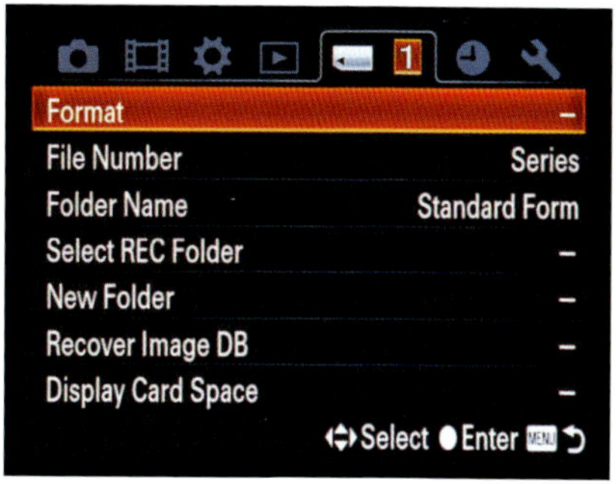

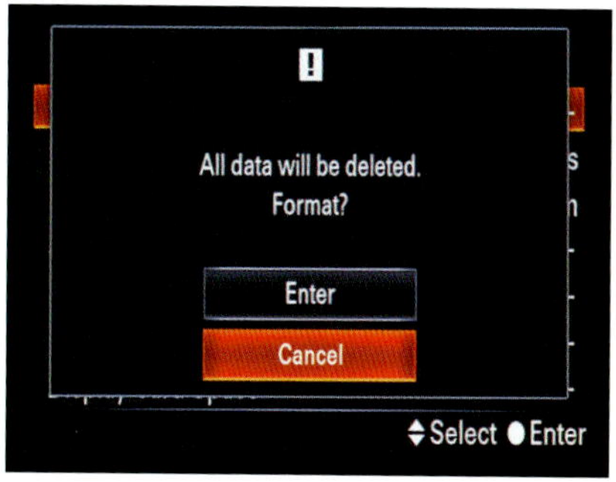

Before you use a memory card, or if it's been used in another camera previously, you should format it first. Formatting will remove any data on the card, including images. If there are any images already saved to the card it is important to copy them to a PC or other storage device before formatting.

Formatting a memory card

1) Press **MENU**.

2) Highlight the tab.

3) **Format** is highlighted by default. Press ● to continue.

4) Highlight **Enter** and press ● to format the memory card or highlight **Cancel** and press ● to return to the main menu screen.

5) Press **MENU** or lightly down on the shutter-release button to return to shooting mode.

› Memory card speed

The higher the read/write speed of a memory card, the faster files can be written to and from it. This is particularly important when using Continuous shooting mode or when you are recording video. The speed of a memory card is often shown as a Class Rating: the higher the Class Rating, the faster the read/write time. Sony recommend the use of a Class 4 memory card or faster to shoot video. Speed is sometimes also shown as a figure followed by an "x." This figure refers to the speed of the card compared to the read/write speed of a standard CD-Rom drive.

SPEED	READ/WRITE SPEED (MB/S)	CLASS RATING
13×	2.0	2
26×	4.0	4
40×	6.0	6
66×	10.0	10

The A77 can shoot either JPEG or Raw image files. Both have their strengths and weaknesses, so the one you choose will depend on the final use to which you'll put your images.

› JPEG files

JPEG is short for Joint Photographic Experts Group, which refers to the development team that originally created the file format. JPEGs are compatible with virtually all software that uses image files, including web browsers and email packages. This makes JPEG ideal if you want to use your images immediately.

The file size of a JPEG is relatively small in comparison to an equivalent Raw file, which is due to the fact that the image data in a JPEG is compressed. The compression works by reducing the amount of detail in the image, degrading it to a greater or lesser degree. This is known as "lossy compression," as image data is lost in the process. The A77 offers three levels of compression: Extra fine, Fine, and Standard. Of these settings, Extra fine compresses the data the least, giving you higher quality images. However, the file sizes will be larger compared to the Fine and Standard settings, so fewer shots will fit onto a memory card.

Each camera manufacturer uses a different method to convert the image data captured at the moment of exposure into a JPEG, but during the conversion process the style of the image (such as sharpening and contrast) will be "baked" into the JPEG file. Once this has been done it is far more difficult to alter these characteristics during post-production.

DETAIL

JPEG compression is most noticeable when there are areas of fine detail in an image. On the far left is an image of a ball of string. The center image is an image converted from a Raw file. The image on the right is a JPEG with Standard compression. Many of the details in the Raw image are smudged on the Standard JPEG image.

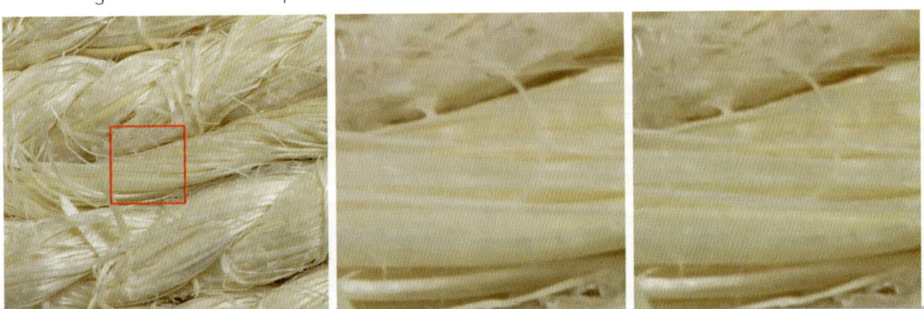

The A77's JPEG rendering, particularly at lower ISO settings, is more than good enough for general use. There is a slight softness to the images, although this can be corrected in post-production. This approach is more effective with the Extra fine compression setting, which retains the greatest amount of detail.

The problem of detail loss is exacerbated when higher ISO settings are used. The A77's built-in noise reduction tends to smear detail, leading to still greater levels of softness. Once detail has been lost in this way it cannot be recovered, even when sharpening is applied in post-production. For critical use, particularly in less favorable lighting, it is recommended to use Raw to extract the maximum amount of detail the A77's sensor is capable of capturing.

ADOBE LIGHTROOM 4
Released in 2012, Lightroom 4 is compatible with the A77's .ARW Raw files.

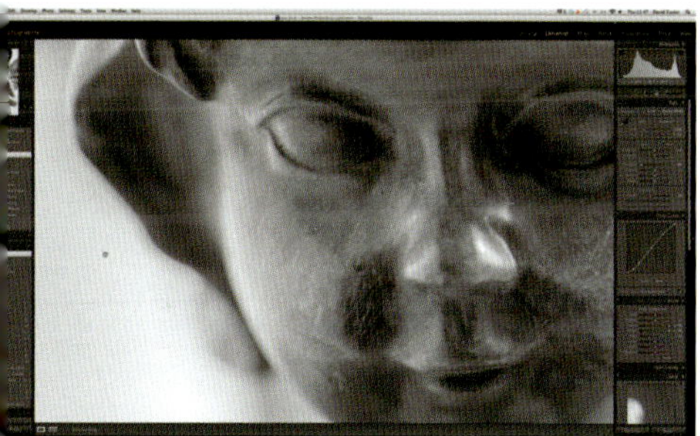

› Raw files

A Raw file is the "uncooked," unprocessed data created by a camera's sensor at the moment of exposure. However, there is no Raw standard and Raw files come in many versions, with each camera manufacturer using a different variation of the format. The A77, for example, uses Sony's .ARW format.

Before a Raw file can be viewed on a computer, a Raw converter such as Image Data Converter (which is supplied with the A77) or a third-party alternative such as Adobe Lightroom must be used to interpret this data: Raw files cannot be used with software other than a Raw converter.

If you want to use your Raw image for general use it will need to be processed and then saved into a more convenient file type such as JPEG or TIFF, so Raw files should be thought of as a "digital negative." It is the first step in the creation of an image, in the way that a negative is necessary to create a print in a darkroom.

Unlike a JPEG, a Raw file retains every detail captured by the camera, so it is up to you to decide how that detail should be processed. This makes shooting Raw files far more labor-intensive than JPEGs. If you shoot Raw you should be prepared to spend time in post-production polishing your images.

A Raw file will always take up more space on your memory card than an equivalent JPEG file, so you will need to be prepared to empty the card more frequently.

2 » LCD and EVF

The A77 allows you to use either the LCD or the EVF to compose, review images, and adjust menu options, and it is down to personal preference which system you prefer to use. In terms of keeping the camera steady when handholding it, the EVF is the preferred choice, as holding the camera against your face makes a far steadier platform for shooting than when the camera is held at arms' length.

However, the LCD comes into its own if you are shooting low down using a tripod, as the screen is articulated, which means it can be pulled away from the camera body and angled outward. Shooting this way is far easier than trying to crouch down to peer through the viewfinder. Setting the **Smart Telecon. Button** on Custom Menu 3 to to **Focus Magnifier** will allow you to check critical focus more easily too. The LCD can also be rotated so that it faces into the camera for protection, and it is recommended that you set it this way to avoid damage when it is not in use.

To begin using the LCD, pull it out gently from the camera. Once it's fully open, rotate it 180° forward, toward the front of the camera. Having done that, push the LCD back into the camera so that it fits snugly with the screen facing outward. This is the orientation that is most useful for "standard" shooting, but the screen can be used at a wide variety of angles, including raising the LCD screen higher than the body of the camera.

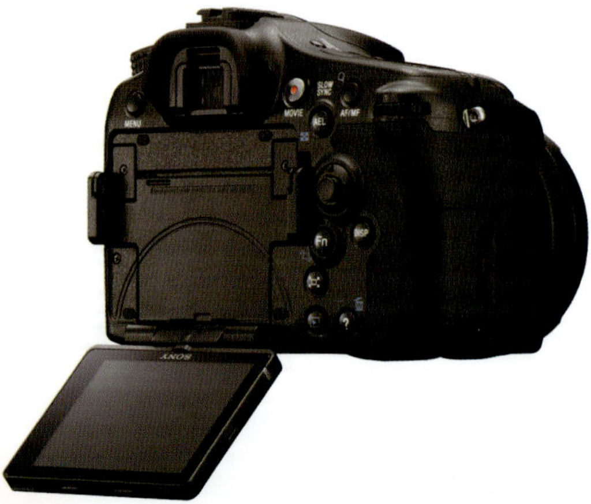

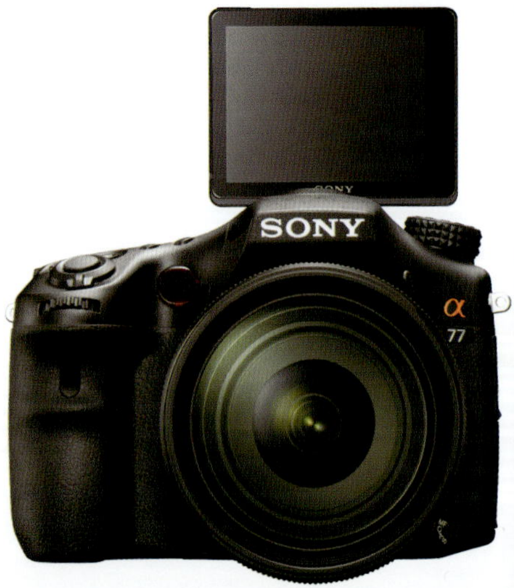

› Level

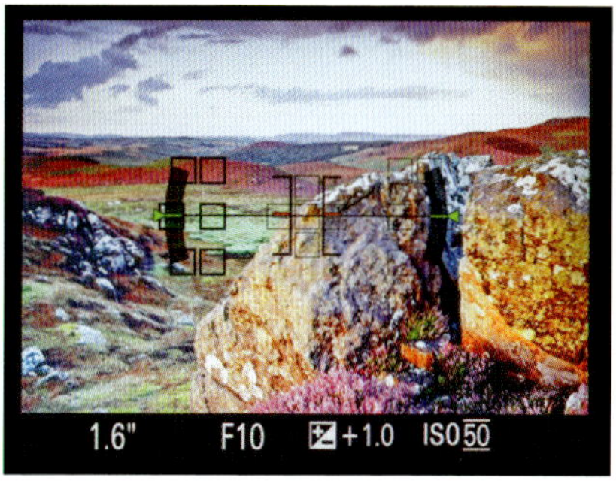

For most shooting situations it won't matter too much if the camera wasn't perfectly level when the image was created. However, there are some types of photography that require more care when it comes to setting the orientation of the camera. Landscape and architectural photography are two styles of photography that often require a methodical approach.

Any scene that involves water also has to be straight, as there's something very off-putting about an image of a body of water that slopes: water should be horizontal and not appear to be running out of the side of the image.

A different problem—"converging verticals"—occurs in architectural photography. This is where buildings appear to be falling either forward or, more commonly, backward. Converging verticals are caused by the camera not being parallel to a building when the image was captured. Fortunately the A77 can help you rectify both these errors by using its Level function.

With Levels switched on, the horizontal line (the roll bar) across the screen shows the angle of the A77 relative to the horizon. When the camera is completely level, the triangles at either end of the bar turn green. When the camera isn't level the triangles remain white and the ends of the roll bar turn orange.

At the center of the screen are pitch indicators that show the vertical orientation of the camera. When the camera isn't level vertically, the pitch indicators turn orange. If you tip the camera upward, the pitch indicators drop lower; tip the camera down and the indicators rise. When the camera is level, the pitch indicators turn green.

CONVERGING VERTICALS
Seen most often when shooting close to buildings, using a wide-angle lens.

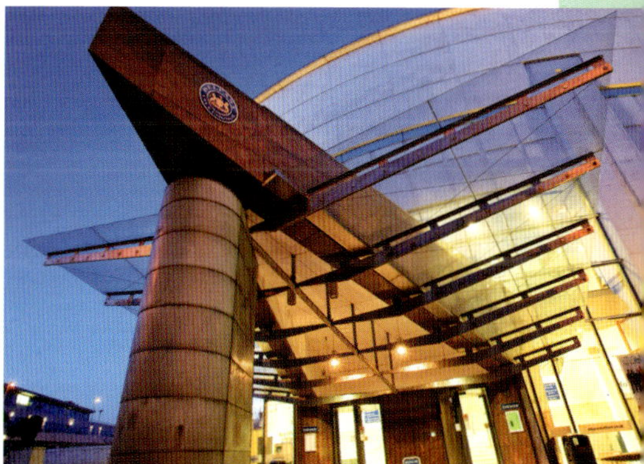

You can set your A77 to automatically display an image after exposure. You can choose between four settings on the Custom 2 menu under **Auto Review**: **2**, **5**, and **10** seconds, or **Off** (with **Off** being the default). If **Auto Review** is set to **Off** you will need to press ▶ to display the last image shot. Once in playback mode you can then use ◀/▶, , or to skip backward and forward through the images stored on the memory card.

There are several different ways to view an image. By repeatedly pressing **DISP** you can view the image with shooting data such as shutter speed and aperture, shooting data, and an RGB histogram, or the image only, without any shooting information.

› Magnify images

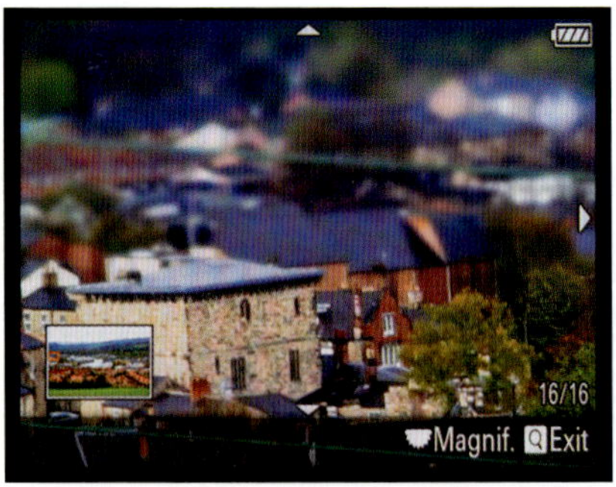

You can magnify images in playback mode, which is useful for checking focus after shooting. To magnify an image, press 🔍 and turn to zoom in or out. At the bottom left of the screen is a white box. Within this box is an orange frame that represents the area of the image that is currently displayed. You can move the area displayed by using ◀/▲/▶/▼. If you want to skip to another image turn , but note that this image will be magnified as well: to exit magnify image mode press 🔍 once more.

› Rotating images

If an image needs to be rotated press the **Fn** button when viewing it in ▶ mode. Then press ● to rotate it 90° counter-clockwise. Pressing ● a further three times will return the image back to its original orientation. Once you are happy with the image orientation press **Fn** to exit or use ◀/▶, , or to review and rotate more images.

> ***Notes:***
> By default, the **View Mode** on the ▶ 1 menu is set to **Folder View (Still)**, but you can set this option so that movies can be viewed.
>
> Images can be viewed on either the LCD or in the EVF.

› Image index

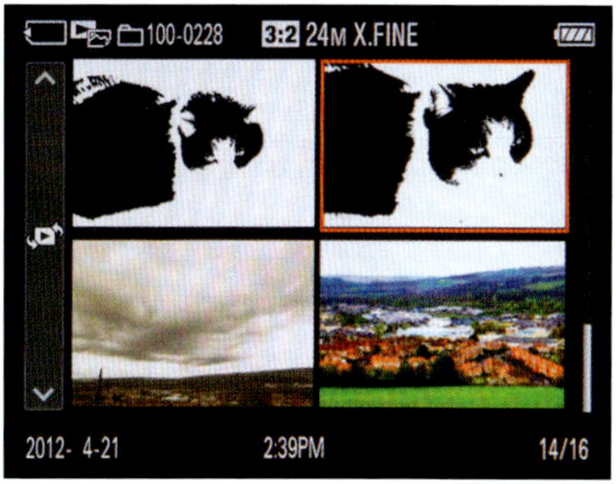

Image index allows you to view either four or nine images on screen simultaneously as thumbnails, which is a good way to skip quickly through a large number of images. To use image index press ▶ and then ⊞. To toggle between four or nine images press **DISP**.

The current image selected is highlighted in orange. Press either ◀/▲/▶/▼, or turn the control dial to highlight a new thumbnail. Alternatively, turn the control dial to move between different pages of thumbnails. Press ⊞ to view the highlighted thumbnail full screen.

The A77 can save images to different folders on your memory card. To navigate between the different folders on the card use ◀/▶ or the control dial to highlight the folder bar at the far left of the image index screen. Press ◀/▶ to select the desired folder.

› Slide show

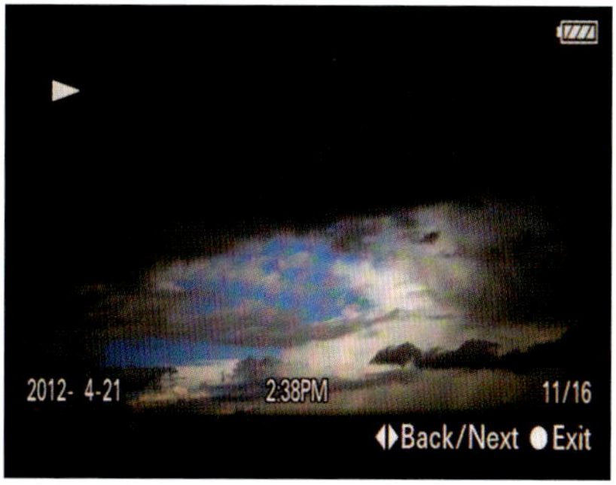

The A77 can display a slide show of the images on the memory card. This can either be viewed on the LCD (or in the EVF), or on a compatible television.

Viewing a slide show

1) Press **MENU**, navigate to ▶ Playback 1 and highlight **Slide Show**. Press ●.

2) Select and set the Slide Show options: **Repeat**—**On** or **Off**, and **Interval** (how long each image remains onscreen) from **1** to **30** seconds—and **Image Type** (**All** or **Display 3D Only**). Then, highlight **Enter** and press ● to begin your slide show, or **Cancel** to return to the ▶ 1 screen.

3) from **1** to **30** seconds—and **Image Type** (**All** or **Display 3D Only**). Then, highlight **Enter** and press ● to begin your slide show, or **Cancel** to return to the ▶ 1 menu screen.

› Deleting and Protecting images

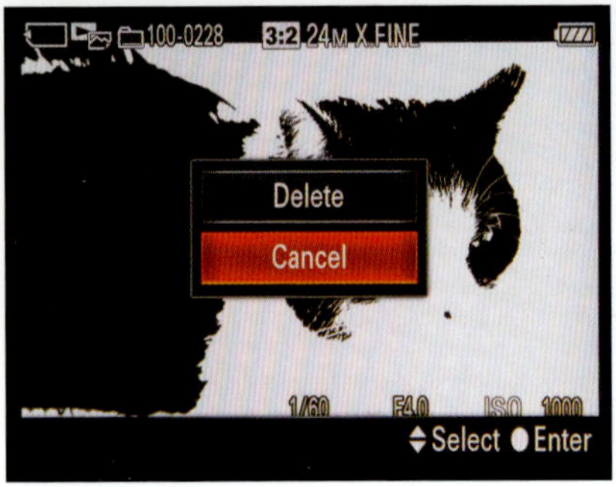

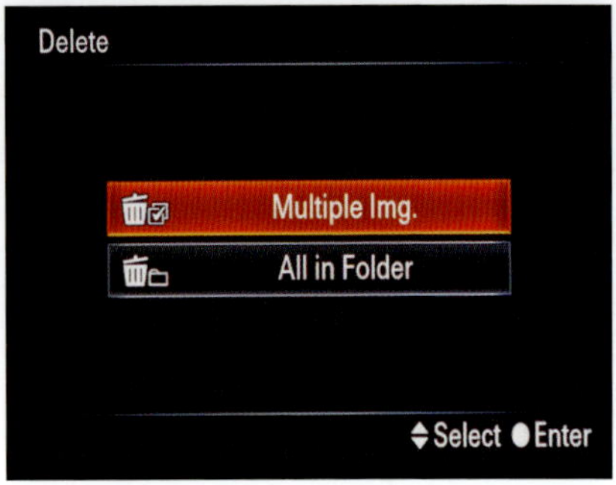

In playback mode you can delete single images, but there are options on the ▶ 1 menu that allow you to delete groups of images, either by selecting a range or by deleting all images in the current folder. Note that once an image has been deleted it cannot be recovered.

Delete single image

1) Press 🗑 and then ▲ to highlight **Delete**. Press ● to confirm deletion.

2) Alternatively, highlight **Cancel** and press ● to return to playback mode.

Delete multiple images

1) To delete a range or all images press **MENU**, navigate to the ▶ 1 menu and highlight **Delete**. Press ●.

2) To select specific images to delete highlight **Multiple Img**. and press ●. Press ◀/▶ or turn the front or rear control dial to skip through the images on the memory card.

3) Press ● to mark the displayed image for deletion. An orange tick symbol will be displayed in a box at the far left of the screen. To deselect the image press ● once more.

4) When you've marked the full range of images you wish to delete, press the **MENU** button. Highlight **OK** and press ● to confirm deletion. Alternatively, highlight **Cancel** and press ● to continue marking images for deletion.

> **Tips**
>
> *When selecting images for deletion or protection, pressing ▶ will exit image selection and return to standard playback.*
>
> *Formatting a memory card will erase all the images on a disk.*

Deleting images in a folder

1) To delete a range or all images press **MENU** navigate to [▶] 1 and highlight **Delete**. Press ●.

2) Highlight **All in Folder** and press ●. Highlight **Delete** and press ● to confirm. Alternatively highlight **Cancel** and press ● to return to playback mode.

› Protecting images

Marking images for protection will make sure that they are not erased accidentally.

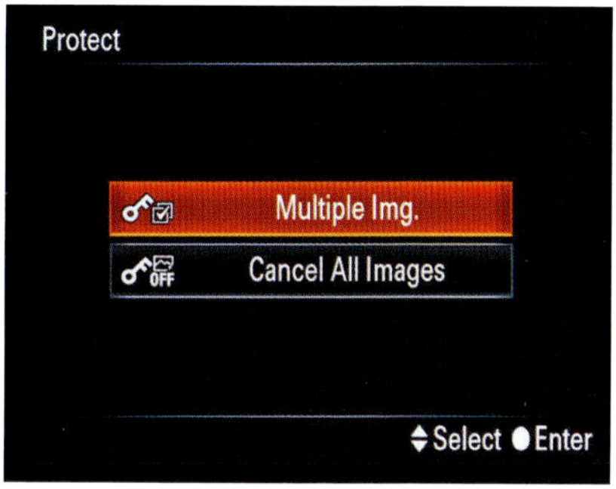

Selecting images for protection

1) To protect a range of (or all) images press **MENU** and highlight **Protect** on the [▶] 1 menu screen. Press ●.

2) To select specific images to protect highlight **Multiple Img.** and press ●. Press ◀/▶ or turn the front or rear dial to skip through the images on the memory card.

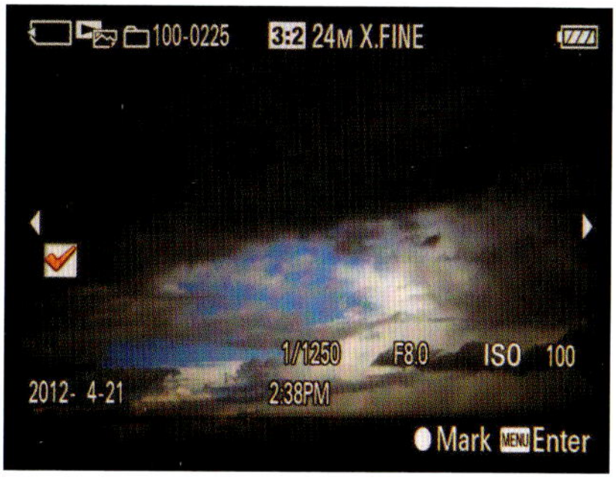

3) Press ● to mark the displayed image for protection. An orange "tick" will be shown in a box at the far left of the screen. To deselect the image press ● again.

4) When you've marked all of the images you wish to protect, press the **MENU** button. Highlight **OK** and press ● to confirm protection. Alternatively highlight **Cancel** and press ● to continue marking images for protection.

> ***Tip***
>
> *Although there's no way on the A77 to recover an image once it's been deleted, all is not necessarily lost. Software is available, such as Digital Pictures Recovery for both Windows and Mac, which will attempt to recover deleted images. What is vitally important is not to save any other images to the card until you have a chance to run the software and recover the "lost" photographs.*

The A77 is compatible with all of the A-mount lenses in the current Sony lineup, as well as third-party lenses designed for the system. Most (but not all) of these lenses are equipped with an AF/MF switch that will allow you to switch between auto and manual focus. If the lens does not have an AF/MF switch, use the focus mode dial on the front of the camera to set the focus mode: this is below the lens release button and allows you to switch between three AF modes and MF.

The AF system in the A77 is generally fast and accurate, but like most AF systems, it's not infallible and there may be times when focus cannot be locked. This is most likely to occur when light levels are low or you are trying to focus on something with insufficient contrast. In these situations the AF system will appear to dither and continuously "hunt" without coming to a final decision. If this happens, you may want to switch to manual focus.

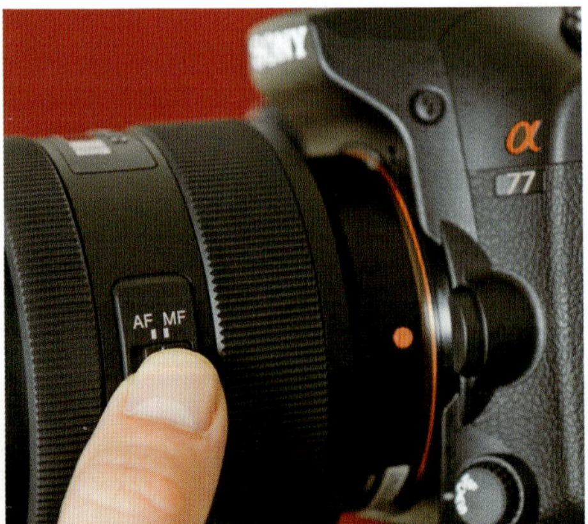

Manual focus

When the lens is set to MF you are entirely responsible for setting the correct focusing distance for your subject. To focus, rotate the focusing ring on the lens.

When Wide AF is selected, the central AF point is lit green when the correct focus has been achieved; in Zone AF, a focus point in the selected zone is lit; and when Local AF is selected, the focus point selected by the multi-selector is used. In all modes, focusing manually is made easier by using the A77's Peaking function.

Warning!

Do not try to force the focusing ring on a lens if it resists turning. Instead, check that the focus mode switch on the lens, or the focus mode dial on the camera, is set to MF.

Note:
Certain autofocus functions are set using the **Fn** menu, including **AF Area, Object Tracking, Face Detection,** and **Smile Shutter.**

Single-shot AF

This AF mode is best suited to stationary subjects. To use this mode, partially depress the shutter-release button to lock AF. The camera will not try to refocus until you release pressure on the shutter-release button. When focus is locked, the green ● confirmation and the active focus point(s) will be lit on the LCD and in the EVF. Focus lock will also be confirmed by a beep unless this has been deactivated in 🔧 Setup 2. Keeping the shutter-release button partially depressed will keep the focus locked, enabling you to recompose the shot.

Continuous AF

Continuous AF mode is ideal for subjects that have directional movement. If Eye-Start has been activated, focus will begin when you bring your camera to your eye, or it will start when you partially depress the shutter-release button.

When the AF system starts tracking your subject the active focus point and the ((●)) confirmation will light on the LCD and in the EVF. The camera will continue to focus until the shutter-release button is depressed fully. Focus lock will not be confirmed by the usual beep.

Automatic AF

Automatic AF is a hybrid of Single-shot and Continuous AF, switching between the two depending on the subject. If the subject is motionless, depressing the shutter-release button will lock the focus; if the subject moves, the AF system will continue to focus until the shutter-release button is depressed fully. The function of the Automatic AF dial position can be altered using **AF-A Setup** on the 📷 Still Shooting 3 menu.

AF status is shown on the LCD and in the EVF by a focus indicator. The grid below shows the messages the indicator conveys.

INDICATOR	MESSAGE
● *(Lit)*	Focus is locked and the shutter can be fired.
((●)) *(Lit)*	Focus is confirmed but not locked. AF will continue to track until the shutter-release button is pressed.
(( ))	AF system is still trying to acquire focus. The shutter cannot be fired.
● *(Flashing)*	Focus can't be locked. Shutter can't be fired.

› Focus area

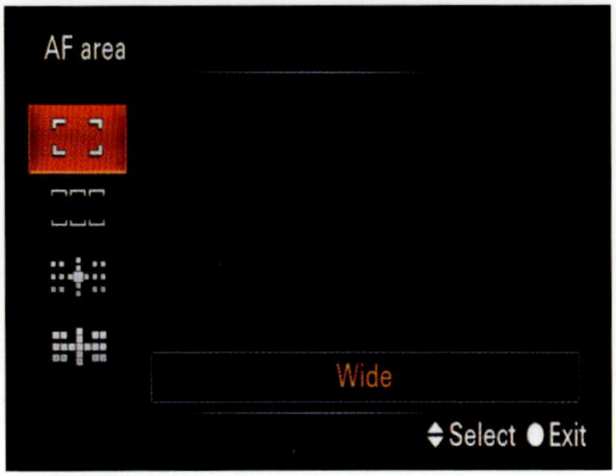

The A77 has 19 AF points clustered around the central area of the image space; six on the left, seven in the middle, and six on the right. You can let the A77 decide which AF point to use when focusing, pick a specific AF point, or divide the AF points into zones of influence—with focusing centered on one zone only. Select the required AF area from the **Fn** menu and use them as described below.

[ ] Wide

Set to [ ], the A77 will automatically decide which of the 19 AF areas is used for focusing. This means you have no control over where the camera focuses—it may be just where you want it but on the other hand it may not.

Zone

This mode splits the AF points into three groups (left, center, and right). You can choose which group the camera uses, but it still chooses which AF point to use within the group. Use ◀ / ▶ to select the group you want to use. This setting is useful if you're shooting off-center subjects.

Spot

The A77 uses the AF point located directly in the center of the EVF.

Local

This mode allows you to choose which of the AF points is used to focus. Use ◀/▲/▶/▼ to move the AF point around the 19 focus points available.

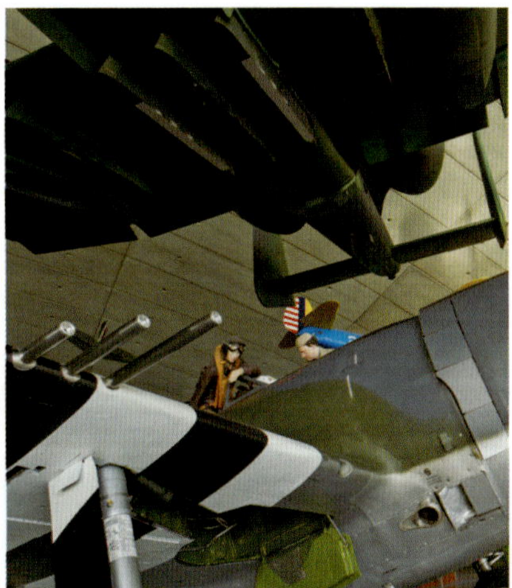

LOCAL »
I used Local AF for this shot, focusing on the two figures to make sure that they were the sharpest part of the image.

› Object Tracking

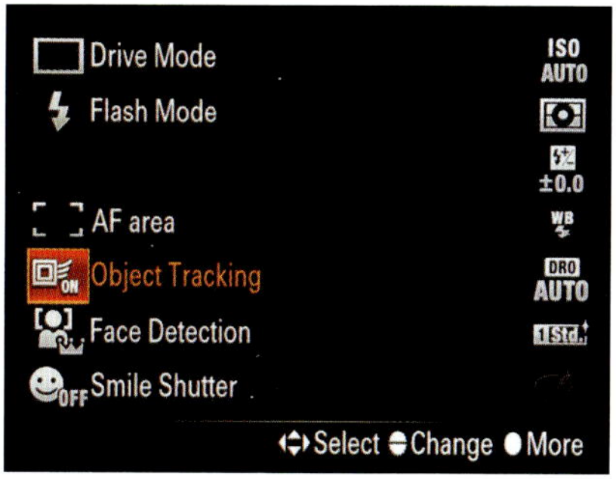

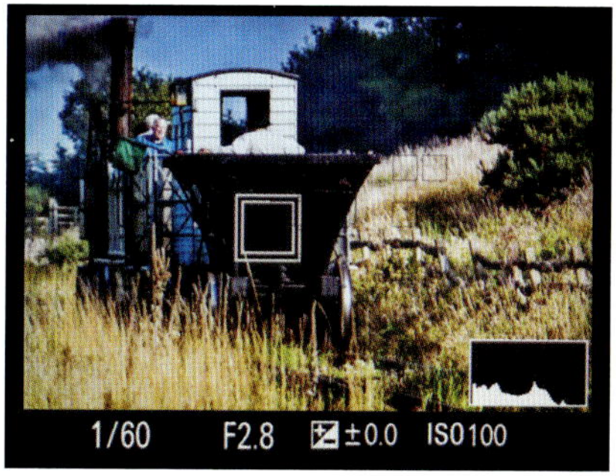

Object tracking is a useful AF function that allows you to indicate to your A77 what you'd like it to keep focusing on. If either the subject or the camera moves, the subject will be tracked and focus maintained, as long as the subject remains under one of the 19 AF points. Object Tracking has its limitations though: fast, jerky movement will defeat it, so your subject (or camera) movement needs to be reasonably smooth and unhurried. Object Tracking is set to **On** by default.

Using Object Tracking

1) If **Object Tracking** is turned **Off**, press **Fn** and highlight ⊡OFF. Press ●.

2) Highlight ⊡ON and press ● again.

3) In shooting mode, move your camera so the subject is in the center of the frame.

4) Press ● twice to start Object Tracking. A white target frame will be displayed on screen, and focus will lock. As your subject moves around the image, the target frame will follow it.

5) Press the shutter-release button to take a photograph, or press ● to cancel **Object Tracking**.

> ***Note:***
> Object Tracking will stop tracking your subject if it leaves the image frame.

› Face Detection

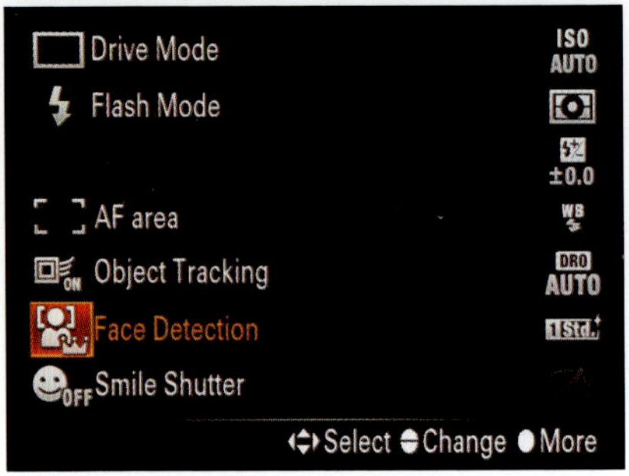

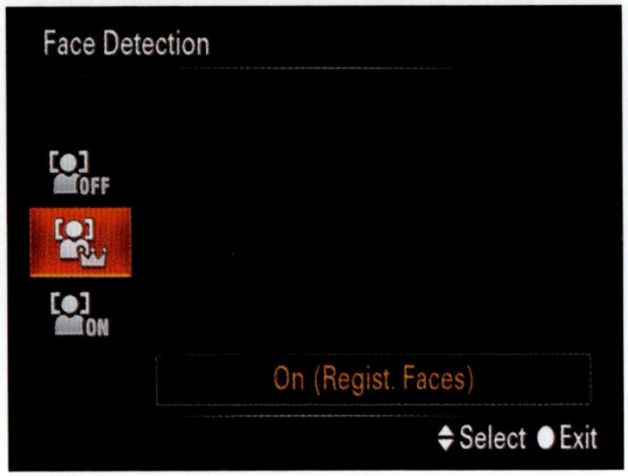

The **Fn** menu offers two modes that aim to help you take technically successful portraits: Smile Shutter and Face Detection. When Face Detection is activated, the A77 will automatically detect up to eight faces that are within your image area. The camera then adjusts the focus, exposure, flash settings, and (in certain shooting modes) the image processing parameters.

When Face Detection is switched to [●] ON , a gray box is drawn around the face when it is detected in shooting mode. If autofocus is possible (if the face is within your lens's focus range) the box will turn white, and when you press the shutter-release button to take the shot, the box turns green. If there is no face present the normal AF points will be displayed and will turn green when focus is achieved.

You can also register faces, so the A77 instantly recognizes them (and can also prioritize them, focusing on them first). If a face has been previously registered and recognized, the focus frame will turn magenta: be sure to set to **On** if you have faces registered.

Tip

Try to keep your subject's hair from covering their face, as this may prevent Face Detection from operating properly.

› Smile Shutter

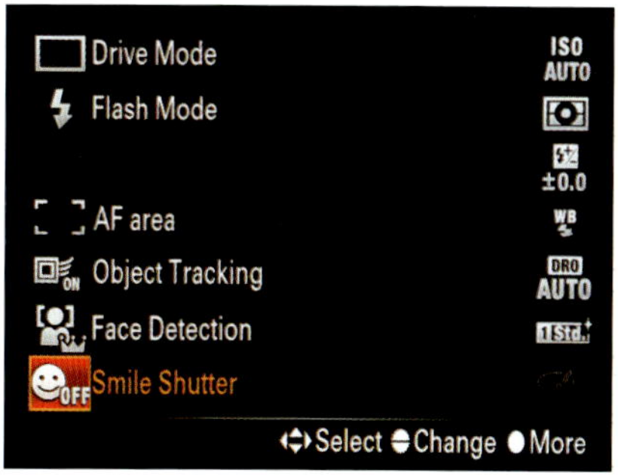

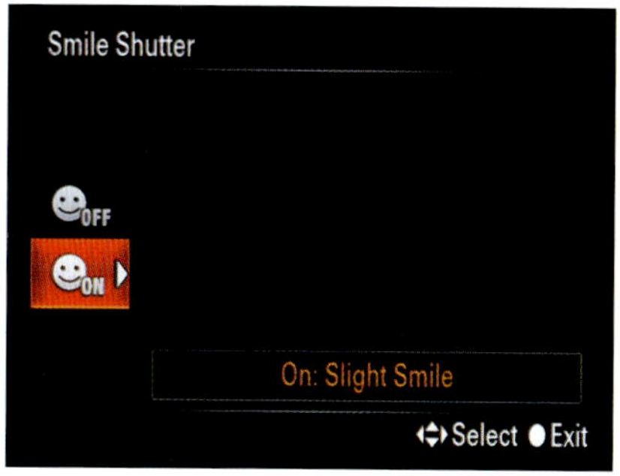

Capturing the exact moment that someone smiles can be a frustrating experience, which often requires careful timing and the ability to be patient at every missed opportunity. By using Smile Shutter, the A77 can automate the firing of the shutter at the exact moment that your subject smiles. The only difficulty for you is making your subject smile.

Using Smile Shutter

1) Press **Fn** and highlight ☻OFF (Smile Shutter is Off by default). Press ●.

2) Highlight ☻ON . You can set the sensitivity of Smile Shutter by pressing ▶ / ◀. You can choose between ☻ON Slight, ☻ON Normal, or ☻ON Big. When set to ☻ON even the smallest smile will trigger the shutter, whereas ☻ON requires a huge smile from your subject.

3) Press ● to return to shooting mode.

4) When the camera detects a face, an orange Face Detection frame is displayed around the face, with the frame turning green when focus is confirmed. On the left side of the screen is a vertical Smile Detection Sensitivity bar. If your subject is smiling, the shutter is fired when the Smile Detection Sensitivity level exceeds the ◀ point on the bar. The bigger the smile, the higher the Smile Detection Sensitivity indicator rises.

5) Press the shutter-release button to take a photograph, or press ● again to cancel Object Tracking.

> **Tip**
>
> *Smile Shutter works well when your camera is mounted on a tripod. After composing the shot, you can then look at your subject directly, which makes it easier to engage with them.*

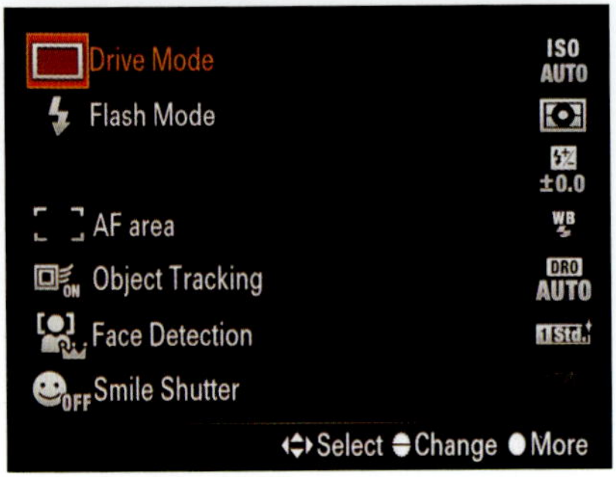

The Drive Mode allows you to choose the speed at which the A77 shoots images when the shutter-release button is pressed.

Single shot

Only one photograph will be taken when the shutter-release button is depressed fully. To shoot another image the shutter-release button must be released and re-pressed.

Continuous Shooting C Hi & Lo

There are two options for Continuous Shooting: Hi or Lo. Both allow you to shoot continuously when the shutter-release button is held down. When set to Lo you can shoot up to three frames per second, while Hi allows you to shoot up to eight frames per second. You can continue shooting until either the memory card or image buffer is full, or when you release the shutter-release button.

Self-timer

This mode allows you to fire the shutter either two or ten seconds after pressing the shutter-release button. When activated, and the shutter-release button has been pressed, the self-timer lamp at the front of the A77 will flash and an audio signal will count down the time until the shot is taken.

Notes:

The maximum frame rate of Continuous Shooting depends on several factors, including the image quality selected, the read/write speed of your memory card, and the shutter speed used.

The image buffer on a camera is a temporary store for images until they are fully written to the memory card. The larger the buffer, the longer the camera can keep shooting at its maximum frame rate. Once the buffer is full, a camera will need to pause in order to empty the buffer by writing the images to the memory card: the read/write speed of the memory card determines the length of time this process takes. The buffer on the A77 is respectable, but after two to three seconds of Continuous Shooting Hi the frame rate will drop noticeably below eight frames per second until the buffer clears.

BRK C Continuous Bracket

"Bracketing" is when you take a number of shots, with a variable changing between each one. This allows you to choose later which of the shots is closest to your requirements. Bracketing is usually applied to exposure ("exposure bracketing"), although the A77 also allows it to be applied to white balance and DRO.

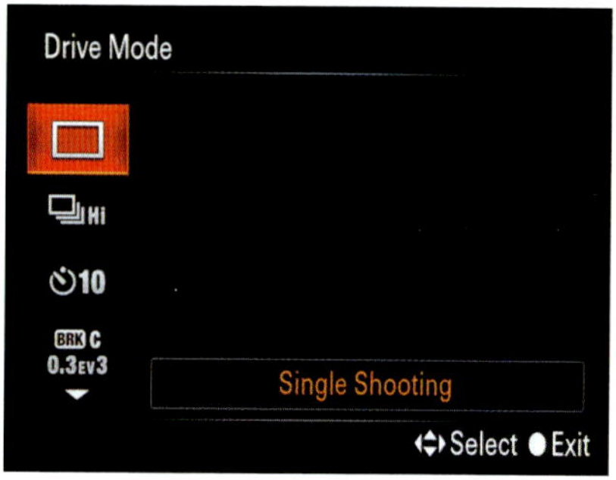

Continuous Bracket allows you to shoot either three or five shots at different exposure levels; the "correct" base exposure, one or two shots "overexposed," and one or two shots "underexposed" with a difference of 0.3, 0.5, or 0.7 stops. You can also shoot three shots bracketed with a difference of 2 or 3 stops. Bracketing your exposures is particularly useful if you plan to create HDR images in post-production.

BRK S Single Bracket

Single Bracket offers the same number of options as Continuous Bracket, but you need to press and release the shutter-release button to take each shot.

BRK WB White Balance Bracket

A similar idea to exposure bracketing, but the white balance is altered over three shots instead. When Lo is selected, white balance is shifted 10 mired between each shot; when Hi is selected this is increased to 20 mired. White Balance Bracket uses Single Shot advance.

DRO Bracket BRK DRO Hi & Lo

This option allows you to bracket the A77's DRO (Dynamic Range Optimization) settings. When Lo is selected, the DRO settings are bracketed using Lv1, Lv2, and Lv3. When Hi is selected, the DRO settings are bracketed using Lv1, Lv3, or Lv5.

Remote Commander

Select this option if you wish to use the RMT-DSLR1 Remote Commander (sold separately) with your A77.

> ***Note:***
> The order of the exposure bracketing sequence can be altered on the 4 menu.

2 » SMART TELECONVERTER

A teleconverter is an optical accessory fitted between a camera and a lens that increases the focal length of the lens by a set factor, such as 2x (which would double the focal length of the lens).

Sony manufacture teleconverters for use with the A77, but the Smart Teleconverter function achieves similar results digitally, simulating the use of both a 1.4x and 2x optical teleconverter by effectively cropping the image.

The drawback of using Smart Teleconverter is that image resolution is reduced. The same effect can also be achieved by cropping in post-production.

Using Smart Teleconverter

1) In Shooting mode press [zoom icon] once to zoom in 1.4x.

2) Press the shutter button to take the shot or press [zoom icon] again to zoom in 2x.

3) Press the shutter button to take the shot or press [zoom icon] a third time to switch Smart Teleconverter off.

4) Once a shot has been taken with the Smart Teleconverter the A77 will return to its standard shooting modes.

Notes:
Smart Teleconverter is unavailable when using Sweep Panorama, 3D Sweep Panorama, or Smile Shutter. It also cannot be used when the image quality is set to Raw or Raw+JPEG.

When Smart Teleconverter is in use, the AF area is set to spot and metering is set to multi-segment.

The recorded image size at 1.4x zoom is equivalent to the medium image size, at 2x zoom it is equivalent to the small image size setting. This is regardless of the image size set on the [camera icon] 1 menu screen.

SMART TELECONVERTER
At 1.4x the focal length of the 70mm lens used to create this image is effectively increased to 98mm and the area in the yellow box is recorded. At 2x, the lens is effectively a 140mm lens and would record the area in the red box.

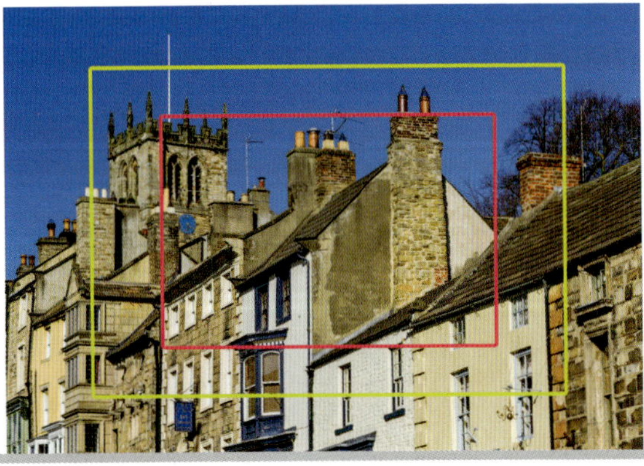

» EXPOSURE METERING

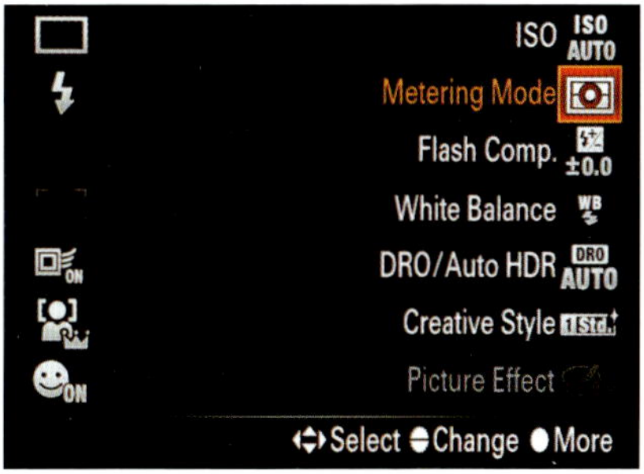

› Metering modes

The A77 offers three different metering modes, each of which is useful in very specific lighting situations.

Multi segment

Multi segment metering is the default on the A77. It's an extremely sophisticated metering system that divides the image into 1200 different zones, each of which is metered independently. The camera then calculates the exposure by comparing the information from each of these zones. This system is generally very accurate and can cope with a wide range of different lighting conditions.

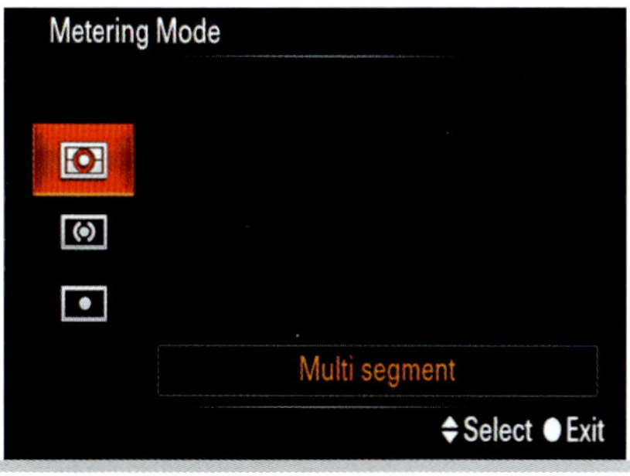

Center-weighted

This metering method measures the light level for the entire scene, but biases the exposure to the center. This is a good metering method to use if your subject is central in the image, and you want accurate exposure for your subject only. This is particularly beneficial if your subject is backlit, though this does run the risk that the background will be grossly overexposed.

Spot

The A77's spot metering mode takes a reading from a small area around the central focus point. Spot metering is a very accurate way of determining the correct exposure value for a small area of the scene and is useful when your subject is spot-lit so that the area around the subject is dark.

> **Tips**
>
> *Multi segment metering is also known as Evaluative or Matrix metering.*
>
> *Spot metering can be assigned to the AEL button, which is a useful way of quickly switching between Multi-segment and Spot metering modes.*

› Exposure compensation

The A77's various metering modes are designed to achieve accurate exposure under most shooting conditions. However, camera meters can be fooled. Using exposure compensation will allow you to override the camera's suggested exposure and choose your own interpretation of the scene. Exposure compensation can be set to a negative value, making the image darker, or a positive value, making it lighter. With the A77 exposure compensation can only be set in the **P**, **A**, or **S** shooting modes, but can be adjusted by ±5 stops in ⅓-stop increments.

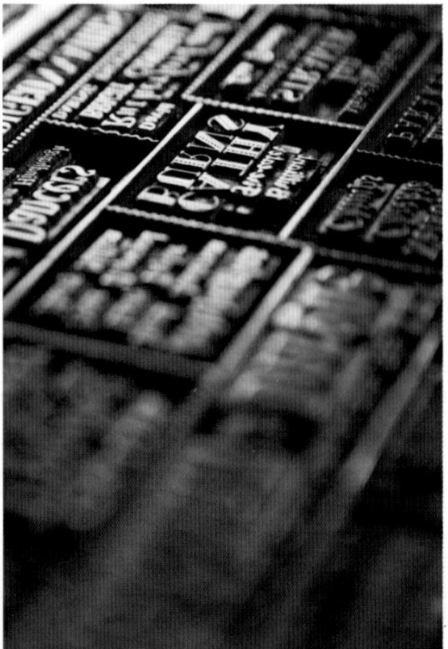

Using exposure compensation

1) Turn the mode dial to **P**, **A**, or **S**.

2) Compose your shot and partially depress the shutter-release button to obtain an exposure reading.

3) Check the exposure level indicator in the EVF or on the LCD to make sure that it is at the center of the exposure scale.

4) Press [±] and then press ◀ or turn either [front dial] or [rear dial] to the left to decrease the exposure, or press ▶ and turn either [front dial] or [rear dial] to the right to increase the exposure. The exposure will decrease or increase in ⅓-stop increments.

5) The exposure compensation effect will be seen on screen if **Live View Display** is set to **Setting Effect On** in the ⚙ 2 menu.

6) Change the level of compensation (if required) and then press the shutter-release button fully to take the photo.

7) Reset the exposure compensation value back to the center point.

TONAL RANGE «

Exposure compensation is most often required with scenes that don't have an "average" tonal range. This is because an excess of dark tones can cause the meter to overexpose; an excess of light tones can cause underexposure.

› Exposure lock

Generally you should find that the exposure your A77 chooses will be correct. However, there may be times when you need to set the exposure and recompose. As soon as you do this, the A77 will re-evaluate the exposure, with the distinct possibility that it then changes. To overcome this, you can lock the exposure by pressing the AEL (auto exposure lock) button. AEL is most effective when used in conjunction with [•] metering. Using [•] metering will allow you to precisely measure a very small area of the scene, without other areas affecting the exposure.

EXPOSURE LOCK
AEL is invaluable when light levels vary across a scene. For this image I spot metered from the lit green leaves, locked the exposure, and then recomposed.

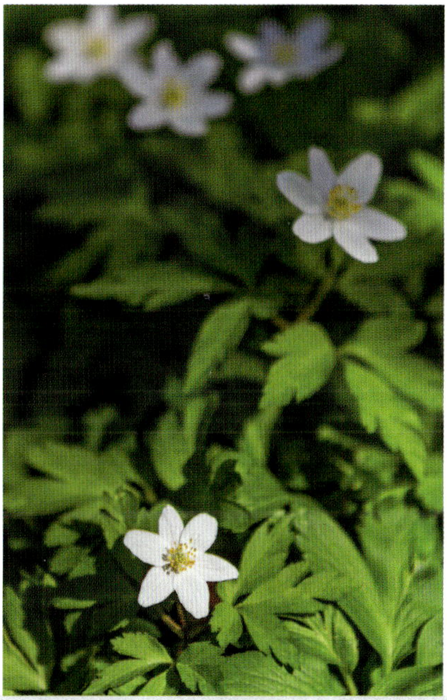

Locking the exposure

1) Press the shutter-release button down halfway to activate the exposure meter in the camera.

2) Press and hold **AEL**. ✱ will be displayed on the LCD or in the EVF to show that AEL has been activated.

3) Recompose and press the shutter-release button down fully to take the shot.

4) Release AEL to revert to non-AEL shooting, or continue to hold it down to take another shot.

Note:
You can modify the behavior of AEL on the ⚙ 3 menu, and set AEL to: **AEL hold** (default); **AEL toggle** (press and release AEL to toggle between AEL and standard exposure); [•] **AEL Hold** (temporarily switches to [•] metering and then locks exposure while AEL is held down); [•] **AEL toggle** (toggles between AEL with [•] metering when AEL is pressed and released).

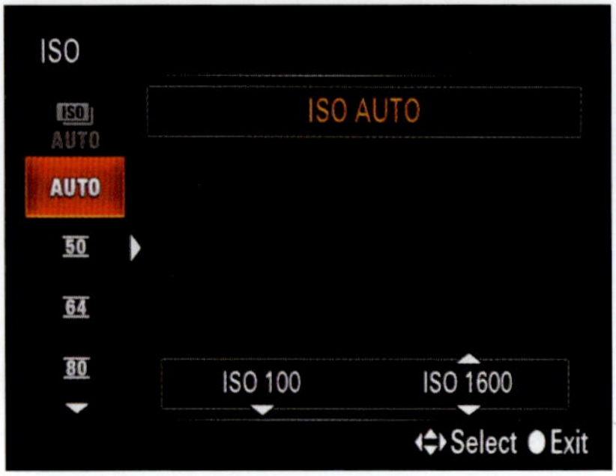

The ISO value controls how sensitive the sensor is to light: the higher the ISO value, the more sensitive the sensor is. This means that with a high ISO setting you can shoot in lower light levels and still maintain a reasonably fast shutter speed or smaller aperture. However, higher ISO values introduce "noise" into an image, reducing fine detail and making pictures coarse.

There are two types of noise: luminance and chroma. Of the two, luminance is usually the less objectionable, as visually it resembles film grain, albeit with a more regular pattern. Chroma noise causes color blotching and is less aesthetically pleasing. It is also more difficult to remove successfully.

Digital sensors produce the best image quality when set to their base ISO, and with the A77 that base ISO is 100. There are, however, ISO settings that are lower than this, with ISO 50 being the lowest value. These settings are useful if you need a longer shutter speed than ISO 100 would allow, but you need to understand that the A77 "cheats" to achieve these settings. The image captured at ISO 50 is actually overexposed by 1 stop, which is then adjusted back to normal. You can achieve the same effect yourself by setting the ISO to 100, setting exposure compensation to +1, and then correcting the exposure in post-production.

The drawback to using IS0 50, 64, or 80 is that the dynamic range is compromised, which means it is more likely that the highlights will be lost. As a result, it is recommended that you only use these settings when the light is relatively soft.

Tips

Doubling the ISO value is equivalent to a 1-stop increase in the sensitivity of the sensor, while halving the ISO decreases sensor sensitivity by 1-stop.

When High ISO NR (noise reduction) is enabled the A77 will attempt to reduce noise in your JPEG images if the ISO is set to ISO 1600 or higher.

FOREVER *(opposite)*
Black-and-white photography has a timeless feel that color can't come close to.

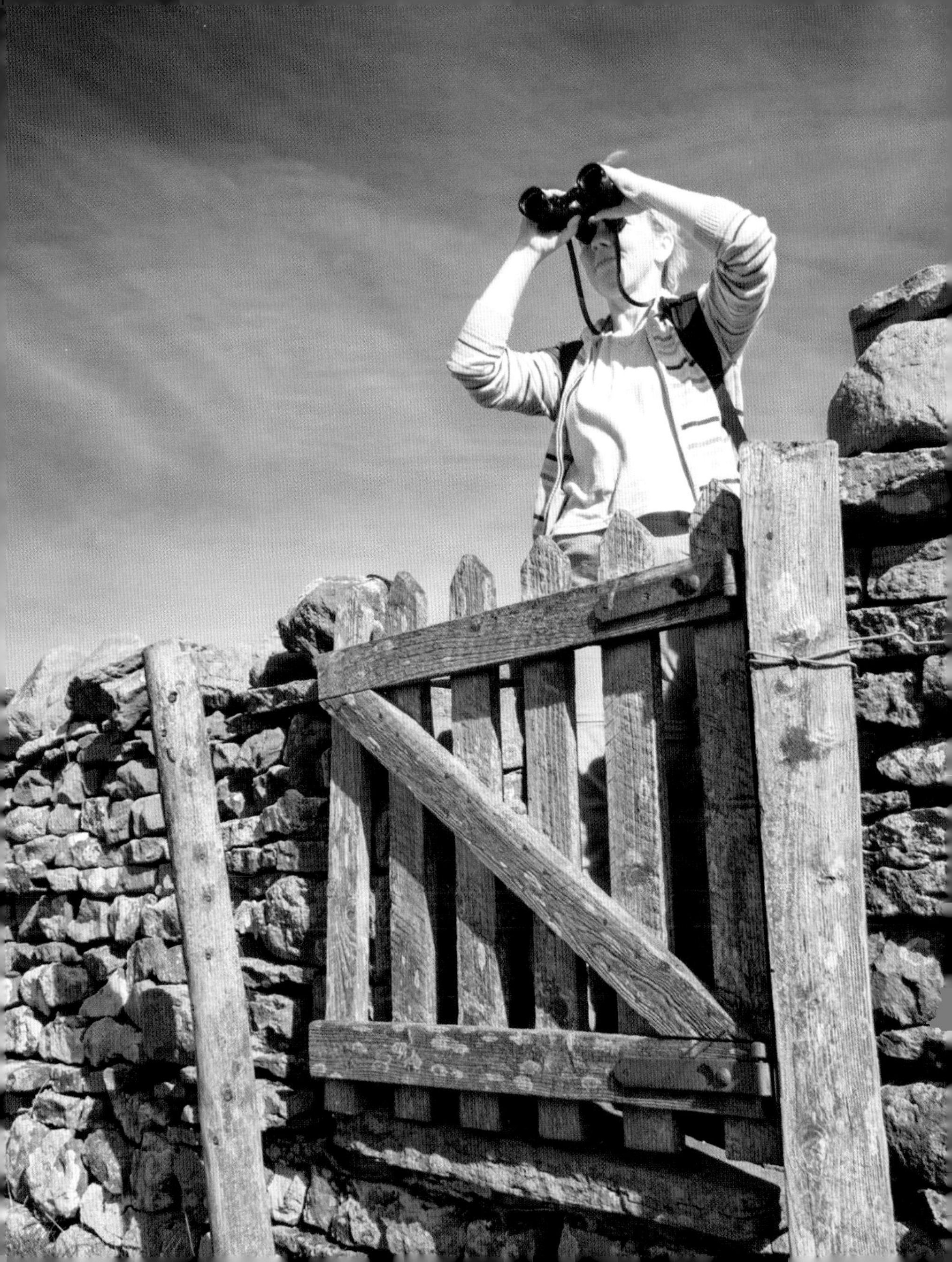

› ISO settings

You can either select the ISO setting manually on your A77; allow the camera to choose the ISO automatically depending on the lighting conditions; or, in certain shooting modes, shoot multiple frames that are combined to reduce the occurrence of noise in the final image. You can choose a higher ISO setting than normal with this latter option.

Setting an ISO value manually

1) Press **Fn** and highlight **ISO**. By default **AUTO** is selected. Press ●.

2) Use ▲/▼ to highlight an ISO value between ISO 50 and ISO 16,000. Press ● again to return to shooting mode.

Setting AUTO ISO

1) Press **Fn** and highlight **ISO**. Press ●.

2) Use ▲/▼ to highlight **AUTO**.

3) You can set the ISO range that the A77 chooses from. If you don't want to set this, press ● to return to shooting mode. Otherwise, press ▶ and then, with **ISO AUTO Minimum** highlighted, use ▲/▼ to set the lowest ISO value you want the camera to use. Use a lower value if you want to prioritize image quality and a higher value to prioritize shutter speed.

4) Press ▶ to highlight **ISO AUTO Maximum**, and use ▲/▼ to set the highest value you want AUTO ISO to use. Use a lower value to restrict the ISO range the A77 chooses from, and a higher value to increase the range.

5) When you've finished, press ● to return to shooting mode.

Multi Frame Noise Reduction

1) Press **Fn** and highlight ISO. Press ●.

2) Use ▲/▼ to highlight **Multi Frame Noise Reduct**.

3) Press ▶ and use ▲/▼ to select an ISO value. The lowest value you can choose is ISO 100, while the highest ISO is extended to ISO 25,600.

4) Press ● to return to shooting mode.

NOISE *(opposite)* »
Changing the ISO can have a dramatic effect on image quality. The image on the opposite page was shot using ISO settings ranging from ISO 100 to ISO 12,800.

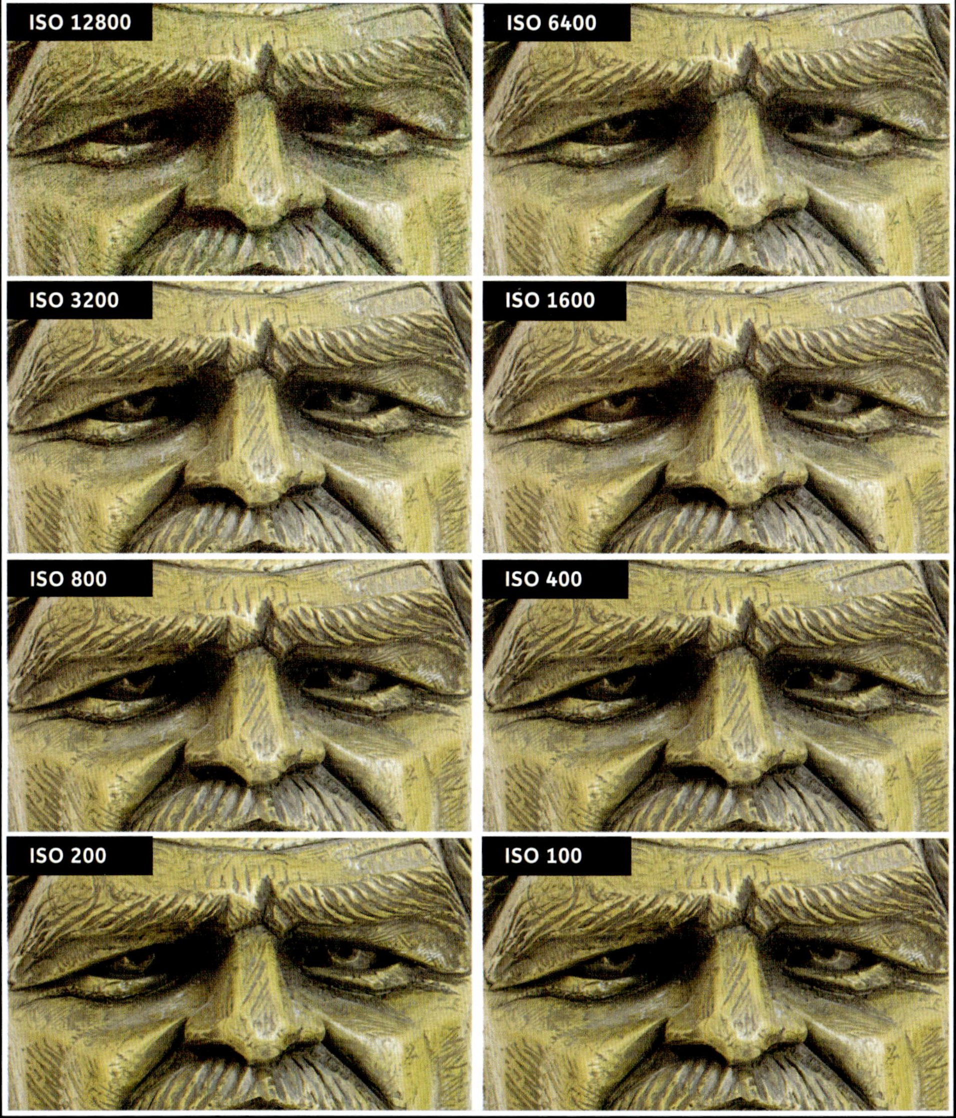
ISO 12800
ISO 6400
ISO 3200
ISO 1600
ISO 800
ISO 400
ISO 200
ISO 100

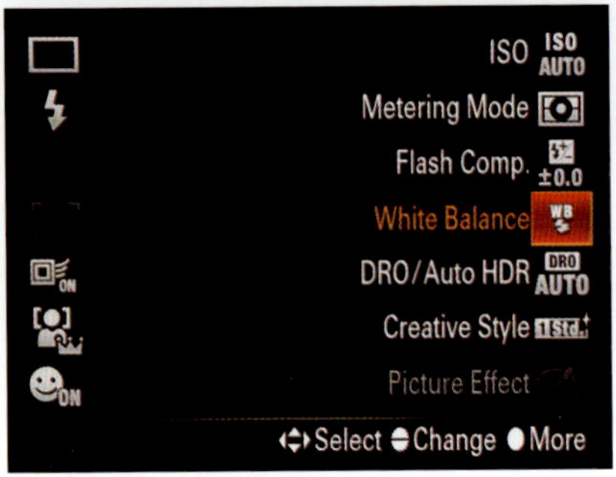

› White balance

What we perceive to be a neutral white light source may be anything but. This is because the human brain is remarkably adept at filtering out any color tint to light, unless that color tinting is extreme.

This variation in the color of light is known as a difference in the color temperature and is measured in degrees Kelvin (K): the lower the Kelvin value, the warmer the light. Candlelight, for example, has a Kelvin value of 1800K, but as the color temperature increases the light cools. Sunlight at midday is relatively neutral, with a color temperature of 5500K, while the light on an overcast day is far cooler, with a color temperature of 6500K.

White balance is the adjustment of a digital image to render white correctly by removing any color tinting caused by the light source: adding blue "cools" warm light, and adding red "warms" cool light. Certain kinds of light, such as fluorescent lighting, have a significant amount of green, and so magenta needs adding to counteract this.

The A77 offers a series of presets to correct white balance when shooting in different lighting conditions. You can also set the A77 to correct white balance automatically, create a custom white balance, or refine the standard presets.

SYMBOL/SETTING NAME	KELVIN	SYMBOL/SETTING NAME	KELVIN
AWB AWB (Auto White Balance)	–	0 Fluorescent: Cool white	4100K
Daylight	5200K	+1 Fluorescent: Day white	4750K
Shade	7600K	+2 Fluorescent: Daylight	5950K
Cloudy	6050K	WB Flash	7050K
Incandescent (tungsten)	2800K	K Specific Kelvin value	–
-1 Fluorescent: Warm white	3150K	Custom white balance	–

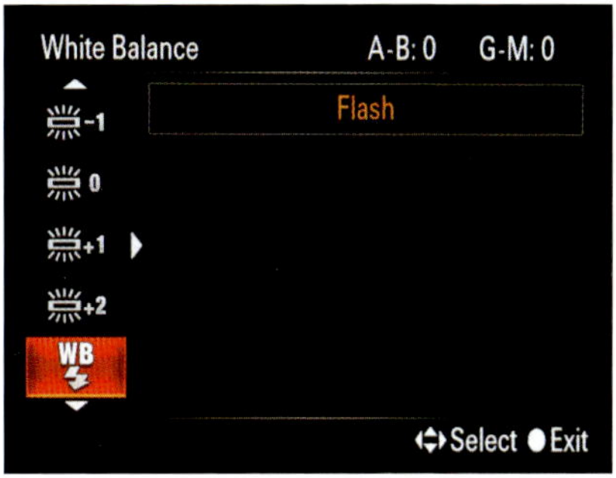

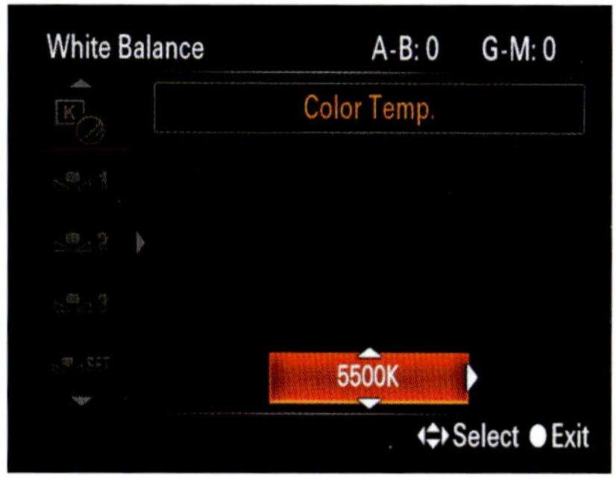

Using the WB presets

1) Press **Fn** and highlight **AWB White Balance** (**AWB** is the white balance preset selected by default). Press ● .

2) Use ▲ / ▼ to highlight a white balance preset. Choose the white balance preset that most closely matches the dominant light source your scene is lit by. As you move down the preset list the change in white balance will be shown immediately on the LCD and in the EVF if **Auto Review** on ⚙ 2 is set to **Setting Effect ON.**

3) Press ● to set the white balance and return to shooting, or press ▶ to fine tune the white balance preset further. When the White Balance Adjustment screen is displayed press ◀ to add more blue to the white balance; ▲ to add more green; ▶ to add amber; and ▼ to add magenta. When you've finished, press ● to set the white balance and return to shooting mode.

The A77 also allows you to set a specific Kelvin value between 2500K and 9900K in increments of 1000K, starting at the default of 5500K. You can also fine tune the white balance by adding blue, green, amber, or magenta, as described previously.

Setting the Kelvin value

1) Press **Fn** and select **AWB White Balance**. Press ● .

2) Use ▲ / ▼ to highlight K and then press ▶ .

3) Press ▲ / ▼ to select the desired Kelvin value.

4) Press ● to set the white balance and return to shooting or press ▶ to fine tune the white balance further.

› Custom white balance

For the greatest level of control over the white balance you should create a custom white balance. Up to three custom white balance settings can be stored on the A77, and it's important to note that a custom white balance should only be used in the lighting setup that has been measured, so if you move to a different lighting setup you should make a new custom white balance.

To set a custom white balance you need to have a neutral-colored surface lit by the same light as the scene you will be shooting. In the cover of this book is a white balance reference card that can be used for this purpose.

Setting a custom white balance

1) Press **Fn** and highlight **AWB White Balance**. Press ●.

2) Use ▲ / ▼ to highlight **SET**. Press ● again.

3) Move the camera so that the center spot is over your neutral-colored reference surface and then press the shutter-release button down.

4) The camera calculates and displays the suggested white balance setting. You can assign this setting to one of the three white balance registers by pressing ◀ / ▶. Press ● to set the custom white balance and return to shooting mode.

5) To use the custom white balance follow the procedure for setting a white balance preset, this time selecting one of the three options.

Notes:
When the mode dial is set to **AUTO** **SCN**, or **AUTO +**, white balance is set automatically.

If in doubt, you can use white balance bracketing to produce several different versions of the same image.

If you shoot Raw files you can adjust the white balance in post-production.

PEOPLE *(opposite)*
Skin tone is something that can look truly hideous when white balance is set incorrectly. Too cool in tone and the subject can look sickly; too warm and the subject will look jaundiced. Getting the white balance right for this image was tricky because the subject's luminous vest caused problems with **AWB**. In the end I made a custom white balance using the technique described above.

4500K

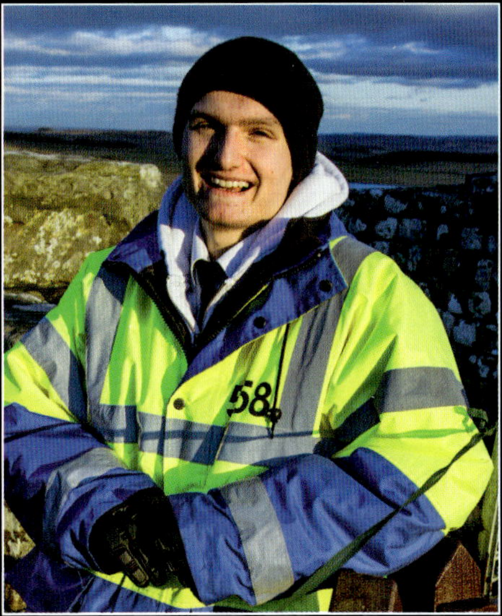

6000K (Custom white balance)

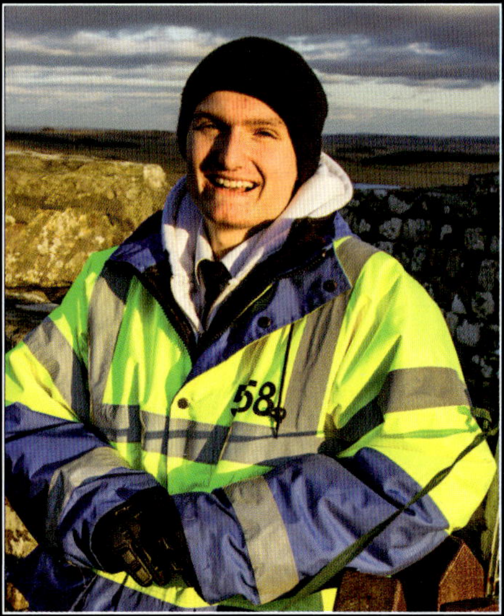

7500K

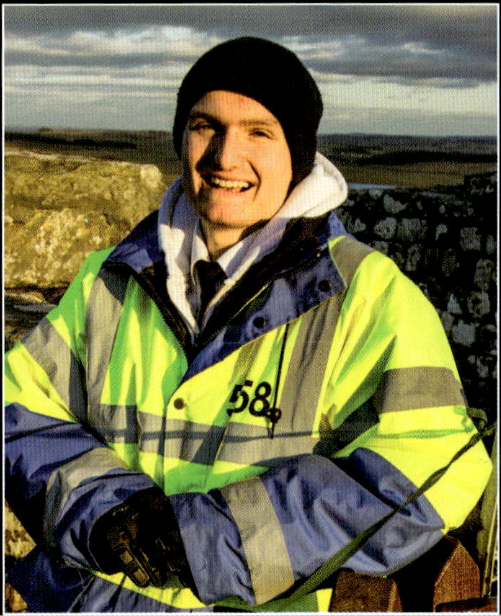

9000K

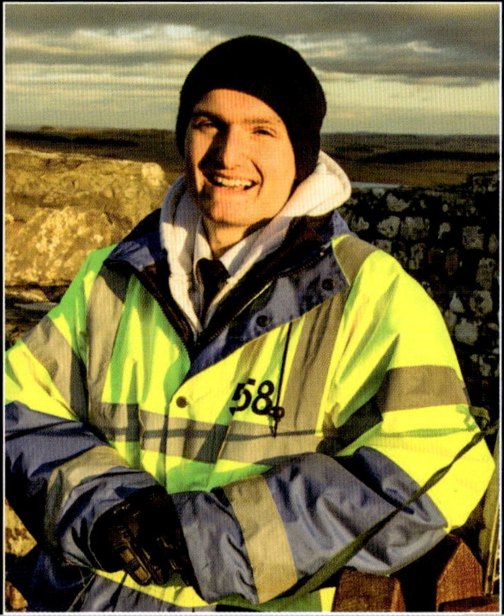

› DRO and HDR

The A77 can apply a certain level of contrast control in high-contrast situations, using what Sony calls Dynamic Range Optimizer (DRO). Although it has its limitations, DRO has its uses, particularly if you're struggling to maintain detail in the shadow areas of your images.

The A77 also has the ability to shoot High-Dynamic Range (HDR) images in-camera. When shooting HDR, three images with different exposures are taken and then merged to create a single image with improved contrast. When shooting HDR it's recommended that the camera is on a tripod to avoid movement as the three frames are shot.

SYMBOL	DESCRIPTION
D-R OFF	DRO is switched off—no optimization is applied to the image.
DRO AUTO	Divides the image into small areas and automatically applies contrast control where it is needed. This process will take time to complete and may reduce the number of images you can shoot consecutively in Continuous Shooting.
DRO Lv	Applies contrast control from weak (Lv 1) to strong (Lv 5).
HDR AUTO	The exposure difference between the individual frames is calculated and applied automatically.
HDR EV	Allows you to set the exposure difference from 1–6EV in 1EV increments. Use a lower value if the contrast range is low, and a higher value if the contrast level is extremely high.

Notes:
When using the A77's Dynamic Range Optimizer, images may exhibit more noise than usual.

The A77's HDR option cannot be selected when shooting Raw files or using AUTO, AUTO+, [panorama], 3D, [12], or SCN modes. It is also disabled when ISO is set to Multi Frame Noise Reduct.

› Creative Styles

When you're recording JPEG files, the A77 allows you to apply one of 13 different Creative Styles to the image, which alter the color, the contrast, or the sharpness of the image. Creative Styles should be used with care though, as they are permanently "baked" into the JPEG image and extreme settings, such as [B/W], will be difficult, if not impossible, to undo in post-production. Because of this, use the [Ntrl] setting if you intend to alter your images post-capture, as this will give you a neutral start point.

If you're shooting Raw, you can use Creative Style and the effects are applied, but they can be undone when the Raw files are converted using Image Data Converter. You can also apply Creative Style effects to Raw images using Image Data Converter.

SYMBOL	DESCRIPTION
[Std.] Standard	Renders the colors of the image as accurately as possible with a small boost to the contrast.
[Vivid] Vivid	The overall saturation and contrast in the image is boosted. This would give the effect of a high-contrast transparency film.
[Ntrl] Neutral	Color is less saturated, so images appear flatter and less intense. This option is ideal if you intend to make changes post-capture.
[Clear] Clear	Colors are boosted even more than Vivid.
[Deep] Deep	Darkens the image to convey a moodier feel.
[Light] Light	Lightens tones in the image so that shadows are less dense and the image feels more airy and (arguably) more romantic.
[Port.] Portrait	Skin tones are rendered as faithfully as possible. Reds will not be as saturated, and sharpness is reduced.
[Land.] Landscape	The saturation, contrast, and sharpness are all boosted to increase the vividness of the image.
[Sunset] Sunset	More emphasis is placed on the reds, oranges, and yellows in the scene, and the overall saturation and contrast are increased.
[Night] Night	Contrast is lowered to help deal with the high contrast found when shooting at night.
[Autm] Autumn/Fall	The vividness of red and yellow is increased so that the colors of fall foliage are more intense.
[B/W] Black & White	Color is removed from the image entirely so that it is rendered purely in shades of gray.
[Sepia] Sepia	Similar in effect to Black & White, but the image is given an overall brown tint.

› Picture Effects

Creating an artistic statement with an image was once only possible using image-editing software in post-production. However, your A77 allows you to apply one of 15 different processed picture effects to your JPEG images (if you choose to), arguably giving them an artistic gloss. The picture effects radically alter the look of your images, in a

SYMBOL	DESCRIPTION
OFF	Picture Effect is switched off.
Toy Camera	Recreates the effect of a Toy Camera lens (which tends to be of very low quality—introducing a vignette around the image corners and altering the colors). Use ◀/▶ to select Normal/Cool/Warm/Green/Magenta.
Pop Color	Boosts colors to create a "Pop Art" look.
Posterization	Creates a high contrast image. Use ◀/▶ to swap between Color and B&W.
Retro Photo	Reduces contrast and adds a sepia color cast to replicate the look of an old photo.
Soft High-Key	Brightens an image so that shadows are open. Creates an airy, romantic feel.
Partial Color	Removes all the colors except one from the image. Use ◀/▶ to swap between B&W+Red, B&W+Green, B&W Blue, and B&W+Yellow.
High Contrast Mono	Creates a high contrast black-and-white image.
Soft Focus	Adds a soft focus feel to your images. Use ◀/▶ to set the soft focus level.
HDR Painting	Three images are shot in rapid succession to create a grungy HDR image (visually different to Auto HDR).
Rich-Tone Mono	Creates a black-and-white HDR image by shooting three images in rapid succession.
Miniature	Recreates the narrow focus of a macro image, making the shot look like a miniature model. Use ◀/▶ to move the sharp zone of the image around the image frame.

way that is impossible to remove afterward, so if you are in doubt, shoot two versions of the image—one with the Picture Effect activated and another with it switched off.

If you're shooting Raw (or Raw+JPEG) you can't use Picture Effects and, unlike Creative Style, they cannot be applied retrospectively using Image Data Converter.

PICTURE EFFECTS

The A77 offers a range of Picture Effects that can be applied to your images.

> ***Notes:***
> Picture Effect is not available when shooting using AUTO+, AUTO, 12, 3D, or panorama shooting modes.
>
> You cannot use Mini or Toy when using Smart Teleconverter.
>
> If ! is displayed on screen after shooting using Soft or Rich BW, the camera wasn't steady during the exposure of the three images. You'll need to reshoot!

Picture Effect Off

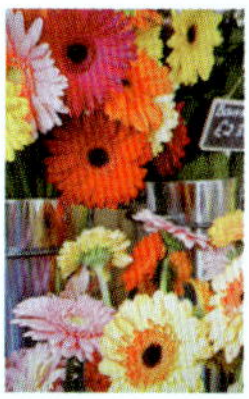

Toy Camera

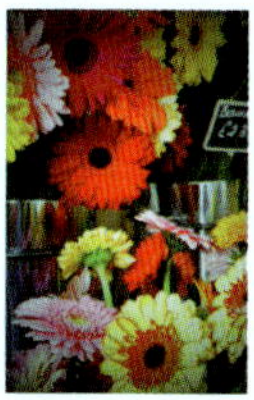

Pop Color

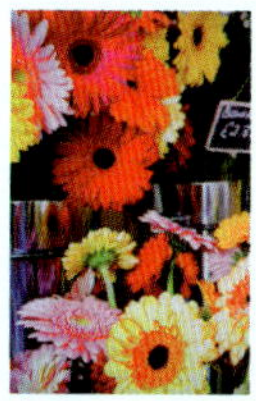

Posterization

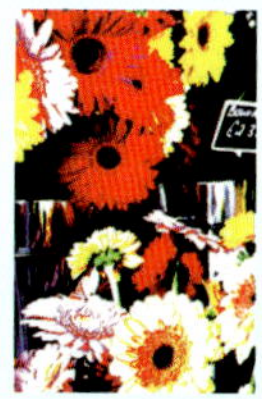

Retro

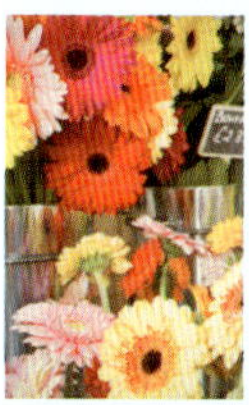

Soft High-Key

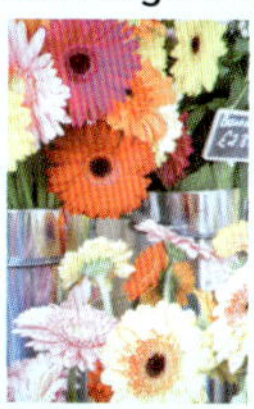

Partial Color (Red)

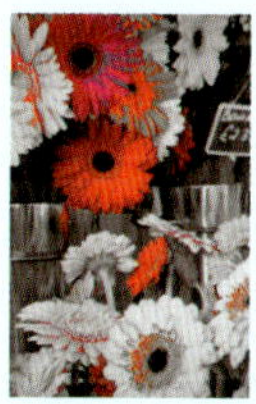

High Contrast Mono

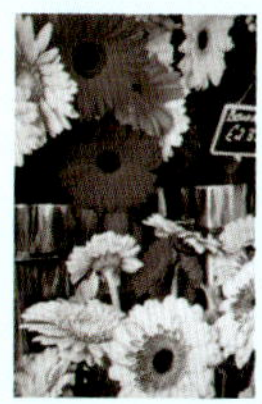

Soft Focus

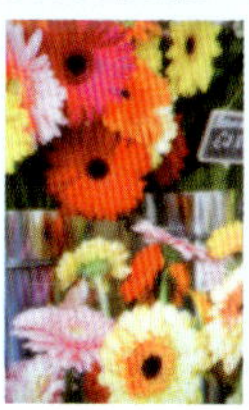

HDR Painting

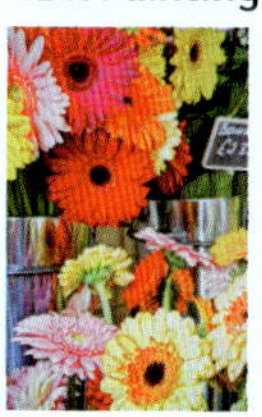

Rich-Tone Mono

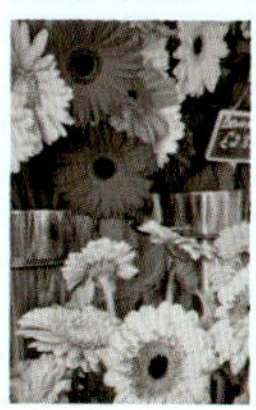

Miniature

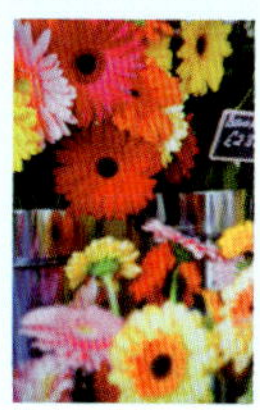

The mode dial allows you to choose from 12 separate shooting modes. Of these, 11 are still image shooting modes (and are covered in the pages that follow), while the last one is an HD video shooting mode, which is covered in detail in chapter four.

The still image modes can be divided into two broad categories: automated modes for specific shooting situations, and a less automated selection of modes that allow greater control over the camera. To select the desired mode, turn the mode dial until the appropriate icon is aligned with the white mark to the right of the dial.

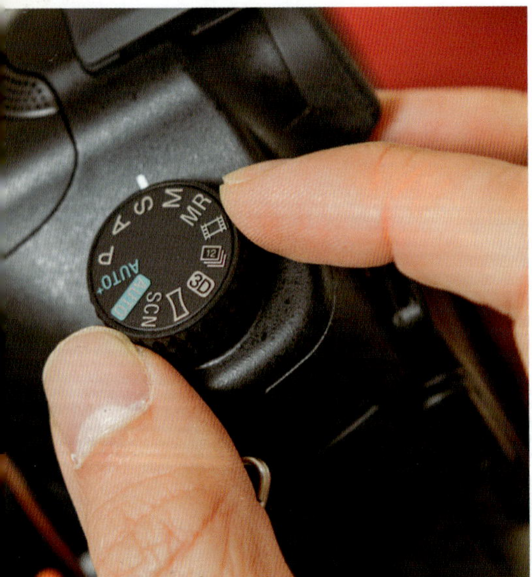

Mode Dial	
Memory Recall	MR
Movie	
Continuous Priority AE	12
3D Sweep Panorama	3D
Sweep Panorama	
Scene Selection	SCN
Auto	AUTO
Auto +	AUTO +
Program Auto	P
Aperture Priority	A
Shutter Priority	S
Manual	M

DAWN *(opposite)*
The colors of dawn are heavily dependant on the amount of cloud. I always check a weather forecast before setting my alarm clock for an early start.

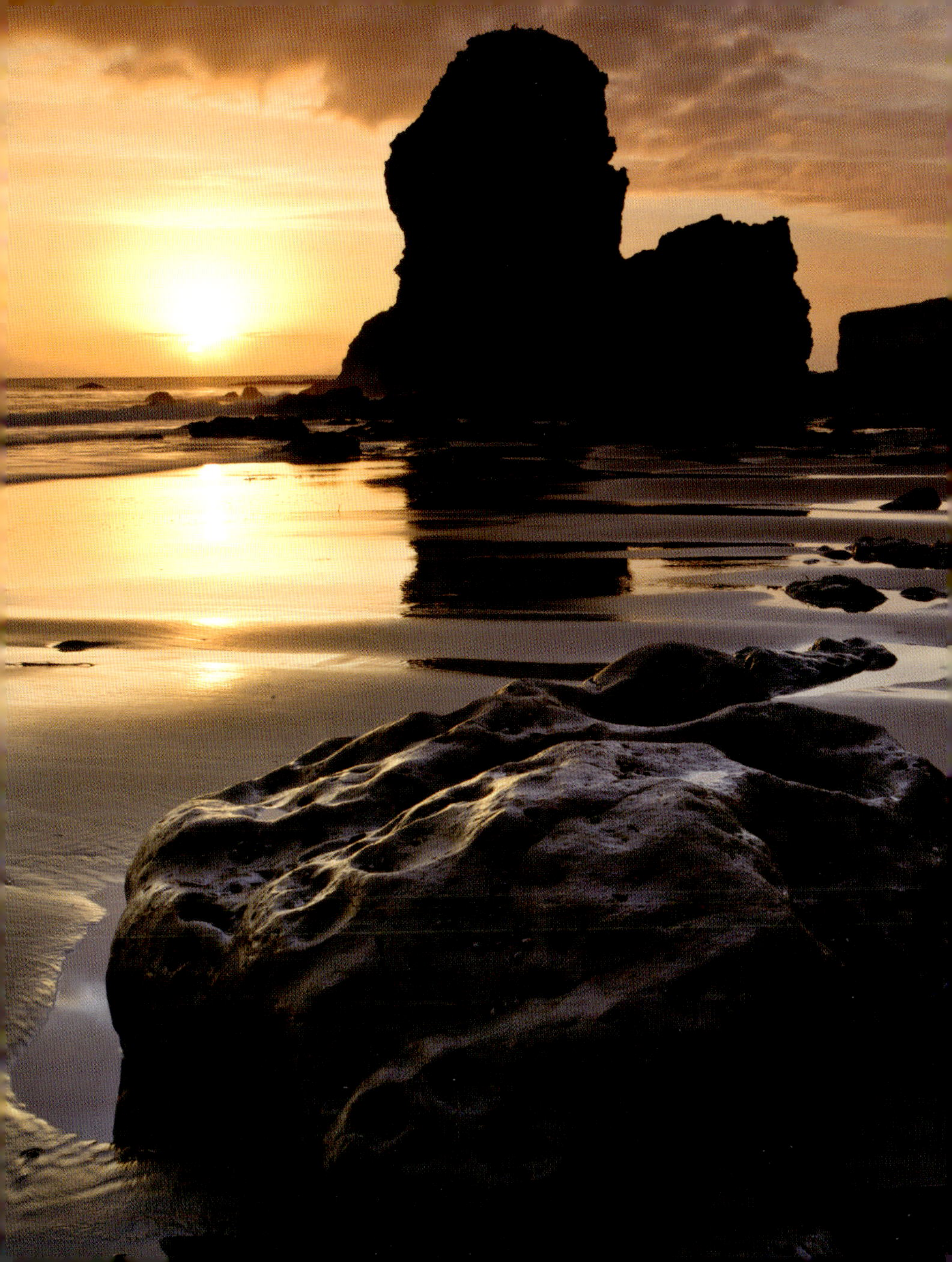

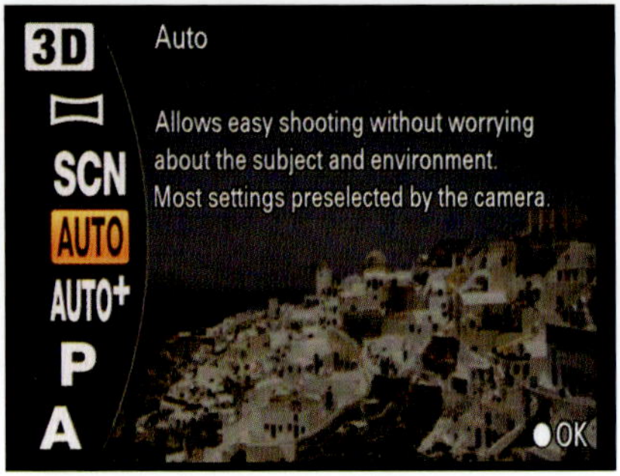

There are times when it's good to have a camera that you can snap with, without worrying about what functions need to be set. Turning the mode dial to AUTO changes your sophisticated A77 into a point-and-shoot camera, with all the work—bar composing the image—done for you.

In AUTO the A77 will automatically adjust its settings to suit the prevailing conditions, which is useful if you are in a fast-moving situation when there is little time to think about the optimum camera settings. The A77 will select the ISO, aperture, and shutter speed and will always try to bias the settings so that you can successfully use the camera handheld. If the built-in flash is activated, it will automatically pop up if required. The catch? If you want any creative input into your shots, AUTO will just get in your way.

> **Tip**
>
> *Set the flash mode to (flash off) in the* **Fn** *menu if you're in a shooting situation where flash would not be appreciated: this will deactivate the A77's flash.*

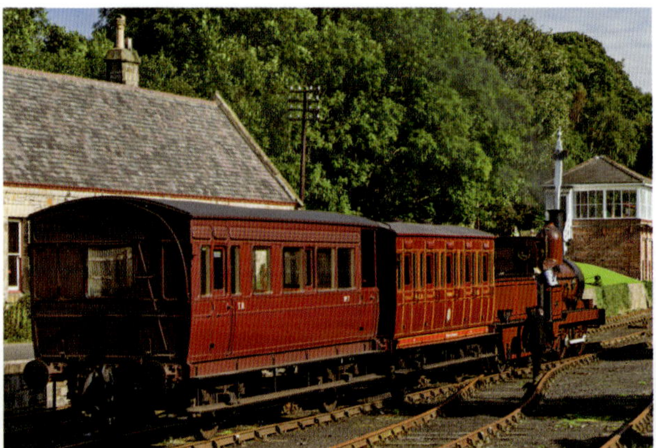

AUTO «
Auto is perfect when you're out for the day and don't want to worry about setting the A77's various controls.

› AUTO+ Auto+

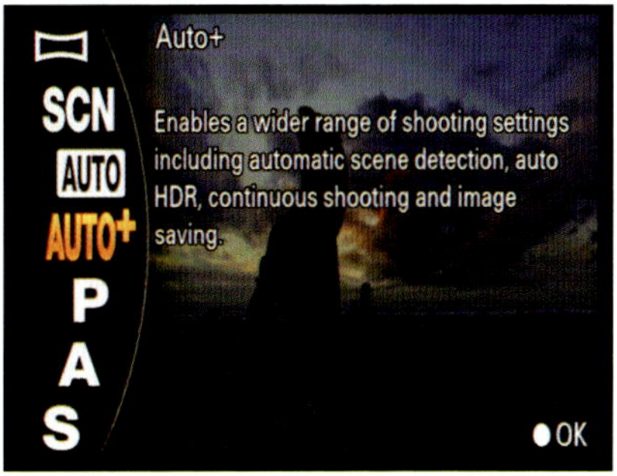

Unsurprisingly, **AUTO+** is **AUTO** with a little bit extra. That little bit extra is the ability to recognize the type of scene you're shooting and alter the shooting parameters to suit. After assessing the scene, the A77 will display an icon on the LCD and in the EVF to show what type of scene it thinks you are shooting. There will also be a short description of the shooting function it will use to achieve the best results.

ICON	DESCRIPTION
Night Scene	*See page 79.*
Backlit Portrait	Biases the exposure to the subject.
Backlit Scene	Biases the exposure to the subject, shooting Auto HDR if backlighting is particularly strong.
Spotlight	Adjusts exposure so that background isn't overexposed.
Handheld Twilight	*See page 79.*
Portrait	*See page 76.*
Macro	*See page 77.*
Low Brightness	Adjusts ISO to cope with subdued lighting.
Landscape	*See page 78.*
Tripod Night Scene	Shoots high-quality, low-light images with tripod support.
Night Portrait	*See page 79.*
Baby	Similar to Portrait.

SHOOTING FUNCTIONS	
Cont. Shooting	Slow Shutter
Daylight Sync.	Auto HDR
Slow Sync.	Handheld Twilight

› SCN Scene Selection

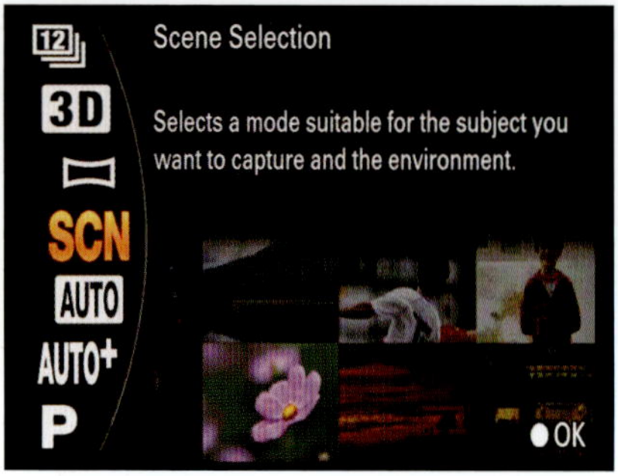

Scene Selection allows you to choose one of eight specific photographic categories. Each represents a commonly occurring photographic situation and the A77's performance is optimized for each of those moments. The camera sets the exposure controls of the camera (the aperture, shutter speed, ISO, and flash, if activated), as well as the drive mode, Creative Style, and white balance. How these controls are set will depend on the Scene Selection category chosen, which is the one big drawback: you give up a lot of creative choice for a more automated way of shooting.

To choose the desired Scene Selection category, turn the mode dial to **SCN** and then press **Fn**. Highlight the Scene Selection icon at the top left of the screen and press **Fn** once more. Press ▲ / ▼ or turn the control dial to highlight the desired category.

As you do this, a guide screen will display an explanation of the currently highlighted category. Once you've highlighted the required category, press **Fn** to return to shooting mode.

Portrait

As the name suggests, Portrait is designed to help you achieve pleasing shots of people's faces. To realize this, the A77 biases the aperture setting so that depth of field is minimized. This means that backgrounds will be relatively soft and so be less distracting; the longer the focal length of the lens, the greater the effect. Using a telephoto lens also creates a more natural perspective for your subject.

EYES

A portrait feels more direct when the subject looks at the camera. When the eyes are averted a more ambiguous feeling is evoked.

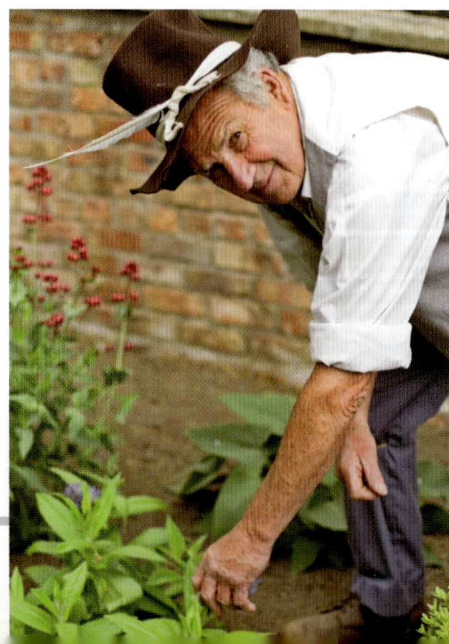

When depth of field is minimized your focusing needs to be accurate, which is why it is recommended that **Face Detection** is switched **On**. Visually, Portrait warms up the image slightly for more natural skin tones, and reduces sharpening so that blemishes or pores in the skin aren't distracting.

Sports Action

Sports Action gives priority to fast shutter speeds at the expense of the aperture (minimizing depth of field). The ISO is also increased, up to a maximum of ISO 1600, making your action images potentially "noisy." The drive mode is set to Continuous Shooting Hi, so keeping your finger on the shutter-release button will allow you to record multiple frames in quick succession.

Capturing fast action successfully isn't just about shooting wildly and hoping that at least one frame works. The most successful sports photographers understand their subject and can anticipate when the peak of action will occur and be ready to shoot at that point. This discipline was often honed by shooting on film, when exposing multiple rolls of film would incur unnecessary expense. If you intend to photograph a lot of sports or action, it's worth training yourself to think this way.

Obviously, digital images are essentially "free," but it can take time to work through hundreds of almost identical images: wouldn't you rather be out shooting other events than staring at a computer screen?

Macro

The Macro option can be confusing if you're used to using a compact camera, which often have a similar mode. When switched to Macro, the A77 is optimized to shoot macro, with the aperture and shutter speed set to minimize depth of field and reduce the risk of camera shake. However, unless you have a macro lens attached to your camera you will not actually be able to shoot macro images.

The 18–55 and 16–50mm kit lenses commonly sold with the A77 are not true macros, although with a minimum focusing distance of only 25cm and 30cm respectively, they will allow you to capture striking close-up images.

ACTION

Sports Action mode is suitable for any subject that moves, including animals and children.

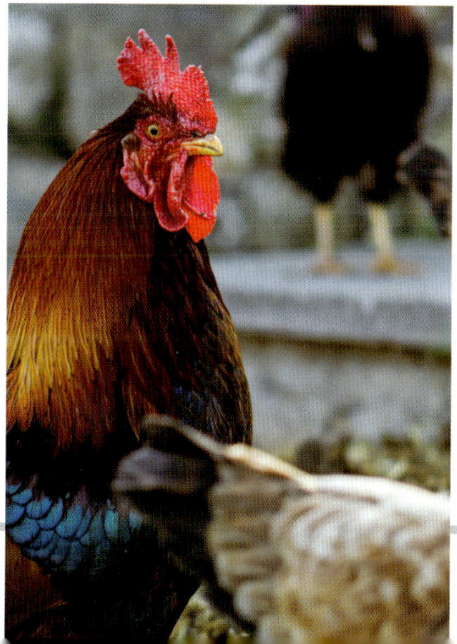

2

Landscape

Landscape Mode on the A77 is designed to enhance your landscape shots by boosting the saturation of greens and blues and increasing the contrast.

Landscape is a genre that embraces many styles. The "classic" approach involves using a wide-angle lens to capture the scale of a landscape, but there's nothing wrong with experimenting with telephoto lenses to capture a more intimate landscape.

The true landscape photography aficionado will be out either early in the morning or later in the afternoon, when the warm, low light helps to produce attractive landscape images. However, there are some subjects that benefit from the softer light found on overcast days. Woodland is one of these subjects. Soft light reduces the contrast range, making it easier to record detail in both the shadows and the highlights.

Sunset

The light from the sun travels more obliquely through the earth's atmosphere the closer it is to the horizon. This means that the light has to pass through a thicker slice of air. Because of this, the shorter blue wavelength component of the sun's light is scattered more, allowing the longer red and yellow wavelengths to dominate. This is what causes the light to appear "warmer" at the ends of the day.

Sunset mode gives nature a helping hand by boosting the reds and yellows in the image. This mode should be used sparingly, though: sunsets can be just as interesting when they are subtle as when they are dramatic.

HEIGHT
Finding a high viewpoint and shooting across a landscape is a good way of conveying a sense of scale.

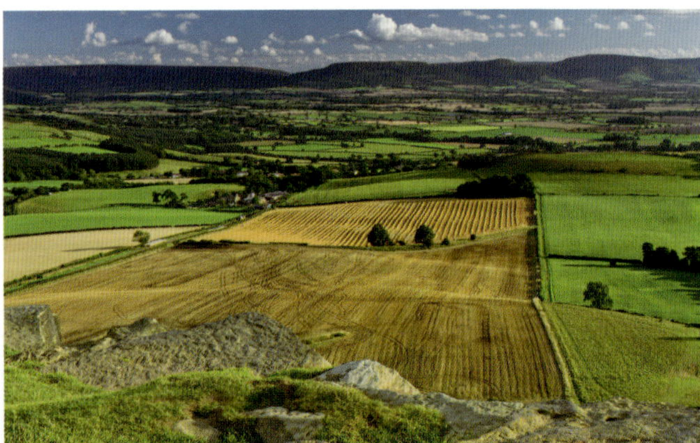

☽ Night Scene

Night Scene is designed for the trouble-free shooting of night scenes. When light levels are low, shutter speed invariably lengthens, so it's advisable to mount your camera on a tripod when using ☽.

Night isn't actually the best time to be shooting night images. This is because it becomes more difficult to distinguish the (usually unlit) roofs of buildings against the dark background when the sky is black. The best time to be out shooting at "night" is at twilight, roughly half an hour after sunset (or before sunrise). This is a time when there is still light and color in the sky.

Handheld Twilight

A tripod is a necessity at night, but what if you don't have a tripod handy and the shot of a lifetime has just presented itself to you? The answer is [Handheld Twilight icon]. When you shoot using [Handheld Twilight icon] the ISO of the camera is increased for a faster shutter speed. The camera then shoots several images in rapid succession before merging them to minimize the appearance of noise. This clever technology can produce impressive results.

Night Portrait

In Night Portrait mode the flash will fire to illuminate your subject, but the shutter will stay open to record the ambient light and expose the background (which won't be illuminated by flash).

Because the shutter speed will be longer at night, mounting your camera on a tripod (or other support) is highly recommended. If the shutter speed drops below 1/4 sec., ask your subject to keep as still as possible during the exposure. If they move during the exposure they will be recorded as a ghostly double image: the first image is lit by flash, the second by ambient light.

TWILIGHT »
This night scene was shot approximately 45 minutes after sunset. Not long afterward the sky was completely black.

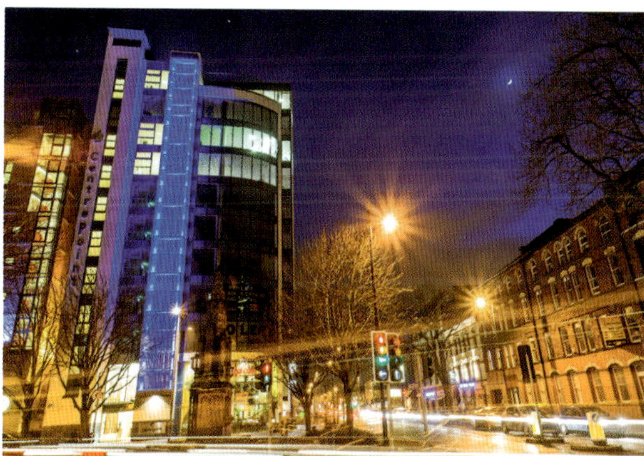

Sweep Panorama / 3D 3D Sweep Panorama

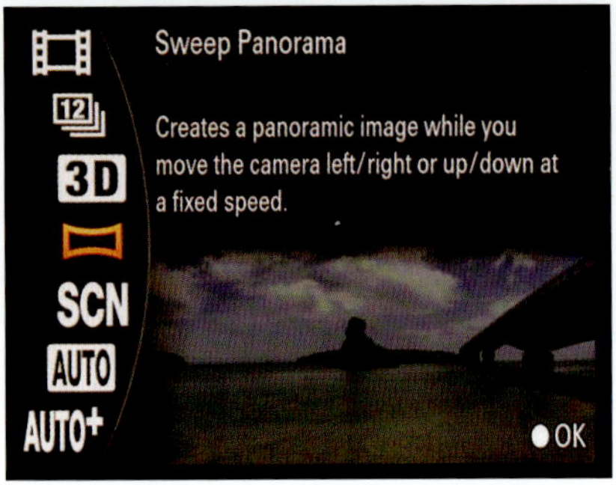

Panoramic photography is an increasingly popular genre of photography and is arguably closer to how we perceive the world than the standard image frame. and 3D allow you to shoot a panoramic image by panning the camera from the start point of the scene to the end point. The panoramic image is created in-camera so that there's no need to use special software afterward.

3D Sweep Panorama creates MPO images suitable for viewing on a compatible 3D HDTV. You can alter the resolution of the panoramic images before you start shooting and can also change the direction that you pan when creating a panorama.

To create a panoramic image set the mode dial to either or 3D. Point the camera at the starting edge of your panoramic image and press the shutter-release button down. Pan the camera smoothly, following the direction of the on-screen arrow until the positioning square reaches the far end of the guidance bar. The camera will take a few seconds to create a panoramic image. If you pan too slowly or too quickly you will be prompted to try shooting the image again.

Because the camera stitches images together, it is a good idea to try and avoid scenes with movement. Running water can be problematical, as can foliage blowing in the wind. If you're creating a panoramic image with people try to persuade them to stay still during the sweep process.

TELEPHOTO
Pan more slowly if you're using a telephoto lens rather than a wide-angle lens.

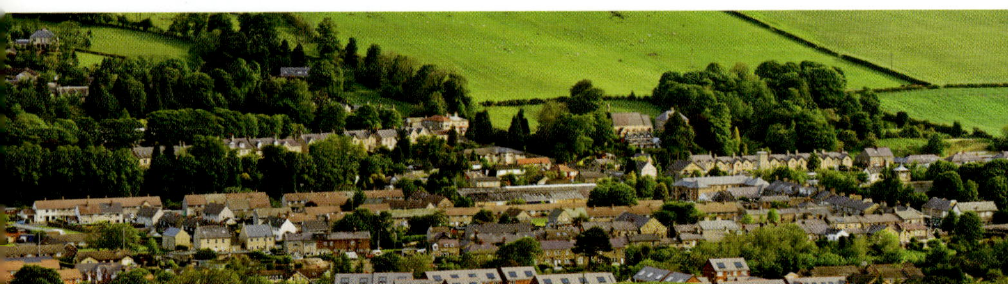

[12] Cont. Priority AE

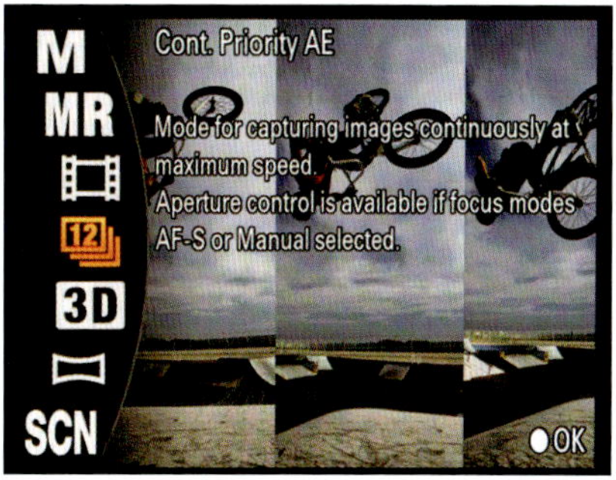

Continuous Priority AE sets your A77 to shoot at its maximum frame rate, which is approximately 12 frames per second: there are few cameras, even professional models, that can match this.

However, your A77 has to process each image as it's created, and generating 12 images per second means there is a lot of data to process. The images then have to be written to the memory card, and this takes time as well—the slower the memory card, the longer it will take. This means that you cannot just keep your finger on the shutter-release button and rattle off hundreds of images shooting in [12] —after a second or two you'll find the frame rate slows. Once you've finished shooting, there may also be a considerable delay as the images are written to the memory card.

Therefore, despite this mode being designed for fast action, there's still a need to anticipate the moment before the peak of the action. That way you can start shooting to capture the decisive moment before the camera is overwhelmed and slows down.

> **Tips**
>
> *When the A77 is set to Continuous AF, both the focus and exposure continue to be adjusted as the camera's shutter fires. ISO can be set before shooting, but the aperture value is fixed and cannot be altered.*
>
> *Using either Single-shot AF or MF allows you to alter both the ISO and the aperture before shooting.*
>
> *Face Detection is not available when using Continuous Priority AE.*

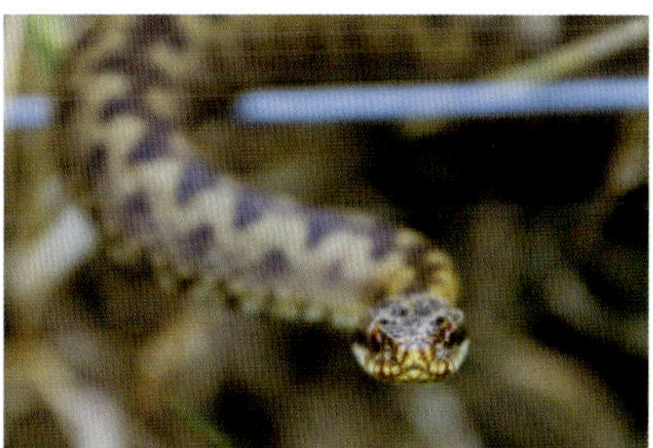

ANTICIPATION «
A good understanding of how your subject will act is the key to successful action photography.

› P Program Auto

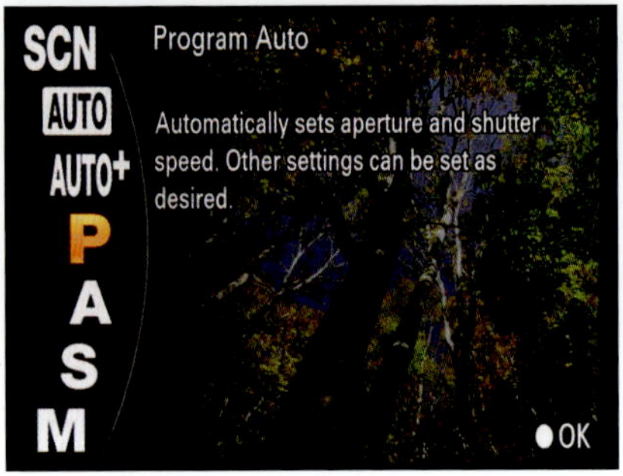

Program Auto is similar to Auto and Auto+ in that it allows you to shoot without needing to worry too much about the shutter speed or aperture. However, you can step in and adjust the exposure if necessary, using either exposure compensation or Program Shift. You are also free to use the full range of creative options on the **Fn** menu screen. Program Auto is a good halfway point between full Auto and modes such as Aperture Priority and Manual described on the following pages.

Although Program Auto sets both the shutter speed and aperture, you don't have to use the combination suggested. Program Shift allows you to "shift" the combination so that either the aperture is wider and the shutter speed faster, or the aperture smaller and the shutter speed longer than the original settings selected by the camera.

Tips

The flash is not automatically raised in Program Auto.

Auto ISO is useful if you're moving between areas where the light level fluctuates.

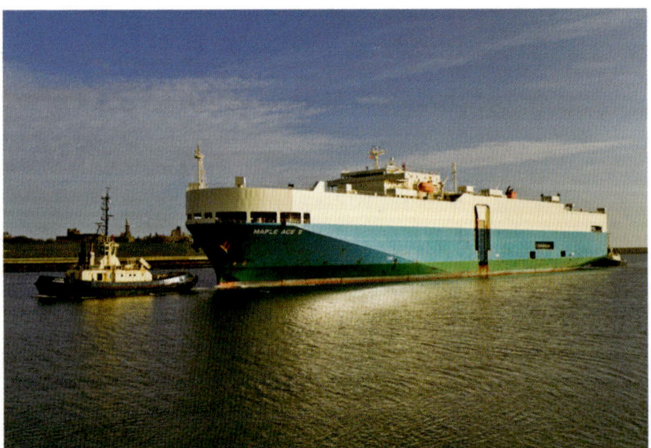

TIMING «
Program Auto is a good point-and-shoot option in rapidly changing situations where you also want to be able to make creative adjustments.

PROGRAM AUTO SETTINGS

The following options are available in Program Auto mode:

Image quality

File formats: Raw, Raw+JPEG, JPEG
JPEG compression: Extra Fine, Fine, Standard
Resolution: Large, Medium, Small
Aspect ratio: 16:9/3:2

Drive modes

Modes: Single shot, Continuous Shooting Hi, Continuous Shooting Lo
Self timer: 2- or 10-second delay
Continuous Bracket: 3 or 5 images at 0.3EV, 0.5EV, or 0.7EV increments
3 images at 2EV or 3EV increments
Single Bracket: 3 or 5 images at 0.3EV, 0.5EV, or 0.7EV increments
3 images at 2EV or 3EV increments
White Balance Bracket: Lo/Hi
DRO Bracket: Lo/Hi
Remote Commander: On/Off

Flash

Flash Off, Fill Flash, Rear Sync., Wireless, Flash exposure compensation

Focus

AF modes: Wide, Zone, Spot, Local,
Object Tracking: On/Off
Face Detection: On/Off

Exposure

Modes: Multi-segment, Center weighted, Spot

Tone

White Balance, DRO, Creative Style, Picture Effect (JPEG only), DR Correction (JPEG only), Shadow Correct (JPEG only), My Colors (JPEG only)

ISO

ISO Auto, ISO Manual (ISO 50–16,000), Multi Frame Noise Reduction

Using Program Auto mode

1) Turn the mode dial to **P**.

2) Point the camera at your subject. To use Program Shift either turn or to shift the exposure settings; **P ✱** will be displayed in the EVF to show that Program Shift is in use.

3) Lightly press the shutter-release button to focus. The focus confirmation symbol and active focus points will light in the EVF when focus is achieved. The exposure settings will also be displayed in the EVF.

4) Depress the shutter-release button fully to take the photograph.

› A Aperture Priority

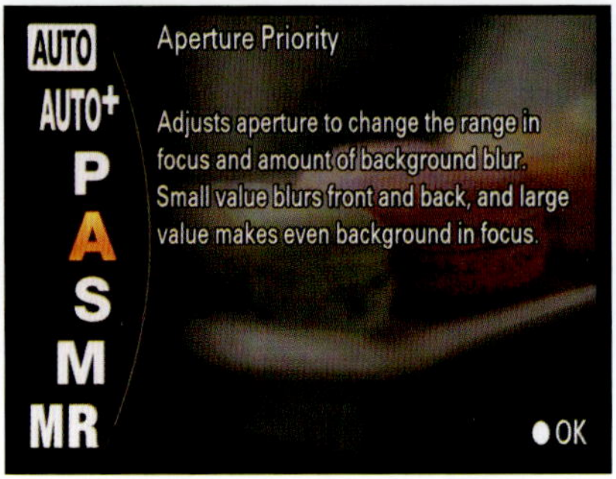

In Aperture Priority mode, you set the aperture that you want to use and the camera selects a suitable shutter speed. The aperture in a lens can be varied in size so that a precise amount of light is let through to the sensor. The size of the aperture is measured in f/stops, represented by f/ and a suffix number. A typical range of whole f/stops on a lens is f/2.8, f/4, f/5.6, f/8, f/11 and f/16—the greater the suffix number, the smaller the aperture. Each whole f/stop value on a lens represents either a doubling or halving of the amount of light, so f/8 will allow in half as much light as f/5.6, but twice as much light as f/11.

If this was all that the aperture did that would be valuable enough, but the size of the aperture also controls the amount of acceptable sharpness in an image. The sharpest part of an image is always at the point of focus, but, by making the aperture smaller, a zone of sharpness known as "depth of field" is extended out from the focus point. Depth of field always extends further back from the focus point than it does in front.

The smaller the aperture you use, the greater the depth of field and the greater the level of apparent sharpness in the image. However, there are two other factors that determine the extent of the depth of field. The first of these is the focal length of the lens, as depth of field is always greater at any given aperture with a wide-angle lens than it is with a telephoto lens.

The second factor is the camera-to-subject distance—the closer your subject is to the camera lens, the less depth of field you will be able to achieve, even with the aperture set to a lens's minimum. This is a particular problem when shooting using the A77's Macro mode.

SOFT
It's tempting to shoot with small apertures to achieve maximum sharpness across the image, but using a larger aperture can help to make your composition less cluttered.

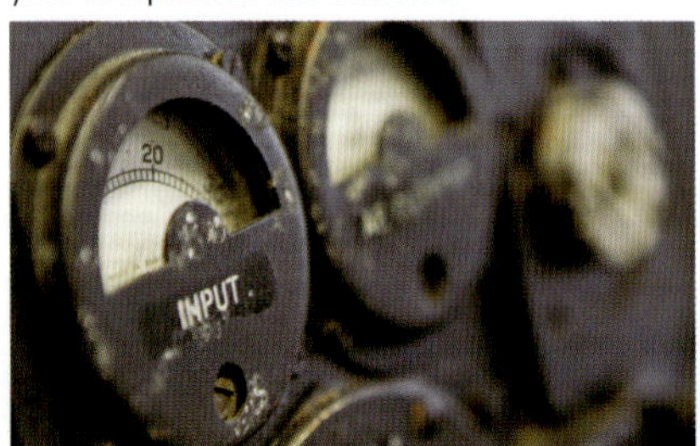

APERTURE PRIORITY SETTINGS

The following options are available in Aperture Priority mode:

Image quality

File formats: Raw, Raw+JPEG, JPEG
JPEG compression: Extra Fine, Fine, Standard
Resolution: Large, Medium, Small
Aspect ratio: 16:9/3:2

Drive modes

Modes: Single shot, Continuous Shooting Hi, Continuous Shooting Lo
Self timer: 2- or 10-second delay
Continuous Bracket: 3 or 5 images at 0.3EV, 0.5EV, or 0.7EV increments
3 images at 2EV or 3EV increments
Single Bracket: 3 or 5 images at 0.3EV, 0.5EV, or 0.7EV increments
3 images at 2EV or 3EV increments
White Balance Bracket: Lo/Hi
DRO Bracket: Lo/Hi
Remote Commander: On/Off

Flash

Flash Off, Fill Flash, Rear Sync., Wireless, Flash exposure compensation

Focus

AF modes: Wide, Zone, Spot, Local,
Object Tracking: On/Off
Face Detection: On/Off

Exposure

Modes: Multi-segment, Center weighted, Spot

Tone

White Balance, DRO, Creative Style, Picture Effect (JPEG only), DR Correction (JPEG only), Shadow Correct (JPEG only), My Colors (JPEG only)

ISO

Auto, Manual (ISO 50–16,000), Multi Frame Noise Reduction

Using Aperture Priority mode

1) Turn the mode dial to **A.**

2) Point the camera at your subject. Turn either [front dial] or [rear dial] to select the appropriate aperture value.

3) Lightly press the shutter-release button to focus. The focus confirmation symbol and active focus points will light in the EVF when focus is achieved. The exposure settings will also be displayed in the EVF.

4) Depress the shutter-release button fully to take the photograph.

› S Shutter Priority

The shutter in your A77 is a light-tight curtain that can be opened for a very precise period of time to expose the sensor behind it to light. The length of time the shutter is open is known as the shutter speed. In Shutter Priority mode you select the shutter speed you would like to use and the camera sets the aperture needed to produce the "correct" exposure. On the A77 you can set the shutter speed from its fastest setting of 1/8000 sec. all the way down to 30 seconds. You would use Shutter Priority when the shutter is more important than the depth of field. This is usually because there is movement in the scene.

The shutter speeds are varied by set amounts, such as 1/500 sec., 1/250 sec., 1/125 sec., 1/60 sec. and so on. The difference between each of these values is referred to as one "stop," with each stop representing either a halving (as the shutter speed gets faster) or a doubling (as it gets slower) of the amount of light that reaches the sensor. For example, a shutter speed of 1/500 sec. lets through twice as much light as 1/1000 sec., but half as much light as a shutter speed of 1/250 sec.

The shutter speed you choose will have a direct bearing on how the movement is captured in the final image and the faster the shutter speed, the more chance there is that the movement in the scene will be "frozen" (the faster the movement, the faster the shutter will need to be).

Slowing the shutter speed will make a moving subject appear more blurred and soft. This is often not a bad thing, as some softness can help to convey a sense of movement more effectively than pin-sharp detail. The slower the shutter speed, the more necessary a tripod or other support will become.

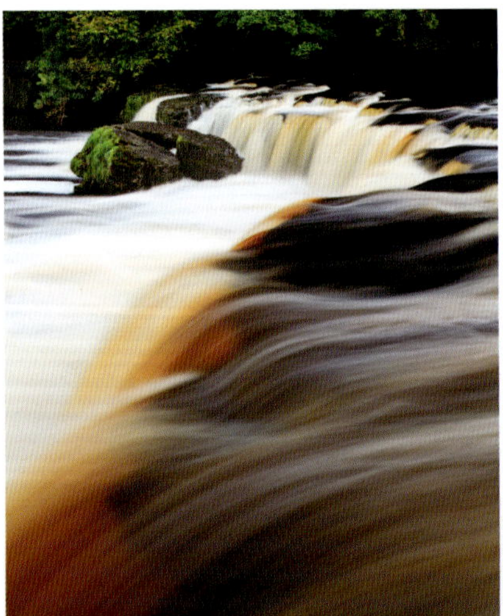

BLURRED «
A shutter speed of 2.5 seconds guaranteed that the water running over this waterfall would appear soft and flowing.

SHUTTER PRIORITY SETTINGS

The following options are available in Shutter Priority mode:

Image quality

File formats: Raw, Raw+JPEG, JPEG
JPEG compression: Extra Fine, Fine, Standard
Resolution: Large, Medium, Small
Aspect ratio: 16:9/3:2

Drive modes

Modes: Single shot, Continuous Shooting Hi, Continuous Shooting Lo
Self timer: 2- or 10-second delay
Continuous Bracket: 3 or 5 images at 0.3EV, 0.5EV, or 0.7EV increments
3 images at 2EV or 3EV increments
Single Bracket: 3 or 5 images at 0.3EV, 0.5EV, or 0.7EV increments
3 images at 2EV or 3EV increments
White Balance Bracket: Lo/Hi
DRO Bracket: Lo/Hi
Remote Commander: On/Off

Flash

Flash Off, Fill Flash, Rear Sync., Wireless, Flash exposure compensation

Focus

AF modes: Wide, Zone, Spot, Local,
Object Tracking: On/Off
Face Detection: On/Off

Exposure

Modes: Multi-segment, Center weighted, Spot

Tone

White Balance, DRO, Creative Style, Picture Effect (JPEG only), DR Correction (JPEG only), Shadow Correct (JPEG only), My Colors (JPEG only)

ISO

Auto, Manual (ISO 50–16,000), Multi Frame Noise Reduction

Using Shutter Priority mode

1) Turn the mode dial to **S**.

2) Aim the camera at your subject. Turn either or to select the shutter speed. If the shutter value flashes, the camera is warning that it cannot set a suitable aperture. When this happens, adjust the shutter speed until the selected value stops flashing.

3) Lightly press the shutter button to focus. The focus confirmation symbol and active focus points will light in the EVF when focus is achieved.

4) Depress the shutter-release button fully.

M Manual

Manual mode puts you fully in the driving seat when it comes to choosing the exposure for your image. You have to set both the shutter speed and the aperture yourself, so if the light changes and the image is over- or underexposed there will be no-one to blame but yourself if you forget to adjust the settings. However, this is also the beauty of Manual mode: you have complete control. This means you can deliberately ignore the exposure suggested by the camera and use whatever settings are necessary to create the image you visualize.

An image doesn't necessarily need to be "perfectly exposed." High-key images have a light, airy feel with few dark tones and open shadows. This means a high-key image could be considered overexposed, but for certain subjects a high-key exposure is appropriate. Portraiture, particularly when conveying a romantic feel, works well with a high-key treatment, for example.

Low-key images have the opposite feel, with few highlights and dark, dense shadows. This makes low-key images more dramatic, brooding, and atmospheric.

Manual exposure also allows you to use the A77's Bulb facility. Bulb enables you to lock the shutter open by holding down the shutter-release button (or using a remote commander with a shutter lock facility). This means the shutter can be open for minutes, or even hours. To use Bulb adjust the shutter speed past the 30-second point.

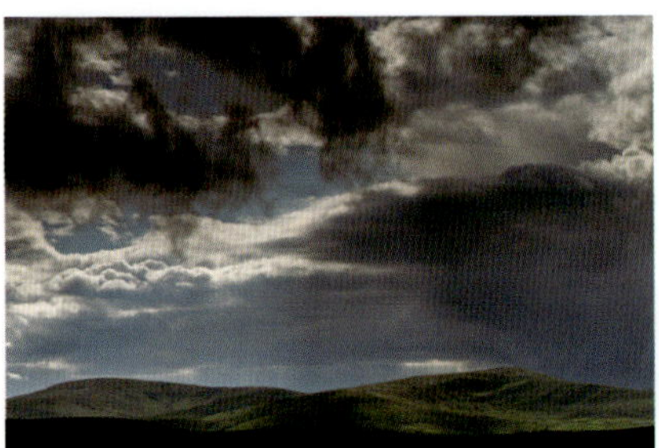

Tips

The  *camera shake warning indicator does not operate when you are in Manual mode.*

In Manual, Auto ISO is not available and will default to ISO 100 if Auto was previously selected.

You can confirm the exposure value (EV) on the LCD, or on the screen of the EVF. A correct exposure will be confirmed by ▼ directly above the 0 in the center of the EV scale. When the ▼ is to the left of 0, the image is likely to underexpose; when it is right of 0 the image is likely to overexpose.

CONTROL «
Use Manual exposure when you need precise control of the tonal range of your image.

MANUAL SETTINGS

The following options are available in Manual mode:

Image quality

File formats: Raw, Raw+JPEG, JPEG
JPEG compression: Extra Fine, Fine, Standard
Resolution: Large, Medium, Small
Aspect ratio: 16:9/3:2

Drive modes

Modes: Single shot, Continuous Shooting Hi, Continuous Shooting Lo
Self timer: 2- or 10-second delay
Continuous Bracket: 3 or 5 images at 0.3EV, 0.5EV, or 0.7EV increments
3 images at 2EV or 3EV increments
Single Bracket: 3 or 5 images at 0.3EV, 0.5EV, or 0.7EV increments
3 images at 2EV or 3EV increments
White Balance Bracket: Lo/Hi
DRO Bracket: Lo/Hi
Remote Commander: On/Off

Flash

Flash Off, Fill Flash, Rear Sync., Wireless, Flash exposure compensation

Focus

AF modes: Wide, Zone, Spot, Local,
Object Tracking: On/Off
Face Detection: On/Off

Exposure

Modes: Multi-segment, Center weighted, Spot

Tone

White Balance, DRO, Creative Style, Picture Effect (JPEG only), DR Correction (JPEG only), Shadow Correct (JPEG only), My Colors (JPEG only)

ISO

Manual (ISO 50–16,000), Multi Frame Noise Reduction

Using Manual exposure mode

1) Turn the mode dial to **M**.

2) Aim the camera at your subject. Turn to select the shutter speed and to change the aperture. You can adjust the aperture and shutter value together by holding down AEL and turning / .

3) Lightly press the shutter-release button to focus. The focus confirmation symbol and active focus points will light when focus is achieved.

4) Depress the shutter-release button fully to take the photograph.

STILL SHOOTING 1	Options
Image size	L:24M; M:12M; S:6M
Aspect Ratio	3:2; 16:9
Quality	Raw; Raw+JPEG; Extra Fine; Fine; Standard
Panorama: Panorama Size[1]	Standard; Wide
Panorama: Direction[1]	Right; Left; Up; Down
3D Pan.: Image Size[2]	16:9; Standard; Wide
3D Pan.: Direction[2]	Right; Left

STILL SHOOTING 2	Options
Long Exposure NR[3]	On; Off
High ISO NR[4]	High; Normal; Low
Flash control	ADI flash; Pre-flash TTL; Manual Flash
Power Ratio[5]	1/1; 1/2; 1/4; 1/8; 1/16
AF Illuminator	Auto; Off
Color Space	sRGB; AdobeRGB
SteadyShot	On; Off

STILL SHOOTING 3	Options
Exposure Step	0.3EV; 0.5EV
AF-A setup	AF-A; DMF
Priority setup	AF; Release
AF w/ shutter	On; Off
Memory	Three registration settings

Notes:

(1) ⌓ mode only. (2) 3D mode only. (3) Set to On in AUTO, **AUTO+** and **SCN** modes. (4) Not available when shooting RAW or when in Sweep Panorama, 3D Sweep Panorama, AUTO, **AUTO+** and **SCN** modes. (5) When Flash control is set to Manual Flash.

MOVIE MENU 1	Options
File format	AVCHD 50i/50p; MP4
Record Setting	50i 24M(FX); 50i 17M(FH); 50p 28M(PS); 25p 24M(FX); 25p 17M(FH)
Audio Recording	On; Off
Wind Noise Reduct.	On; Off
SteadyShot	On; Off

CUSTOM MENU 1	Options
Eye-Start AF	On; Off
FINDER/LCD Setting	Auto; Manual
Red eye Reduction	On; Off
Release w/o Lens	Enable; Disable
Auto+ Cont. Shooting[6]	Auto; Off
Auto+ Image Extract. [6]	Auto; Off

CUSTOM MENU 2	Options
Grid Line	Rule of 3rds Grid; Square Grid; Diag. + Square Grid; Off
Auto Review	10 Sec; 5 Sec; 2 Sec; Off
DISP Button (Monitor)	Graphic Display; Display All. Info; No Disp. Info.; Level; Histogram; For viewfinder
DISP Button (Finder)	Graphic Display; Display All. Info; No Disp. Info.; Level; Histogram
Peaking Level	High; Mid; Low; Off
Peaking Color	Red; Yellow; White
Live View Display[7]	Setting Effect ON; Setting Effect OFF

Notes:
(6) **AUTO+** mode only. (7) **P**, **A**, **S**, **M** and modes only.

2

⚙ CUSTOM MENU 3	Options
Func. of AEL button	Sets the function of the AEL button
ISO Button	Sets the function of the ISO button
AF/MF button	Sets the function of the AF/MF button
Preview Button	Shot Result Preview; Aperture Preview
Focus Hold Button	Focus Hold; D.O.F Preview
Smart Telecon. Button	Smart Telecon.; Focus Magnifier

⚙ CUSTOM MENU 4	Options
Ctrl dial setup	(front dial) SS (rear dial) F/no.; (front dial) F/no. (rear dial) SS
Dial exp. Comp	Off; (front dial) Front Dial; (rear dial) Rear Dial
Exp. comp set[8]	Ambient & Flash; Ambient Only
Bracket order[9]	0 - +; - 0 +
AF drive speed	Fast; Slow

⚙ CUSTOM MENU 5	Options
Lens Comp.: Shading	Auto; Off
Lens Comp.: Chro. Aber.	Auto; Off
Lens Comp.: Distortion	Auto; Off
Front Curtain Shutter	On; Off
Face Registration	New Registration; Order Exchanging; Delete; Delete All

Notes:
(8) **P**, **A**, **S**, **M,** (movie) and (12 continuous) modes only.
(9) **P**, **A**, **S**, **M** and (movie) modes only.

PLAYBACK 1	Options
Delete	Multiple Img.; All in Folder
View Mode	Folder View (Still); Folder View (MP4); AVCHD View
Slide Show	Repeat; Interval; Image Type
3D Viewing	–
Protect	Multiple Img.; Cancel All Images
Specify Printing	DPOF Setup; Date Imprint

PLAYBACK 2	Options
Volume Settings	0 (off) to 7
Playback Display	Auto Rotate; Manual Rotate

MEMORY CARD MENU 1	Options
Format	-
File Number	Series; Reset
Folder Name	Standard Form; Date Form
Select REC Folder	-
New Folder	-
Recover Image DB	-
Display Card Space	-

CLOCK MENU 1	Options
Date/Time Setup	Daylight Sav.: On/Off; Date Format: Y-M-D; D-M-Y; M-D-Y
Area Setting	Set time zone; Daylight Sav.

SET-UP MENU 1	Options
Menu start	Top; Previous
LCD Brightness	Auto; Manual
Viewfinder Bright.	Auto; Manual
GPS Settings	On; Off
Power Save	0 Sec; 20 Sec; 1 Min; 5 Min; 30 Min
HDMI Resolution	Auto; 1080p; 1080i
CTRL FOR HDMI	On; Off

SET-UP MENU 2	Options
USB Connection	Auto; Mass Storage; MTP
Audio signals	On; Off
Cleaning Mode	–
Delete confirm.	"Delete" first; "Cancel" first
AF Micro Adj.	On; Off

SET-UP MENU 3	Options
Version	–
Language	English, French, Spanish, Italian, German, Portuguese, Dutch, Russian, Swedish, Danish, Norwegian, Finnish, Polish, Czech, Hungarian, Greek, Turkish
Mode Dial Guide	On; Off
Demo Mode	On; Off
Initialize	Reset Default; Rec mode reset; Custom reset

» DEFAULT SETTINGS

Selecting *Initialize* on 🔧 Setup 3 will restore your A77 to the following factory settings:

GENERAL SHOOTING FUNCTIONS (*Reset with* Reset Default & Rec mode reset)	
Exposure compensation	±0.0
Drive mode	Single shot
Flash mode	Fill-flash (depending on whether built-in flash is open or not)
AF area	Wide
Object Tracking	On
Face Detection	On (Regist. Faces)
Smile Shutter	Off
ISO	AUTO
Metering mode	Multi-segment
Flash Comp.	±0.0
White Balance	AWB (Auto white balance)
Color Temp./Color filter	5500K, Color filter 0
Custom white balance	5500K
DRO/Auto HDR	DRO Auto
Creative Style	1/Standard
Picture Effect	Off
Scene Selection	Portrait
Movie Mode	P

📷 **STILL SHOOTING MENUS** (*Reset with* Reset Default & Rec mode reset)	
Image size	L:24M
Aspect ratio	3:2
Quality	Fine
Panorama: Size	Standard
Panorama: Direction	Right

3D Pan.: Image Size	Standard
3D Pan.: Direction	Right
Long exp. NR	On
High ISO NR	Normal
Flash control	ADI flash
Power Ratio	1/1
AF illuminator	Auto
Color Space	sRGB
SteadyShot	On
Exposure step	0.3 EV
AF-A setup	AF-A
Priority setup	AF
AF w/ shutter	On

MOVIE SHOOTING MENUS (*Reset with* **Reset Default & Rec mode reset**)

File Format	AVHCD 60i/60p, AVCHD 50i/50p
Record Setting	60i 17M (FH), 50i 17M (FH)
Audio Recording	On
Wind Noise Reduct.	Off
SteadyShot	On

CUSTOM MENUS (*Reset with* **Reset Default & Custom reset**)

Eye-Start AF	On
FINDER/LCD Setting	Auto
Red eye Reduction	Off
Release w/o Lens	Disable
Auto+ Cont. Shooting	Auto
Auto+ Image Extract.	Auto
Grid Line	Off

Auto review	Off
DISP Button (Monitor)	Display All Info./No Disp. Info./Level/ Histogram
DISP Button (Finder)	No. Disp Info/Level/Histogram
Peaking Level	Off
Peaking Color	White
Live View Display	Setting Effect ON
AEL button	AEL hold
ISO Button	ISO
AF/MF button	AF/MF Control Hold
Preview Button	Shot Result Preview
Focus Hold Button	Focus Hold
Smart Telecon. Button	Smart Telecon.
Ctrl dial setup	SS F/no.
Dial exp. comp	Off
Exp. comp set	Ambient only
Bracket order	0 - +
AF drive speed	Fast
Lens Comp.: Shading	Auto
Lens Comp.: Chro. Aber	Auto
Lens Comp.: Distortion	Off
Front Curtain Shutter	On

▶ PLAYBACK MENUS (*Reset with* **Reset Default**)

View Mode	Folder View (Still)
Slide show—Interval	3 sec
Slide show—Repeat	Off
Specify Printing—Date imprint	Off
Volume Settings	2
Playback Display	Auto rotate

MEMORY CARD MENU (*Reset with* Reset Default)

File Number	Series
Folder Name	Standard Form

SETUP MENUS (*Reset with* Reset Default)

Menu start	Top
LCD brightness	Auto
Viewfinder Bright.	Auto
GPS Settings:	
GPS On/Off (A77V only)	Off
GPS Auto Time Cor. (A77V only)	-
Power Save	1 Min.
HDMI Resolution	Auto
CTRL FOR HDMI	On
Upload Settings	On
USB connection	Auto
Audio signals	On
Mode Dial Guide	Off
Demo Mode	Off
Delete confirm.	"Cancel" first
AF Micro Adj.	Off

SETUP MENUS (*Reset with* Reset Default)

Recording information on LCD	Display All Info.
Recording information in Viewfinder	Level
Playback display	Single-image screen (plus recording information)

Note:
Restoring your A77 to factory default is a drastic step, particularly if you've spent time customizing the camera's various settings. Only reset your A77 if you have good reason.

COMPOSED

One of the keys to successful composition is knowing what needs to be excluded from a shot as much as what needs to be included. In this instance I framed the shot to exclude elements such as tree branches that would have proved distracting.

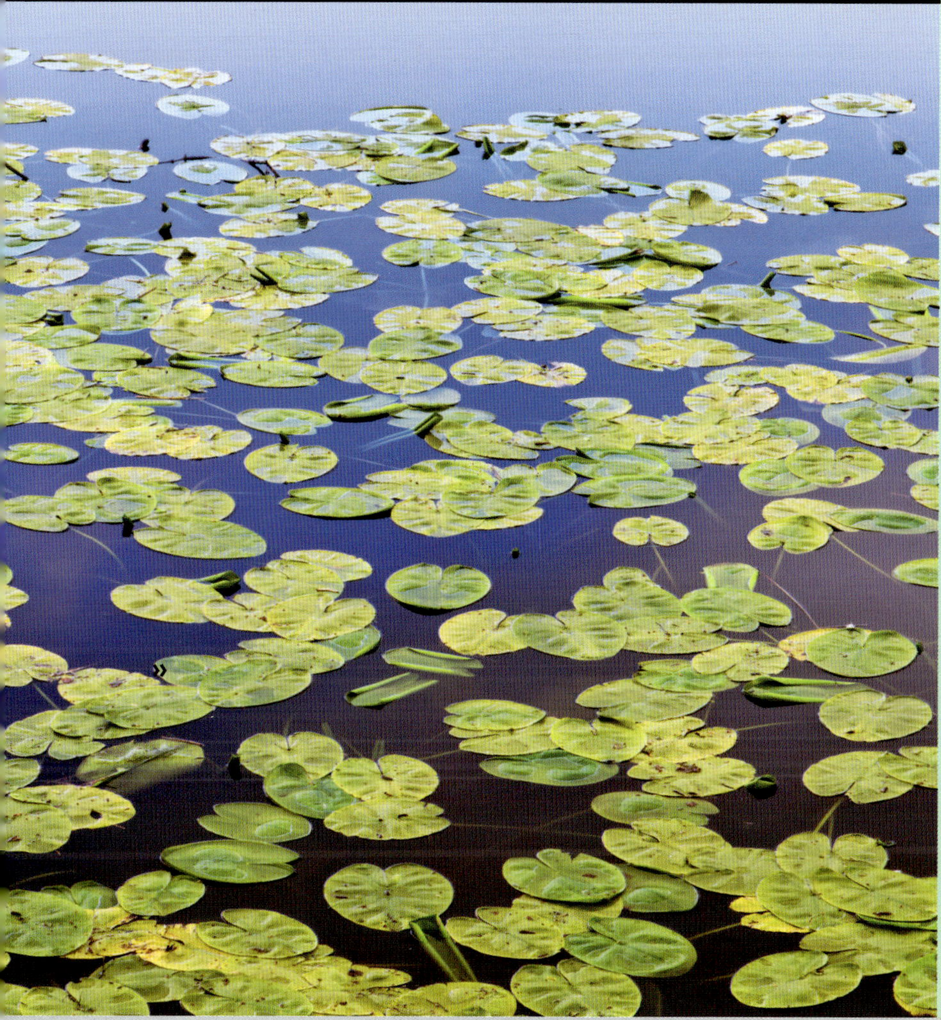

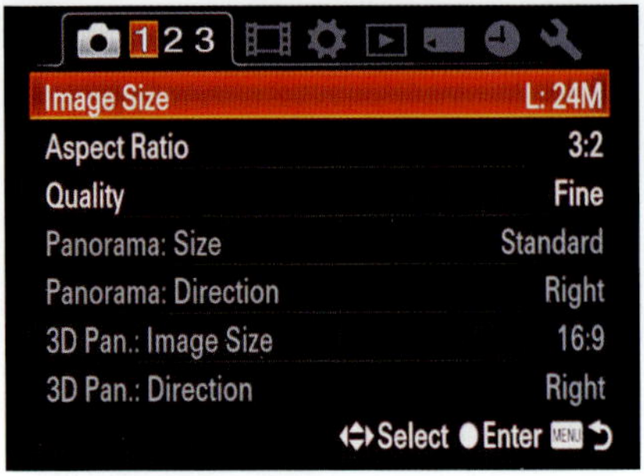

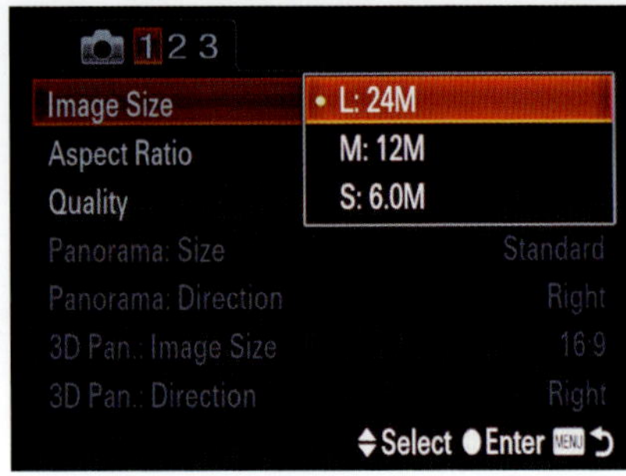

› Image Size

If your A77 is set to capture Raw files they will be saved at maximum image size. However, if the camera is set to shoot JPEGs you have the option of shooting at a lower image size. Shooting at a lower image size reduces the number of pixels in the image, which will also reduce the file size. However, a reduced image size will limit the acceptable size of prints made from the images later. There are three image sizes available: Large (**L**), Medium (**M**), and Small (**S**).

The size and quality of a print created from a digital image is specified by the Pixels Per Inch (ppi) value used. It is an arbitrary value assigned to an image using editing software such as Adobe Photoshop.

A ppi value commonly used when printing is 300ppi, which means that every 300 pixels in the image will equal one inch on a print. Using 300ppi, a print measuring 20 x 13.3 inches could be made from the largest image size captured by the A77 (6000/300 x 4000/300). If you change the resolution to 150ppi (without increasing or decreasing the image size) the print size doubles to 40 x 26.6 inches. However, there will be a drop in quality as the pixels in the image are "spread" across a greater distance.

ASPECT RATIO	LARGE	MEDIUM	SMALL
3:2	24mp 6000 x 4000 pixels	12mp 4240 x 2832 pixels	6mp 3008 x 2000 pixels
16:9	20mp 6000 x 3376 pixels	10mp 4240 x 2400 pixels	5.1mp 3008 x 1688 pixels

› Aspect Ratio

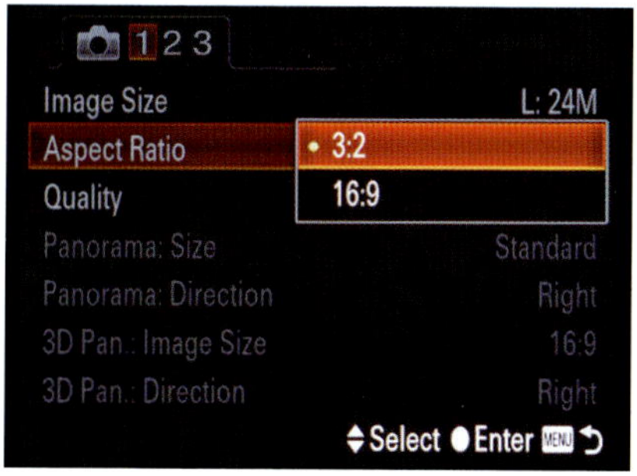

The aspect ratio of an image is the ratio of the width of an image to its height. The A77 offers a choice of creating images with an aspect ratio of **3:2** or **16:9**. The default setting is 3:2, which matches the aspect ratio of 35mm film. The 16:9 aspect ratio matches the standard used for HD video. When shooting in 16:9 the full resolution of the sensor is not used. Shooting at 3:2 and cropping in post-production will achieve the same effect as using 16:9.

Notes:

A larger print generally requires a greater viewing distance. Using a lower resolution (ppi) will reduce the quality of a print when examined closely, but this drop in quality is often not noticed at the correct viewing distance.

Image Size is not available when *Quality* is set to *Raw*.

› Quality

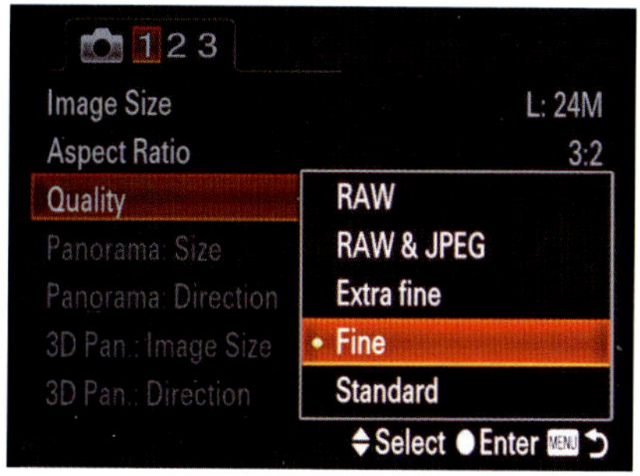

The A77 offers five quality settings: **Raw, Raw & JPEG, Extra Fine, Fine**, and **Standard**. Raw files offer the most scope for alteration in post-production, but they are less instantly usable. Raw files also take up more room on a memory card than an equivalent JPEG. If your memory card is particularly large, then Raw & JPEG saves both files to the card at the moment of capture, giving you the best of both worlds.

When shooting JPEG only, three levels of JPEG compression are available. Extra Fine has the least amount of compression applied, so image quality is maintained at the expense of the room taken up by each image on the memory card. At the opposite end of the scale Standard has the greatest amount of compression, giving the lowest quality but the greatest reduction in file size. Fine is between the two.

› Panorama: Size

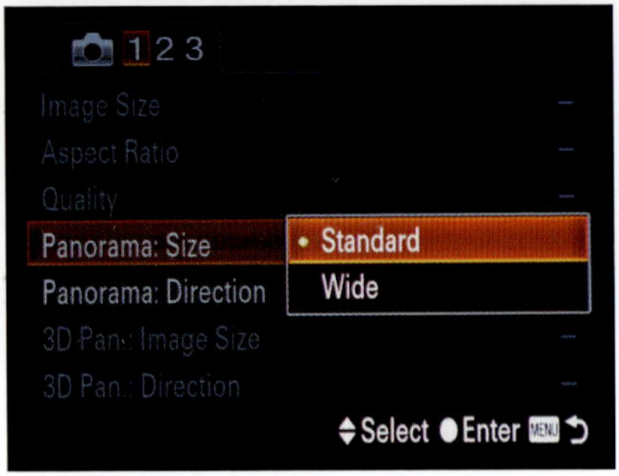

This option allows you to set the size of a panoramic image when using the Sweep Panorama shooting mode. The final size will also depend on the direction chosen to create the panoramic image.

When **Panoramic: Direction** is set to either **Up** or **Down, Standard** will create an image 3872 x 2160 pixels and **Wide** will create an image 5536 x 2160 pixels.

When **Panoramic: Direction** is set to either **Left** or **Right**, **Standard** will create an image 8192 x 1856 pixels and **Wide** will create an image measuring 12,416 x 1856 pixels.

› Panorama: Direction & 3D Pan.: Direction

Sets the direction that Sweep Panorama and 3D Sweep Panorama images are captured. The direction you choose affects the final size (in pixels) of the panoramic image when shooting in Sweep Panorama mode. Sweep Panoramas can be shot from the left

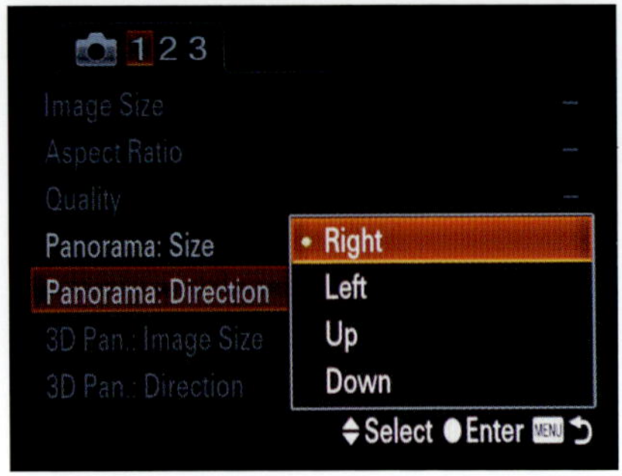

or right, up or down, but with 3D Sweep Panoramas you can only shoot from the left or right.

› 3D Pan.: Image Size

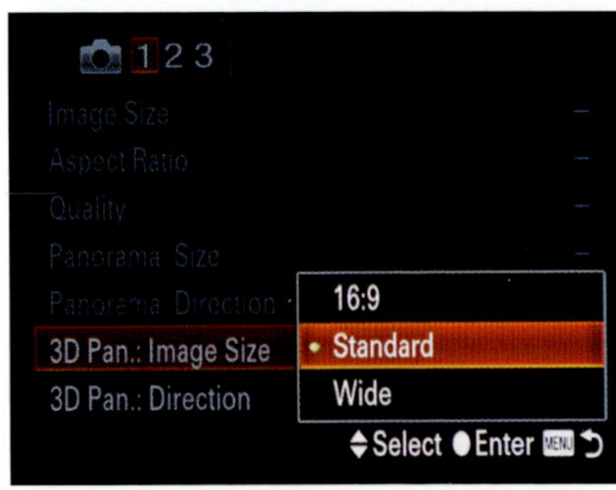

Sets the size of the image for the 3D Sweep Panorama shooting mode. There are three choices; **16:9**, which gives an image size of 1920 x 1080 pixels (the same size in pixels as an HDTV display); **Standard** for an image size of 4912 x 1080 pixels; and **Wide** for an image size of 7152 x 1080 pixels.

» STILL SHOOTING MENU 2

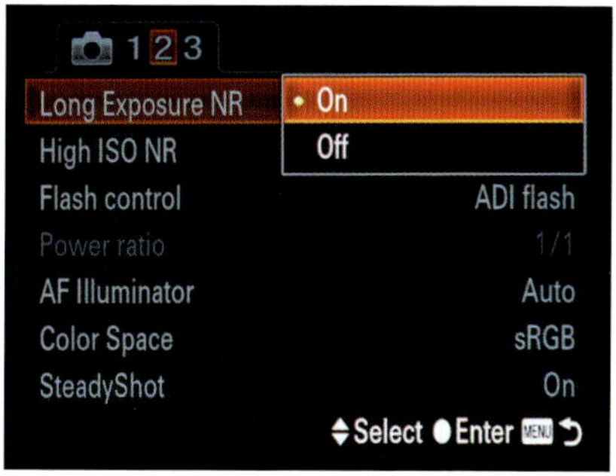

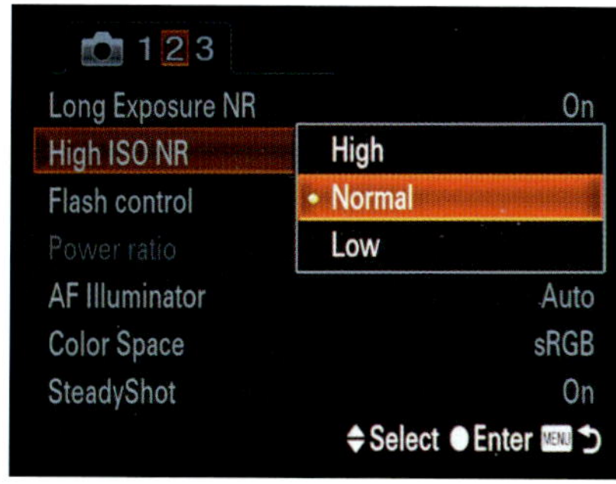

› Long Exposure NR

When the shutter speed is 1 second or longer you have the option of applying noise reduction to the image. The processing time taken equals the length of the original shutter speed, and during this processing time you cannot shoot.

Noise invariably builds up in an image during a long exposure, as heat and the camera's electronics affect the purity of the image data. However, this noise is actually fairly well controlled on the A77 and what noise there is can be removed in post-production. In most cases setting **Long Exposure NR** to **Off** will not be detrimental and will enable you to carry on shooting without pause.

› High ISO NR

When **High ISO NR** is set to **High**, the use of high ISO values will activate noise reduction. This noise reduction process may take a few seconds to complete and during this time you will not be able to shoot any more images. Set **High ISO NR** to **Normal** or **Low** to reduce the amount of noise reduction applied to your images, and to prioritize shooting speed.

› Flash control & Power ratio

See page 174 for more information.

> ***Note:***
> Using extremely long shutter speeds with **Long Exposure NR** set to **On** is a big drain on your camera's battery. Use a fully charged battery when shooting this way and carry a spare charged battery if possible.

› AF Illuminator

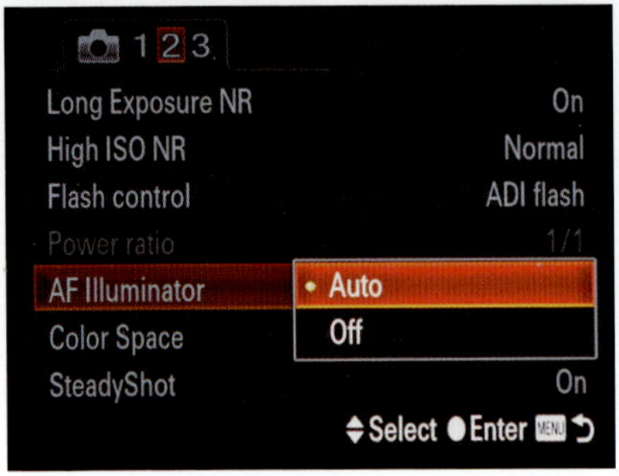

When the light levels are low, the A77's AF system can struggle to achieve accurate focus. When set to **Auto**, the AF illuminator will pulse light to illuminate the subject and assist AF. If you are using an external flash, the AF illuminator of the external flash is used instead.

The AF illuminator will not operate when the AF mode is set to **Continuous** or when the subject is moving and the AF is set to **Automatic**. It will also not operate when the AF area is set to **Local** or **Zone** and the center area is not selected, or when **Smile Shutter** is set to **On**.

Some subjects may be distracted by the AF illuminator, so if a more candid approach is required, switch **AF Illuminator** to **Off.** If the AF struggles, switch the lens to manual focus; bracket the focus; or use a small aperture to increase the depth of field.

› Color Space

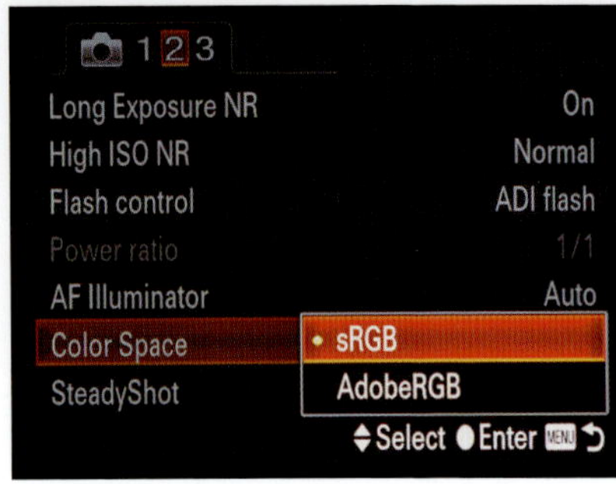

Color space refers to the range of colors a digital device can either record or reproduce. Devices such as printers typically operate with a far smaller color space than computer monitors or cameras. The A77 can record JPEGs using either the sRGB or Adobe RGB color space. Raw files will also be assigned the selected color space, but this can be altered (without a loss of quality) at the import stage.

sRGB is a far smaller color space than Adobe RGB, resulting in images that look "punchier." This makes them ideal for immediate use on the Internet, or printing, without the need for much post-processing. Adobe RGB is the better choice if you intend to extensively post-process your images.

› SteadyShot

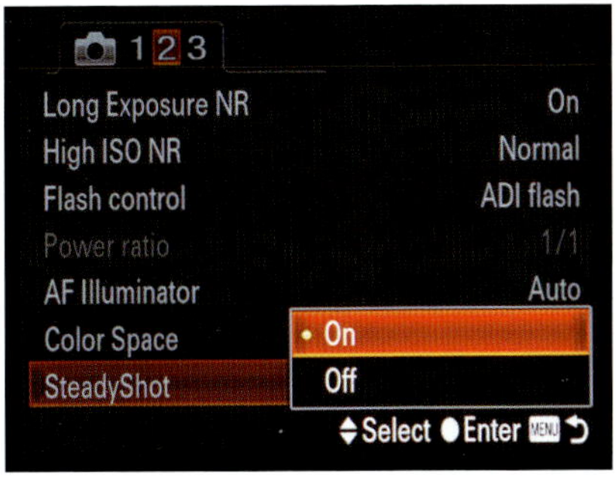

Using SteadyShot can help to reduce the effect of camera shake by the equivalent of 2.5–4 stops of shutter speed. The A77's SteadyShot system is a sensor-based stabilization method in which movement is detected by the camera and is then compensated for by rapidly shifting the sensor in the opposite direction. When **SteadyShot** is set to **On**, image stabilization is activated.

If the shutter speed lengthens to a point where SteadyShot is ineffective, will be displayed. At this point camera shake is likely and it is advisable to mount your camera on a tripod. If you do use a tripod, switch **SteadyShot** to **Off**.

Avoiding camera shake

Camera shake occurs if the camera moves during an exposure; the longer the shutter speed the greater the chance that this will happen. The lowest shutter speed that a camera can be handheld varies from person to person, and it also depends on the focal length of the lens used: the longer a lens, the faster the shutter speed should be to avoid camera shake. A very rough guide is to match the shutter speed to the focal length of the lens, so if you use a 500mm lens, try to use a shutter speed of 1/500 sec. or faster.

Another way to avoid camera shake is to assume the correct posture. Stand as vertically as possible, with your feet shoulder-width apart, and tuck your elbows lightly against your body. With one hand, grip the camera firmly. Use other hand to support the lens. If you wish to shoot from a kneeling position, steady your upper body by resting your elbow on one knee.

Notes:

The SteadyShot function may not be fully effective immediately after the A77 has been switched on or when the shutter-release button has been pressed all the way down without pausing halfway.

The camera shake warning indicator is displayed only in shooting modes that automatically set the shutter speed, although SteadyShot will still be active in other modes.

2 » STILL SHOOTING MENU 3

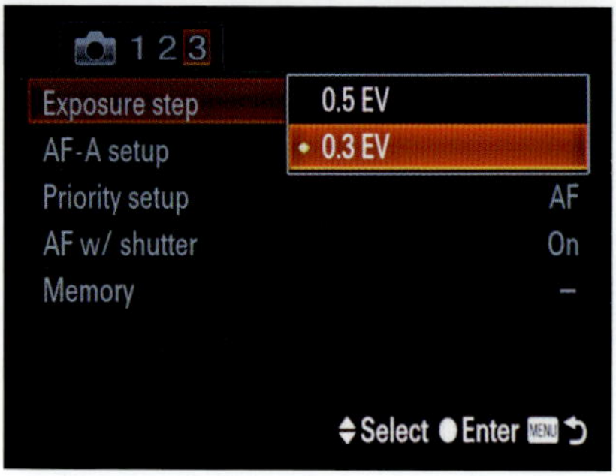

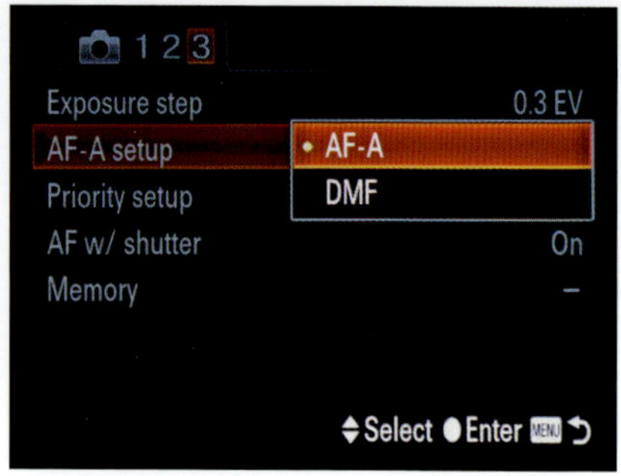

› Exposure step

This menu option allows you to specify how fine or coarse the exposure adjustments are—including exposure and flash compensation. You can choose between **0.3EV** and **0.5EV**, although choosing one over the other won't make a big difference to your exposures.

It is marginally quicker to move through exposure adjustments when **Exposure step** is set to **0.5EV** as there will be fewer steps to move through, but the **0.3EV** setting will give you slightly finer control over your exposures, which may be useful if you're shooting for HDR or other post-production techniques.

> ***Note:***
> DMF stands for Direct Manual Focus. It is always available on SSM lenses, regardless of how ***AF-A setup*** is configured. SAM lenses cannot use DMF, so ***AF-A setup*** is not available.

› AF-A setup

The A77's AF system is good, but it's not perfect, particularly if you're shooting subjects that require pinpoint focus accuracy. Set **AF-A setup** to **DMF** and when the camera focus dial is set to AF-A, the AF system is disengaged once the camera has focused. This allows you to adjust the focus manually. Used in combination with focus peaking this is a powerful tool that will help you achieve perfect focus every time.

› Priority setup

When this shooting option is set to **AF**, the A77 won't allow you to fire the shutter if focus cannot be confirmed. Set to **Release**, you'll be able to fire the shutter regardless of whether focus has been achieved. The latter option is most useful in fast moving situations, where the ability to fire quickly is more important than focus accuracy.

› AF w/ shutter

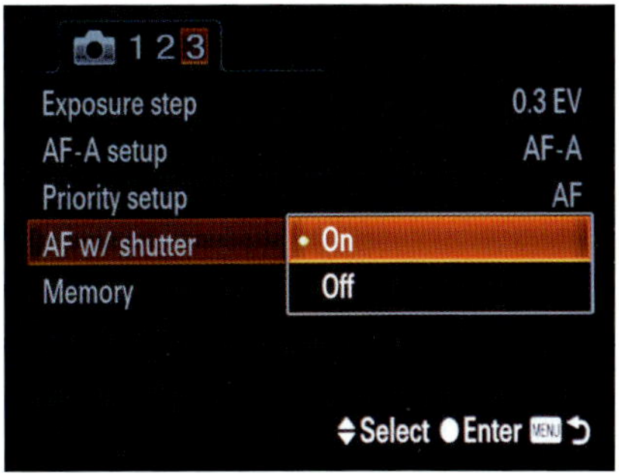

Switched to **Off**, the shutter-release button no longer activates the AF when you press it halfway down. This is useful when you don't want the focus distance to alter as you're shooting. This option works well when **AF/MF button** on ⚙ 3 is set to AF lock. Pressing AF/MF will then activate the AF when required.

› Memory

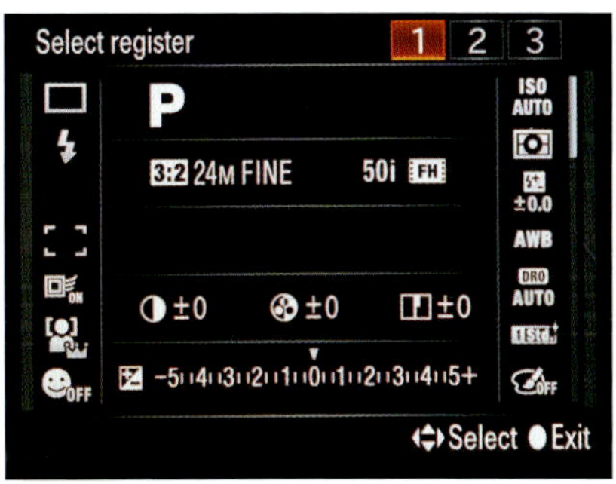

The Memory option is a useful time saver, allowing you to save three different camera configurations. So, for example, you could have one configuration with the camera ready for fast-paced action; a second configuration for landscape work; and a third, portrait configuration with the aperture set to maximum for a shallow depth of field.

Setting a configuration

1) Set the mode dial to the required mode and configure the camera settings. The items you can set include: still/movie shooting modes, the current aperture and shutter speed (**A**, **S**, and **M** modes only), drive mode, ISO, white balance (including custom white balance), exposure compensation, Face Detection, Smile Shutter, Picture Effect, metering mode, DRO, Auto HDR, Creative Style, flash mode (including flash compensation), Object Tracking, AF area, and all 📷 Still Shooting menu options.

2) Press **MENU**, highlight Memory on 📷 3, and press ●.

3) The current configuration is displayed on screen. Select which number you want to allocate the current configuration to by using ◀/▶. Press ● to exit the menu.

Recalling a configuration

1) Set the mode dial to MR. Press **Fn**, highlight **Memory recall**, and press ●.

2) Select the number corresponding to the configuration you want to use by pressing ◀ / ▶ and then press ●.

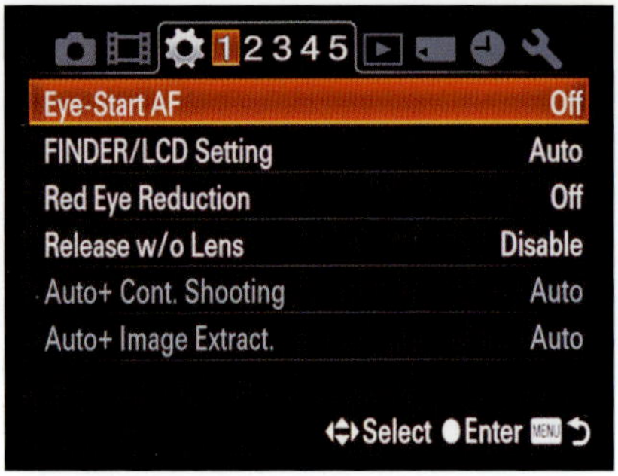

› Eye-Start AF

Above the EVF is an infrared (IR) sensor that detects when something is close to it. Usually this would be your eye, but it can be anything solid and opaque. When **Eye-Start AF** is switched to **On** (it is **Off** by default), the act of bringing your eye close to the EVF will be detected by the IR sensor and the A77's AF system is activated (assuming the AF/MF switch is set to AF).

The benefit of Eye-Start AF is that the amount of time before the camera is ready to shoot is reduced, which is useful when you're shooting in a rapidly changing situation with fast-moving subjects.

The problem with Eye-Start AF is that it can be accidentally activated by anything that passes in front of the sensor above the EVF. This can mean wasted battery power if the lens is constantly focusing. To reduce this risk, set **Power Save** on Setup 1 to **10 Sec** if you decide to use Eye-Start AF.

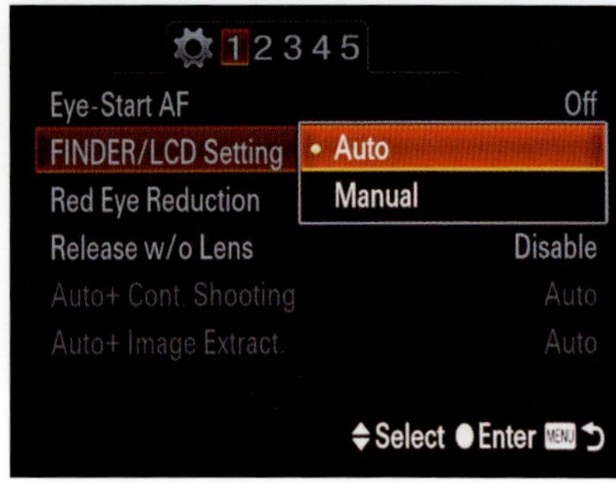

› FINDER/LCD Setting

The IR sensor is also used to switch off the LCD and activate the EVF when you bring the A77 to your face. By default **FINDER/LCD Setting** is set to **Auto**. When set to **Manual**, the switch between the LCD and EVF only occurs when you press FINDER/LCD on the top plate of the A77. If you have the EVF selected it will only activate when the IR sensor detects something close to it.

› Red Eye Reduction

This option reduces the risk of red eye, commonly seen when shooting portraits using flash.

› Release w/o Lens

If you plan to mount your camera to a telescope, reversing ring, or bellows, you'll need to use an M42 lens mount adapter (or similar). This is a non-Sony adapter, which won't have the required electrical contacts.

As far as the A77 is concerned, there won't be a lens attached and you won't be able to fire the shutter. Setting **Release w/o Lens** to **Enable** will allow you to use a non-Sony adapter on your camera. Set this function back to **Disable** when shooting with A-Mount lenses.

When using a non-Sony adapter you won't be able to control the aperture of the lens using your A77—instead you will need to set it manually on the lens itself. Because of this, shoot in **M** mode and adjust the shutter speed on the camera until the correct exposure is achieved.

› Auto+ Cont. Shooting

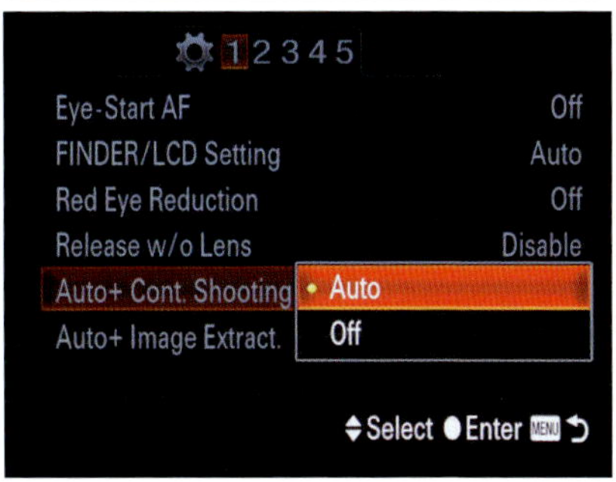

Along with the following option, this is only available when you're shooting in **AUTO+** mode. When **Auto+ Cont. Shooting** is set to **Auto**, your A77 will shoot continuously if it decides that the subject is moving. This can result in a large number of images that are shot rapidly, with little say from you, other than to take your finger off the shutter-release button. Set to **Off**, your A77 won't behave so imperiously.

› Auto+ Image Extract.

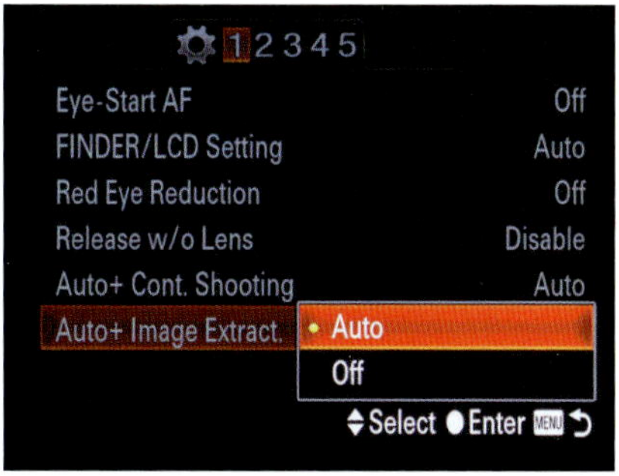

Set **Auto+ Image Extract**. to **Auto** and the A77 will edit the images shot automatically using Auto+ Cont. Shooting. It will decide whether each shot is sharp enough to keep, discarding any that are judged to be unsharp. When set to **Off,** all of the images will be kept when continuous shooting is activated.

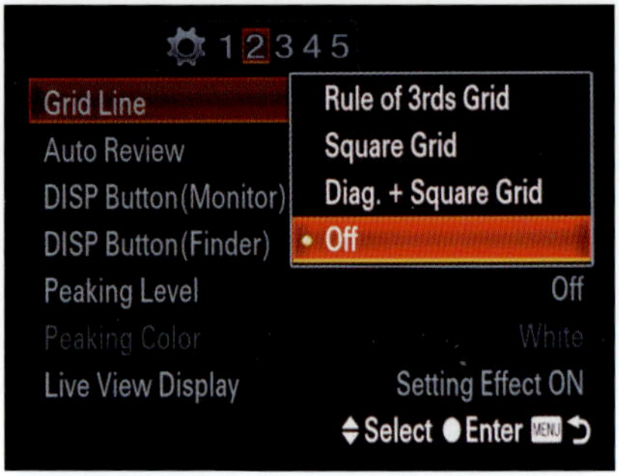

› Grid Line

The **Grid Line** function overlays three different types of grid on the screen, which can be used as an aid to composition or as a visual check that elements in the scene are straight relative to the camera. By default **Grid Line** is set to **Off.**

Rule of 3rds Grid divides the screen into nine equal rectangles by using two vertical lines and two horizontal lines. The Rule of Thirds is a composition device and the idea is that an image has more interest if the subject is placed on, or at, the intersection of the lines. A good example where this would work is when shooting landscapes. Having the horizon line dead center may make the image appear too symmetrical, but moving the horizon up would make more of the foreground, and moving it down would make more of the sky. However, repeatedly using the rule of thirds can make your images repetitive and formulaic.

Square Grid divides the screen into twenty-four squares. This is useful when shooting architectural subjects that need to be square to the camera. Used in conjunction with the Level there is no excuse for sloping buildings!

Diag. + Square Grid adds two diagonal lines running from the top to bottom corners. These lines are useful compositional aids, as diagonals (whether real or implied) add energy to a composition.

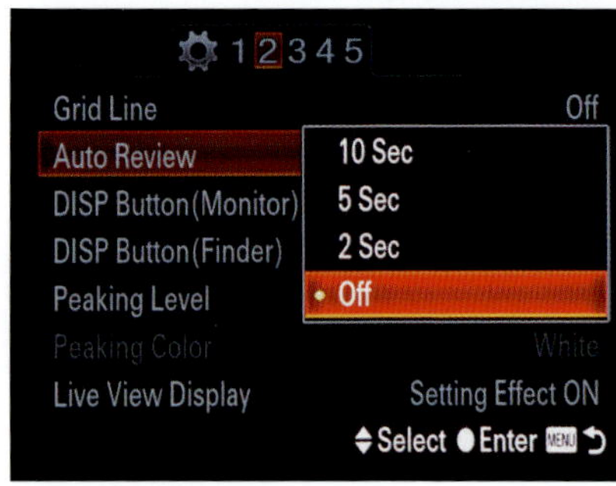

› Auto Review

By default, **Auto Review** is set to **Off**. This means that after shooting the still image you've just captured will not be displayed on screen. To view the image you will need to press ▶. If you want to view images immediately after capture, set **Auto Review** to **10 Sec**, **5 Sec**, or **2 Sec**. Post-capture, the image will be displayed for the selected length of time before the camera returns automatically to shooting mode.

› DISP. Button

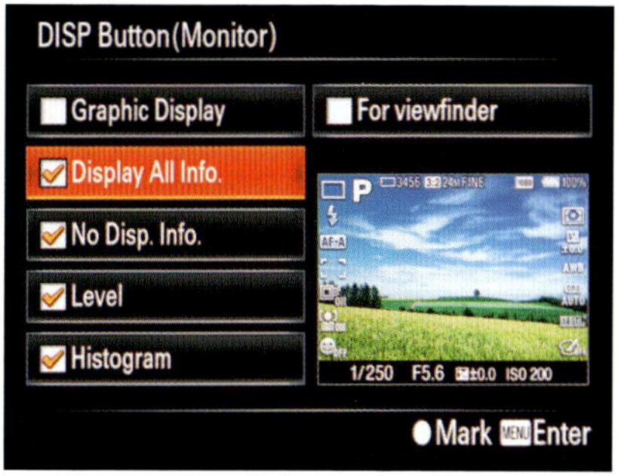

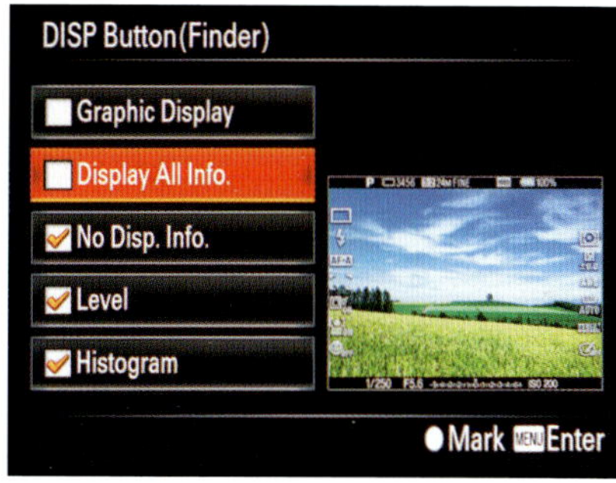

You can configure what information is overlaid on both the LCD and EVF displays in shooting mode. The different categories of information you choose to view are displayed with each successive press of DISP.

The LCD and EVF displays can be configured separately by selecting **DISP Button (Monitor)** and **DISP Button (Finder)** on the ⚙ Custom 2 menu.

Choosing the information to display

1) Highlight **DISP Button (Monitor)** or **DISP Button (Finder)** and press ●.

2) Use ◀/▶ to highlight the required option and press ● to select or deselect the highlighted option.

3) On **DISP Button (Monitor)** selecting **For viewfinder** will display an information-only screen at the end of the sequence when pressing **DISP**. This option is not available on **DISP Button (Finder).**

4) Press **MENU** to save your settings and return to the main ⚙ Custom 2 menu, or lightly press down on the shutter-release button to return to shooting mode, without saving the settings.

OPTION	DESCRIPTION
Graphic Display	Exposure information comparison
Display All. Info	Shows all current **Fn** screen settings
No Disp. Info.	No overlaid information (except AF focus areas)
Level	Spirit level only
Histogram	Live histogram of current scene
For viewfinder	Current camera status information

› Peaking Level

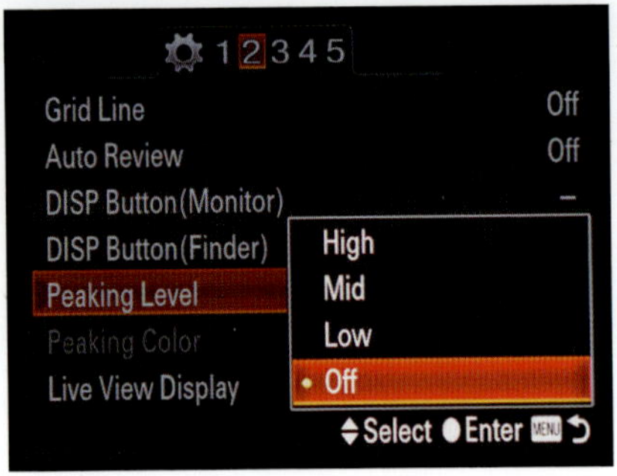

When focusing manually, "focus peaking" is an incredibly useful tool. The idea is derived from similar systems found on camcorders. With focus peaking active, the A77 will turn the outline of the sharpest point of the image red (or yellow or white, depending on how **Peaking Color** is set). The intensity of the **Peaking Level** can be set to **High**, **Mid**, **Low**, or **Off**.

The drawback with using focus peaking is that it relies on contrast to detect sharpness so it may be less effective, or possibly not work at all if you're shooting a low contrast scene, such as a misty landscape.

> ***Notes:***
> In Manual exposure mode, the display will brighten or darken depending on the exposure settings you use.
>
> You can't switch to Setting Effect OFF in AUTO, AUTO+, , 3D, , or **SCN** modes.

› Peaking Color

Sets the color of focus peaking. You can choose between **Red**, **Yellow**, or **White**. If you're shooting Raw, choosing the Black & White Creative Style (with **Live View Display** set to **Setting Effect ON**) makes it far easier to see the Red setting, particularly if the scene you're shooting is colorful. You'll need to reset the Raw file back to color in post-production, but this is a small price to pay for accurate MF.

› Live View Display

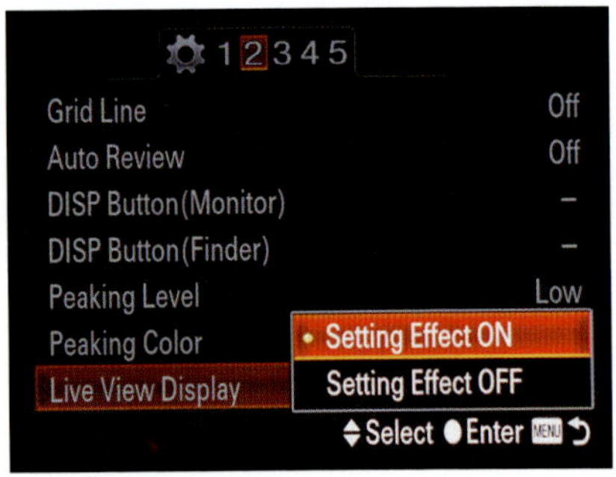

Switching **Live View Display** to **Setting Effect ON** enables you to see the results of exposure settings such as exposure compensation, Creative Style, and others before you press the shutter-release button. When switched to **Setting Effect OFF** the display is always correctly exposed and is shown without any effects applied.

» ✲ CUSTOM MENU 3

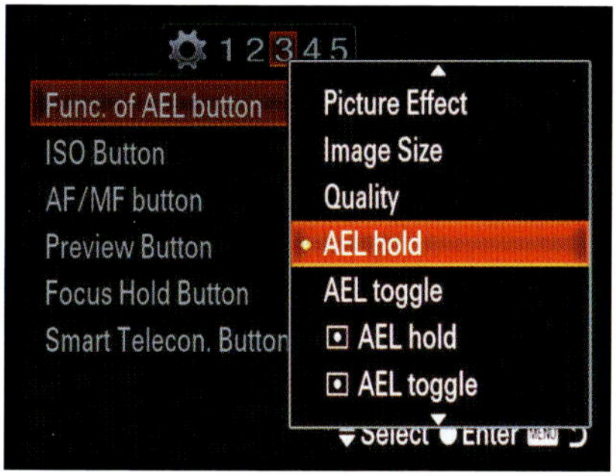

› Func. of AEL button

By default **Func. of AEL button** is set to **AEL Hold**, but you can assign any one of the following functions to this button if you prefer:

Exposure Comp., Drive Mode, Flash Mode, AF Area, Face Detection, Smile Shutter, ISO, Metering Mode, Flash Comp. White Balance, DRO/Auto HDR, Creative Style, Picture Effect, Image Size, Quality, AEL hold, AEL toggle, [●] AEL Hold, [●] AEL toggle, AF/MF Control Hold, AF/MF Control Toggle, Object Tracking, AF Lock, Aperture Preview, Shot. Result Preview, Smart Telecon., Focus Magnifier, Memory.

> ***Note:***
> You could assign the same function to all three buttons, but it's a good idea to choose different options that you use most commonly.

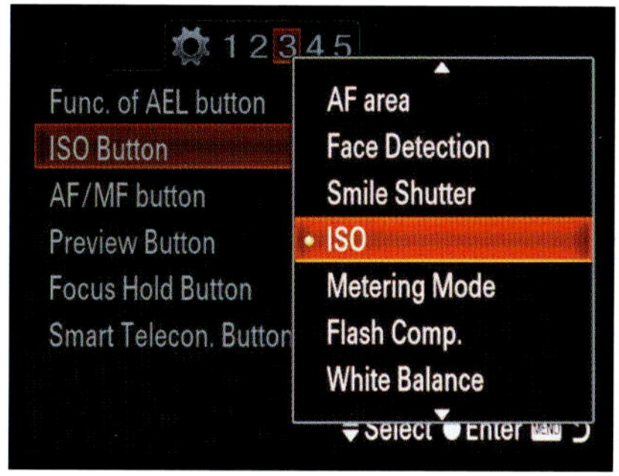

› ISO Button

By default, **ISO Button** is set to **ISO**. You can, however, assign any of the functions listed previously to the **ISO button** instead.

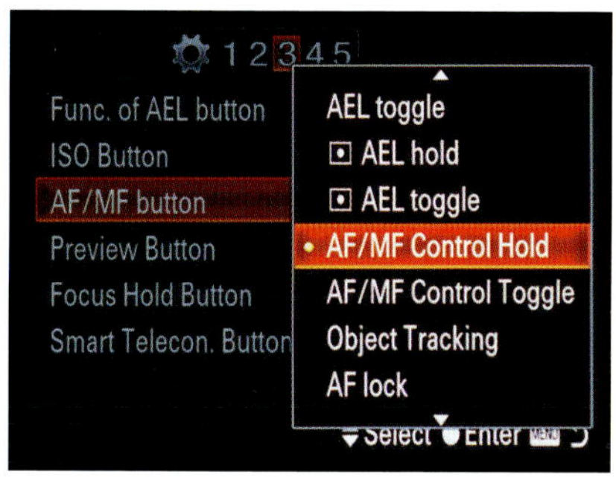

› AF/MF button

By default, **AF/MF button** is set to **AF lock**. Again, you can change this and assign any of the functions listed previously to the **AF/MF button**.

› Preview Button

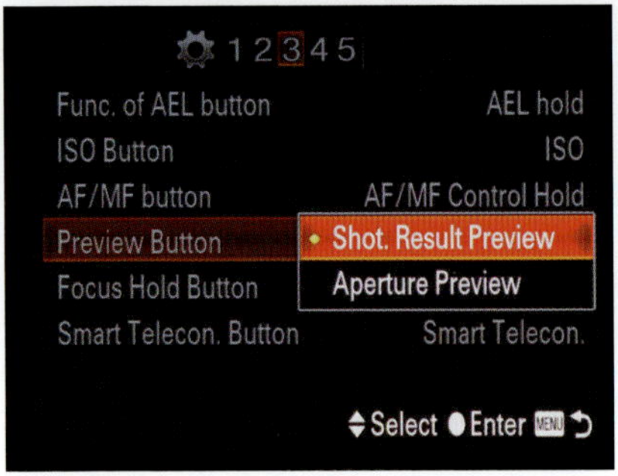

The lens mounted on your A77 is always set to maximum aperture until the moment you press the shutter-release button to take a shot. It's only then that the aperture closes to the selected setting. Maximum aperture is used this way so that there is always sufficient light hitting the sensor for a good Live View image. The drawback is that you are always seeing an image with minimal depth of field, making it hard to judge what your final photograph will look like.

However, with **Preview Button** set to **Aperture Preview**, pressing the Preview button next to the lens will close the aperture so that you can accurately judge depth of field. Set to **Shot Result Preview**, pressing the Preview button will show you how the image will look with effects such as DRO applied.

› Focus Hold Button

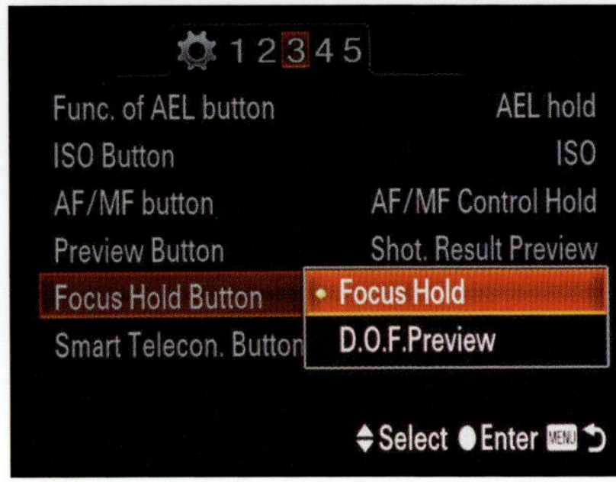

If your lens has a Focus Hold button, this function will control its behavior. Set to **Focus Hold** the button will act as normal, but set to **D.O.F Preview** the aperture will stop down for a depth of field preview in the same way as the Preview Button function described previously.

› Smart Telecon. Button

You can re-assign the Smart Teleconverter button to act as a **Focus Magnifier** instead. This allows you to zoom into the Live View image before you make your exposure, so you can check fine focus. This option is particularly useful if you're shooting macro or close-up subjects that require critically accurate focusing.

» CUSTOM MENU 4

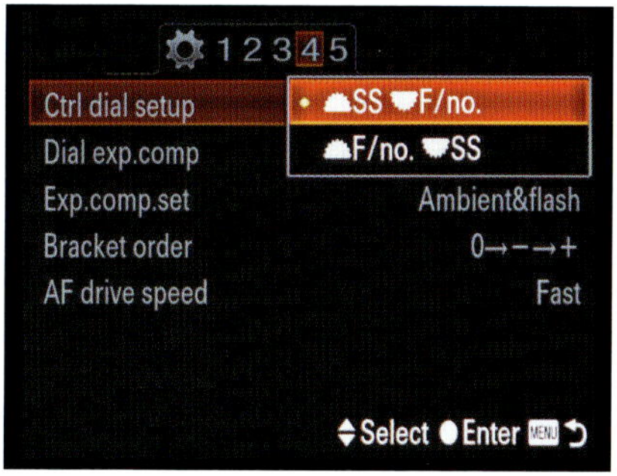

› Ctrl dial setup

In Manual exposure mode, is used to set the shutter speed and sets the aperture when **Ctrl dial setup** is set to **SS F/no**. The functions of the two dials can be swapped by setting this option to **F/no. SS.** There is no advantage to setting this function either way, other than for personal preference.

› Dial exp. comp

When set to **Off**, exposure compensation (in **P**, **A**, and **S** modes) is achieved by pressing and turning either or . However, setting **Dial exp. comp** to **Front dial** or **Rear dial** means that exposure compensation is only set using the appropriate control wheel, while the opposite wheel is used for altering the exposure settings.

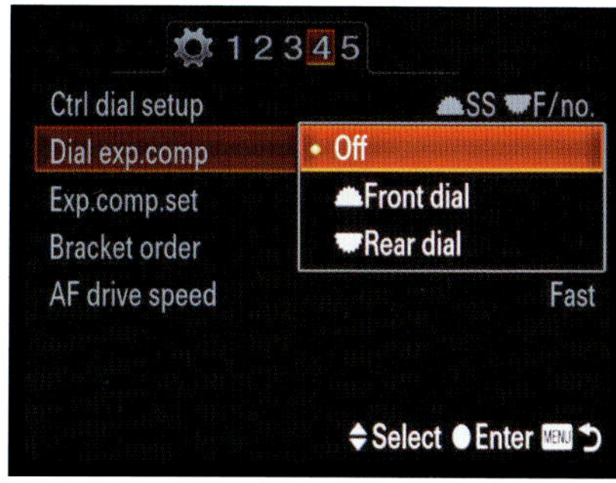

› Exp. comp set

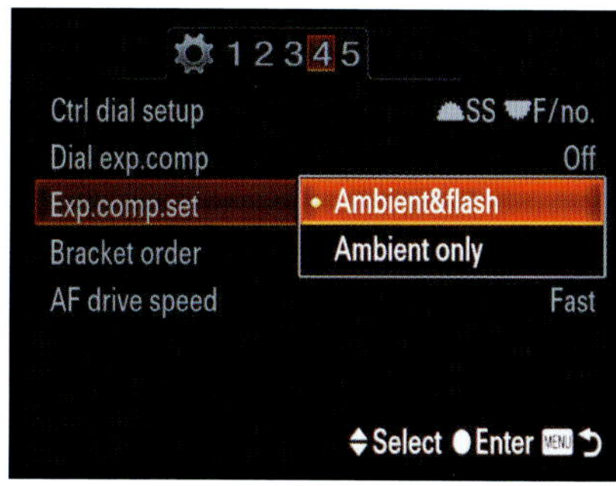

There are two separate ways to compensate the exposure on the A77: exposure compensation and flash compensation. When this option is set to **Ambient only**, only the ambient exposure is changed using , but set to **Ambient & Flash** both and are altered when is used. It's generally not a good idea to lock these two options together, so **Ambient only** is the recommended setting.

› Bracket order

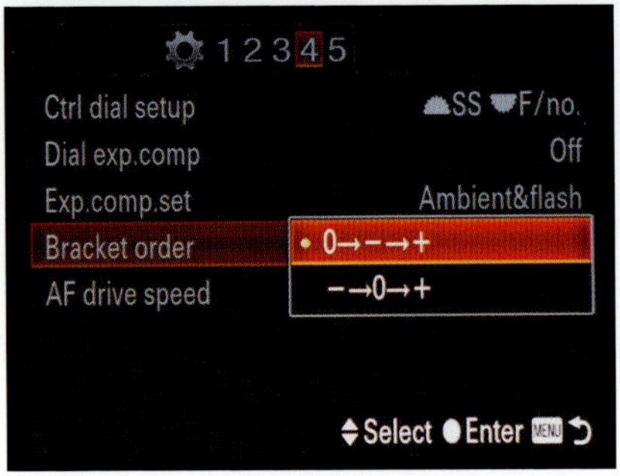

This option sets the order in which bracketed sequences (exposure and white balance) are shot. By default, the "correct" image is shot first, followed by a negatively-corrected image, and then a positively-corrected image (**0–+**). However, you can choose to shoot the negatively-corrected image first, then the "correct" image, followed by the positively-corrected image (**–0+**). There is no real advantage to either setting, although it is possibly a little more comforting to know that the correct image is shot first.

› AF drive speed

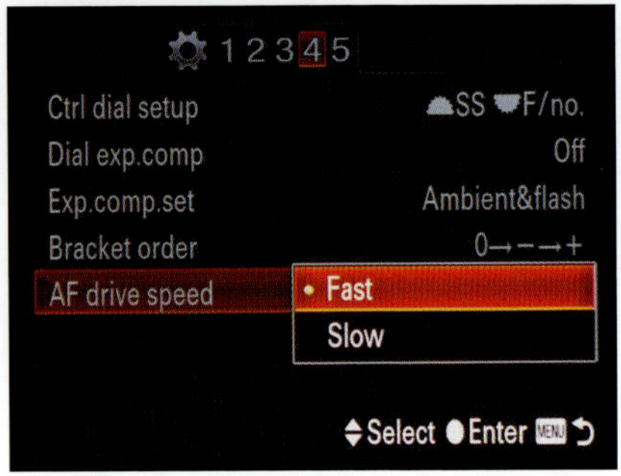

This option possibly shows a slight lack of faith in the A77's AF system on Sony's part. The choice is between **Fast**—with the implication that AF will be quick, but not necessarily accurate—or **Slow**, providing less speedy but more accurate AF. It's worth experimenting with your various lenses to see which option works best for you.

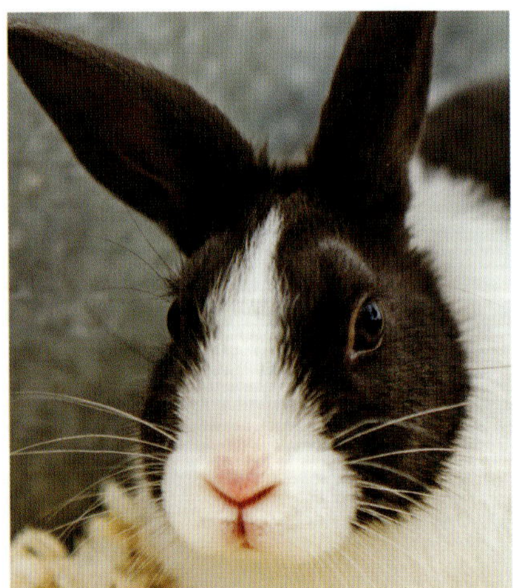

PET PORTRAIT »
With twitchy, fast-moving subjects, AF speed should be prioritized over accuracy.

» CUSTOM MENU 5

Unfortunately there is no such thing as the perfect lens. There are lenses that come close, but these are invariably expensive and often far heavier than a similar "consumer" lens. The good news is that a particular lens design has a quantifiable set of defects that can be cured by processing an image in a way that corrects it.

The A77 has a number of lens profiles built in, so if the lens you use is listed, the A77 can be set to remove (or at least reduce) its defects. The range of lens profiles expands every time Sony issues a firmware update for the camera, although to date the only lenses covered are Sony's own. The following three Custom functions can be used together or independently to automatically cure lens defects.

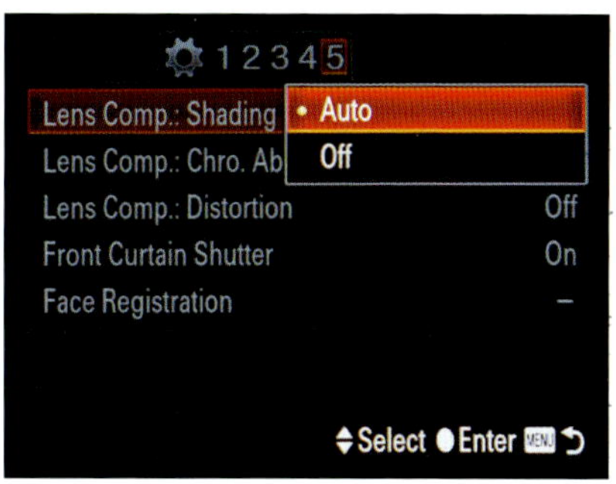

› Lens Comp.: Shading

Shading, more commonly known as vignetting, is the darkening of the corners of an image compared to the center. Most lenses will display a certain amount of vignetting at maximum aperture, but this is reduced as the lens is stopped down. Wide-angle lenses tend to suffer more from vignetting than telephotos.

When **Lens Comp.: Shading** is set to **Auto** it will automatically reduce vignetting. The downside to using this function is that noise may be more apparent in the corners of the image as they need to be lightened relative to the center.

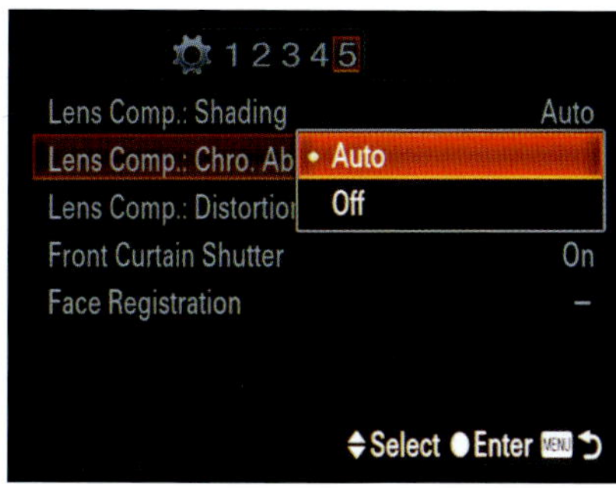

› Lens Comp.: Chro. Aber.

Chromatic aberration (or achromatism) is caused by the inability of a lens to focus the various wavelengths of colored light to the same point. This results in colored fringing along the boundaries of light and dark areas of an image. When it is set to **Auto, Lens Comp.: Chro. Aber**. will attempt to reduce the achromatism exhibited by certain lenses.

› Lens Comp.: Distortion

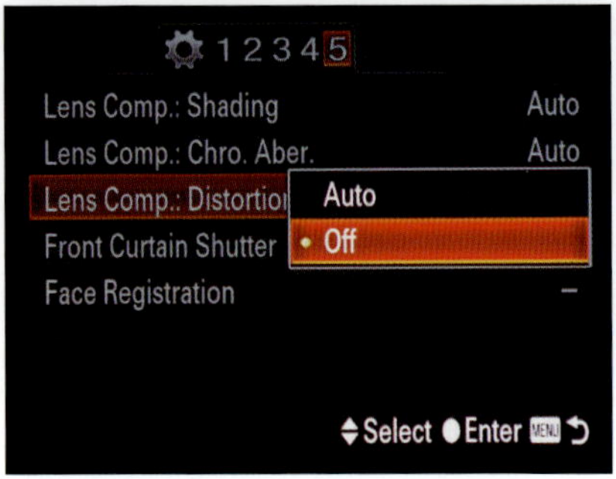

"Pincushion" and "barrel" accurately describe the types of distortion created by lenses. Pincushion distortion results in straight lines appearing to bow inward, toward the center of an image, while barrel distortion causes straight lines to bow outward from the center. If you're using a zoom lens, you will typically see barrel distortion at the widest focal length setting and pincushion at the longest.

When **Lens Comp.: Distortion** is set to **Auto**, your A77 will apply the opposite amount of distortion to correct that caused by the lens. This will degrade the image slightly. However, with many subjects distortion is not noticeable, so correcting it may not be something you need to do very often. If this is the case, set **Lens Comp.: Distortion** to **Off**, as this will retain maximum image quality.

Compatible lenses (Version 1.05)

16–50mm f/2.8 SSM (SAL-1650)
16–80mm f/3.5–4.5 DT Carl Zeiss Vario-Sonnar T* (SAL-1680Z)
16–105mm f/3.5–5.6 DT (SAL-16105)
18–55mm f/3.5–5.6 DT SAM (SAL-1855)
18–250mm f/3.5–6.3 DT (SAL-18250)
24mm f/2.0 Carl Zeiss Distagon T* (SAL-24F20Z)
35mm f/1.8 SAM (SAL-35F18)
50mm f/1.8 SAM (SAL-50F18)
55–200mm f/4–5.6 DT SAM (SAL-55200-2)
70–300mm f/4.5–5.6 G (SAL-70300G)
85mm f/1.4 Carl Zeiss Planar T* (SAL-85F14Z)
135mm f/2.8 (T4.5) STF (SAL-135F28)

› Front Curtain Shutter

The shutter in most cameras comprises two light metal curtains, one in front of the other, that are designed to travel upward at the same speed. When the shutter-release button is pressed, the front curtain begins to rise, exposing the sensor to light. After an appropriate delay, the rear curtain also begins to rise, stopping light from hitting the sensor. The delay between the two curtains rising is the shutter speed used.

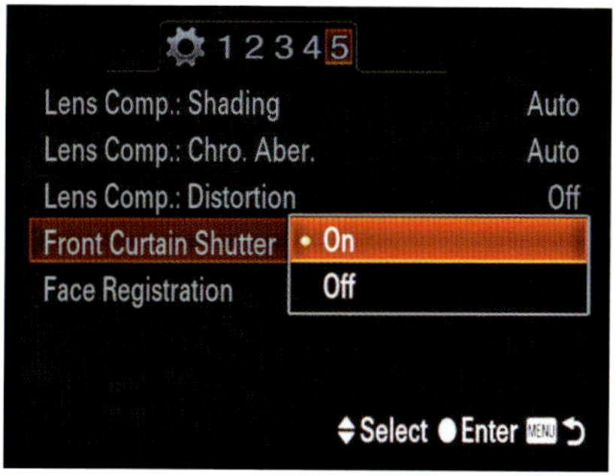

However, while the A77 has a mechanical shutter, the shutter has to stay open to allow for Live View. Set to **On, Front Curtain Shutter** forces the sensor to act as an electronic front curtain when the shutter-release button is pressed, cutting out the need for the mechanical shutter to close before the exposure can begin. At the end of the exposure the shutter closes to stop light from reaching the sensor, before reopening to allow Live View to begin again.

This means that the mechanical shutter only operates once instead of twice, which should extend the life of the shutter and make the exposure process marginally faster. However, some older lenses may cause overexposure using **Front Curtain Shutter**, in which case you need to set this function to **Off**.

› Face Registration

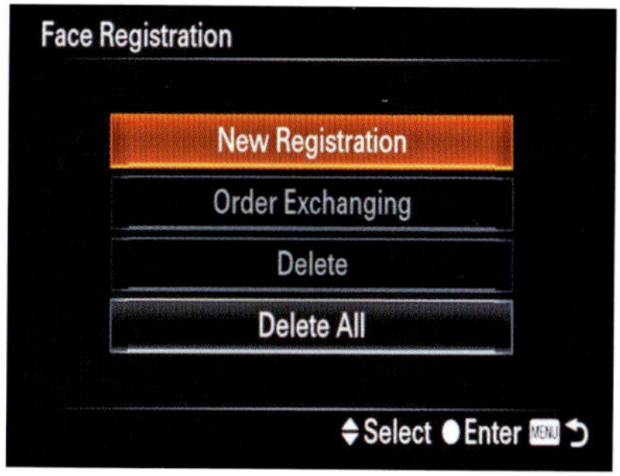

You can add up to eight faces to the A77's **Face Registration** function, so that when you use Face Detection the A77 will prioritize focus on one of those eight faces if they're present in the scene. You can also order the faces registered so that if several registered faces are in the scene, the face with the highest priority will be focused on first, the second highest second, and so on.

Registering a face

1) Highlight **Face Registration** on ⚙ Custom 5 and then press ●.

2) Highlight **New Registration** and press ● once more.

3) Move the camera until the face you want to register is within the white guide box and press the shutter-release button.

4) Highlight **Enter** and press ● or highlight Cancel and press ● to retry.

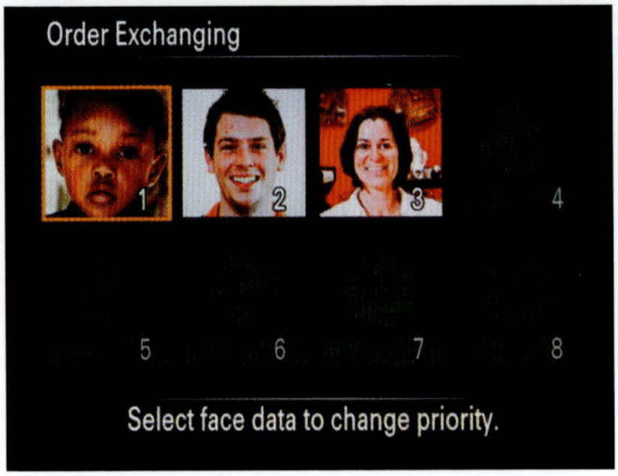

Ordering the registered faces

1) Highlight **Face Registration** on ✿ Custom 5 and then press ●.

2) Select **Order Exchanging** and press ● again.

3) Choose the face you want to move up or down the priority list (face number 1 has the highest priority, number 8 has the lowest priority). Press ●.

4) Move the vertical orange bar using ▲ / ▼. Moving the bar left will move the face higher up the priority list, moving it right will move the face lower down the list. Press ● to change the face's priority, or **MENU** to return to the main Face Registration menu without altering the priority list.

Delete a face

1) Highlight **Face Registration** on ✿ Custom 5 and then press ●.

2) Choose **Delete** to delete individual faces from the list or **Delete All** to remove all faces from the list. Press ● again.

3) If you selected **Delete**, use ◀/▲/▶/▼ to highlight the face you want to delete. Press ● to delete the face, highlight **Delete**, and press ● again or highlight **Cancel** and press ● to continue selecting which face to delete.

4) If you selected **Delete All**, highlight **Delete** and press ● to delete all the faces or **Cancel** and ● to return to the Face Registration page.

> ***Tip***
>
> *When registering a face, make sure that your subject looks directly at the camera and isn't wearing sunglasses or a hat.*

» ▶ PLAYBACK MENU 1

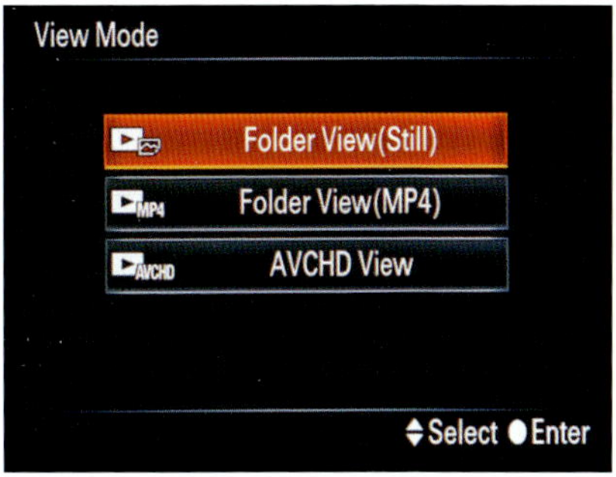

› View Mode

Use this option to choose which image type will be available for viewing when you press ▶. **Folder View (Still)** is used to view still images, **Folder View (MP4)** for MP4 movies, and **AVCHD View** for AVCHD movies.

› Delete

See page 46.

› Slide Show

See page 45.

› 3D Viewing

See page 230.

› Protect

See page 47.

› Specify Printing

See page 232.

» ▶ PLAYBACK MENU 2

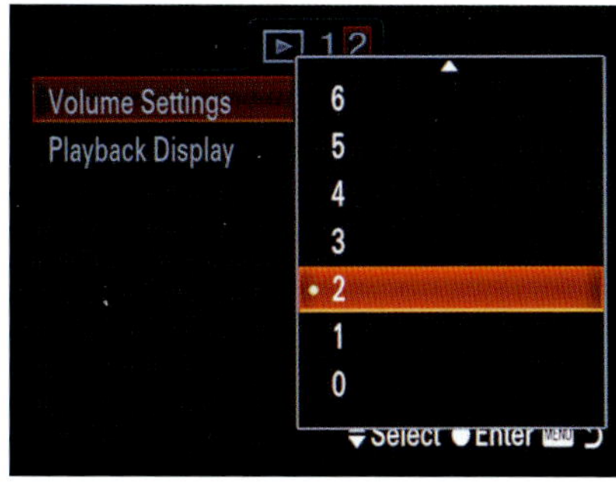

› Volume Settings

This option controls the sound level when movies are played back on your A77 (it does not control the volume of operational sounds). The volume can be set from **0** (off) through to **7** (maximum).

› Playback Display

When this function is set to **Auto Rotate**, vertical images are automatically rotated during playback. This means that they are shrunk still further to fit them into the vertical size of the screen compared to horizontal images. If you'd rather vertical images filled the entire screen (requiring you to turn A77 on its side to view the images in their correct orientation) select **Manual Rotate**.

MEMORY CARD MENU 1

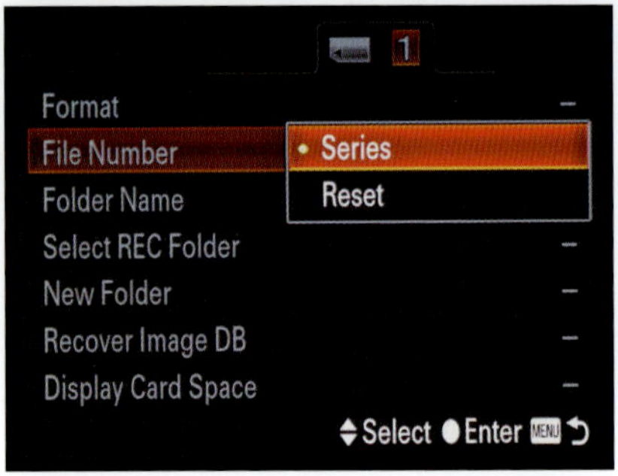

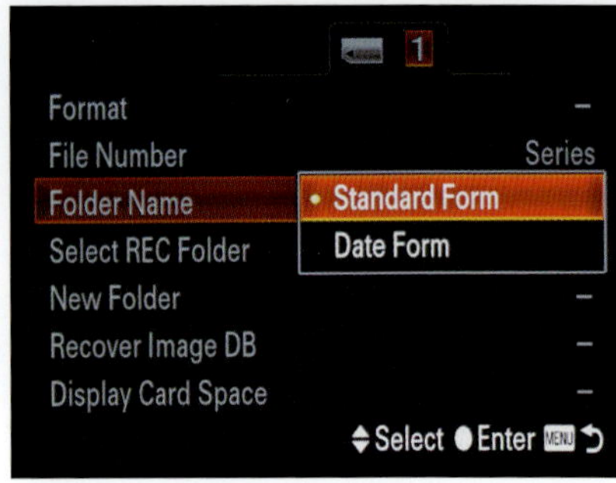

› Format

See page 39.

› File Number

Every still image created by the A77 is assigned a file name before being saved to the currently selected folder. The file name is composed of the prefix DSC0 followed by a four-digit number and a suffix denoting the file type (.JPG for a JPEG and .ARW for a Raw file). The four-digit number is a count of the number of images you've shot with the camera, starting from 0001.

If you select **Series**, when the file number reaches 9999 the counter will be reset and start from 0001 again. Selecting **Reset** forces the A77 to reset the count back to 0001 whenever the folder format is changed, when all the images in the folder are deleted, when the memory card is replaced, or whenever the memory card is formatted.

› Folder Name

Still images are stored in folders on the memory card within the main DCIM folder. You can create new folders on the memory card using the New Folder option, as discussed on the page opposite. **Folder name** allows you to choose between two naming conventions whenever a new folder is created:

Standard Form creates folders with a unique three-digit number followed by the letters MSDCF.

Date Form creates a new folder with a three-digit number followed by a further five numbers. The first three numbers are the unique folder name number; the fourth number is the last digit of the year; the next two numbers indicate the month; and the final two are the day. For example, 10021105 would be folder number 100 created on 5 November 2012.

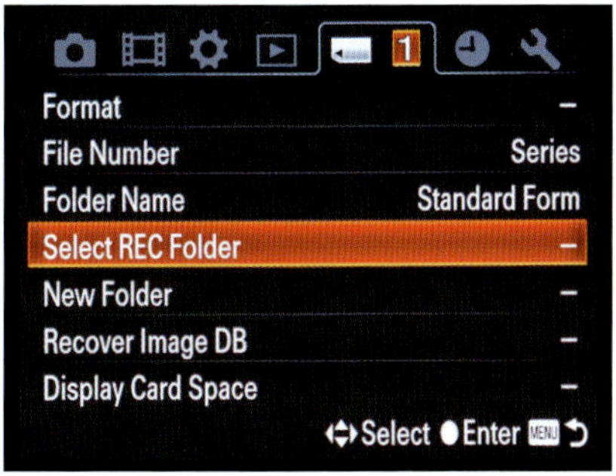

› Select REC Folder

Select REC Folder allows you to choose which of the image folders on the memory card you want to use. That folder will then be used by the A77 to store images as they are created.

Selecting a folder

1) Scroll down to **Select REC Folder** and press ●.

2) Press ▲ / ▼ to move up and down the folders on the memory card and then press ● when the required folder is highlighted.

› New Folder

Creates a new folder on the memory card. That folder will then become the current folder. Any still images you shoot subsequently will be stored in this folder, unless you change folders using **Select REC Folder** (above). The new folder is created using the naming convention chosen in **Folder Name**.

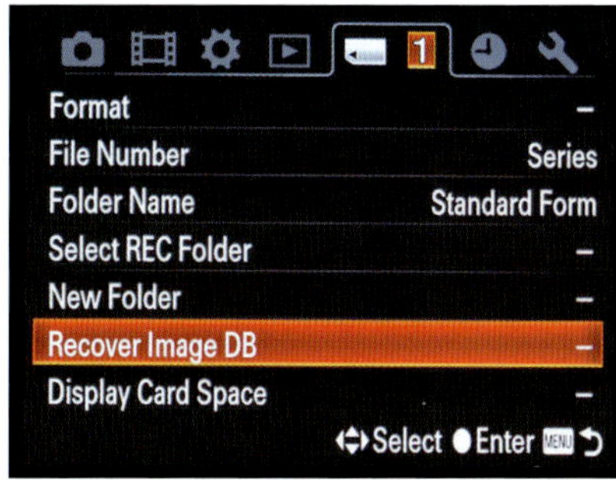

› Recover Image DB

Memory cards can be corrupted and the database of images on the card can become scrambled. Selecting **Recover Image DB** will ask your A77 to rebuild the database to repair any errors. However, **Recover Image DB** does not repair individual images if they become corrupted.

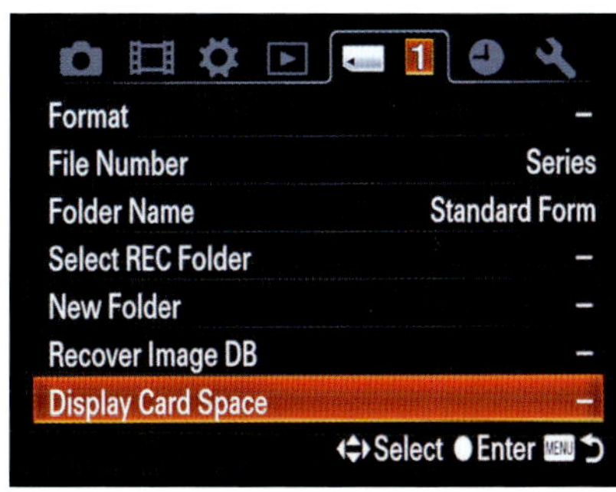

› Display Card Space

This option shows the number of images or length of movie that can be fitted onto your memory card.

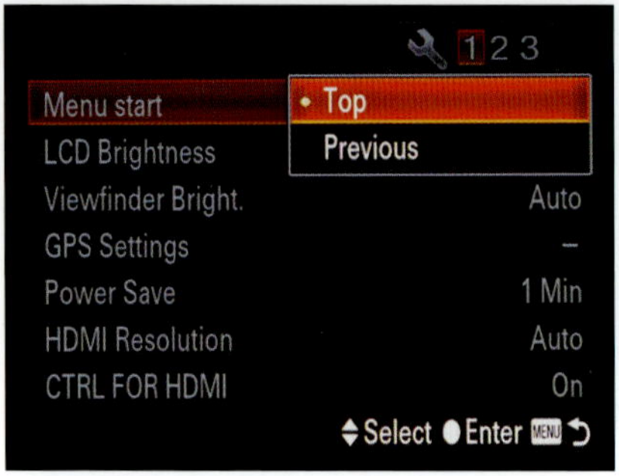

› Menu start

The setting you use for this option is very much a personal preference. Set to **Top**, the menu screen displayed after pressing **MENU** is **Still Shooting 1**; set to **Previous** you will return to the last option you highlighted when **MENU** is pressed.

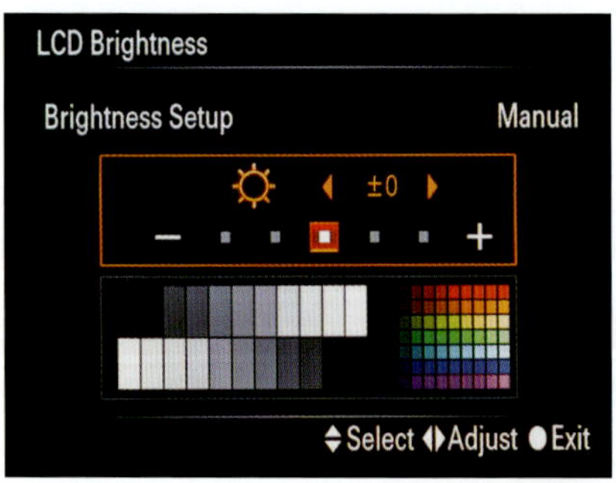

› LCD Brightness

The A77 has an ambient light sensor near the bottom left corner of the LCD. When **LCD Brightness** is set to **Auto**, the brightness level of the LCD is adjusted to suit the ambient lighting, which helps to conserve battery power: the brighter the LCD, the more power it consumes. However, if the brightness level of the LCD fluctuates according to the ambient light level, it's harder to judge an image's exposure.

Setting the LCD brightness manually

1) Highlight **LCD Brightness** and press ●.

2) Scroll to **Brightness Setup** press ● again, and then press ● a third time.

3) Highlight **Manual** using ▼ and then press ●.

4) Use the ◀/▶ control buttons to move the slider to the left to darken the display or to the right to lighten the display. Ideally, the brightness level should be set to a point where every tone in the color charts can be distinguished individually.

5) Press ● to return to the main menu.

› Viewfinder Bright.

The steps that apply to setting the LCD Brightness also apply to the EVF: set **Viewfinder Bright.** to **Manual** and adjust it to a brightness level that is comfortable for you.

Notes:
Using the live histogram is the best way to assess the exposure of an image, but looking at the LCD offers a useful rough and ready guide.

Don't cover up the sensor on the LCD when LCD Brightness is set to Auto.

When the A77 is powered by the PW10AM AC adapter, the LCD is set to maximum brightness.

› GPS Settings

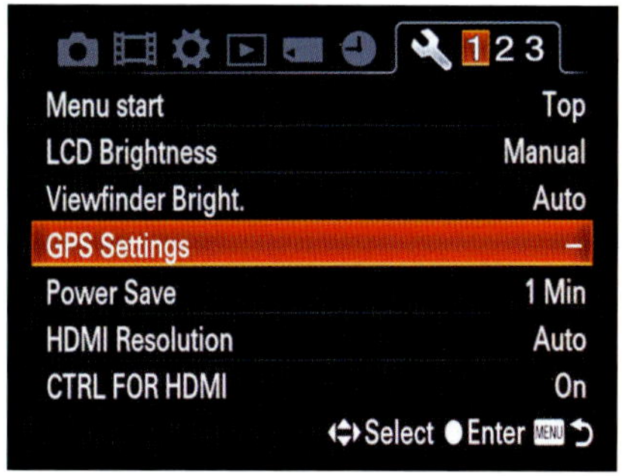

There are two A77 models: the "vanilla" A77 and the A77V, which has a built-in GPS receiver. If a GPS signal can be acquired, the A77V can record the position in which a particular image was shot into the image's metadata. Using GPS-compatible software, you can then view a map showing the exact geographical location of the image.

The GPS function will use more of your A77's battery power when switched **On**, than when it is switched **Off**. The GPS status of the camera is shown on the LCD using the symbols shown below. When **GPS Auto Time Cor.** is switched **On**, it will correct your A77's internal clock using the time code from GPS satellites. **Use GPS Assist Data** will help shorten the GPS location search when you connect your A77 to an Internet-enabled computer and run the GPS Support Tool in PMB (Windows only).

OPTION	DESCRIPTION
No symbol	GPS is switched off.
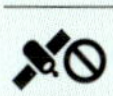	GPS signal can't be found. Generally this occurs when you're shooting indoors or when surrounded by tall buildings or trees.
	Acquiring GPS signal.
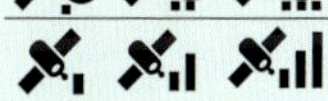	GPS signal acquired. The number of bars next to the symbol indicates signal strength: the more bars, the stronger the signal. Location information will be written to the image metadata.
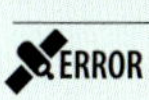	GPS error.

› Power Save

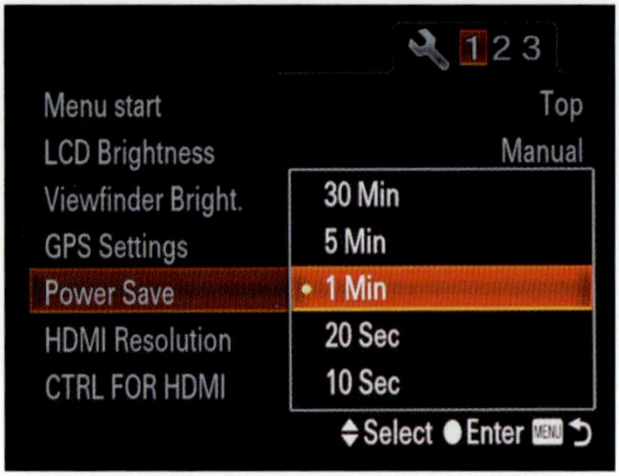

There are five **Power Save** options: **30 Min**, **5 Min**, **1 Min**, **20 Sec**, and **10 Sec**. These refer to the length of time the camera has to be inactive before it goes to "sleep," at which point power consumption is greatly reduced. To wake the camera, all you need to do is press the shutter-release button.

Slightly ironically, switching the camera on and off consumes more power than letting it sleep, as every time you switch the camera off various functions such as sensor cleaning are activated, all of which consume battery power. Specify the least frustrating amount of time for you before **Power Save** is activated.

› HDMI Resolution

Images and movies from your A77 can be played on an HDTV via an HDMI cable. Unfortunately the world of digital high-definition TV isn't as simple as analog: although all HDTVs have a 16:9 aspect ratio, the pixel resolution can be 1280 x 720 pixels, 1366 x 768 pixels, or 1920 x 1080 pixels. Not only that, but HDTVs also vary in frame rate. If you live in Europe your HDTV will have a frame rate of 25 or 50fps, but if you are in North America it will have a frame rate of 24, 30, or 60fps.

To make things even more confusing, the displays can either be progressive or interlaced. Progressive systems draw each line of pixels down the screen in sequence over the course of a single frame, before returning to the top for the next frame (1080p), while interlace systems draw all the odd lines first, before drawing all the even lines (1080i).

The A77's **HDMI Resolution** option lets you to set either of these two scanning systems, depending on the requirements of your HDTV. Generally, **Auto** will work perfectly well.

› CTRL for HDMI

When the A77 is connected to a compatible Sony television, the television's remote control can be used to control certain playback functions on the camera. If the camera starts to perform erratically when connected to a non-Sony television check that **CTRL FOR HMDI** is **Off**.

» SETUP MENU 2

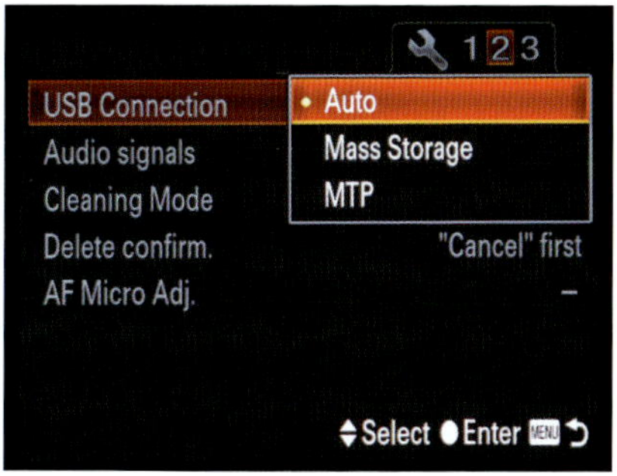

› USB connection

Connecting your A77 to other compatible USB devices requires you to specify the type of USB connection required. **Auto** will allow the A77 to decide the most suitable setting, while **Mass Storage** is the standard mode for connecting the camera to a computer. Using **Mass Storage** means that your A77 will behave in the same way as a standard external drive when it's connected to a computer, allowing you to copy files to and from the camera to the computer.

MTP stands for Media Transfer Protocol and is a new Microsoft standard. If you're connecting your A77 to a PictBridge printer or to a PC running Windows 7, set **USB Connection** to **MTP**.

› Cleaning Mode

See page 199.

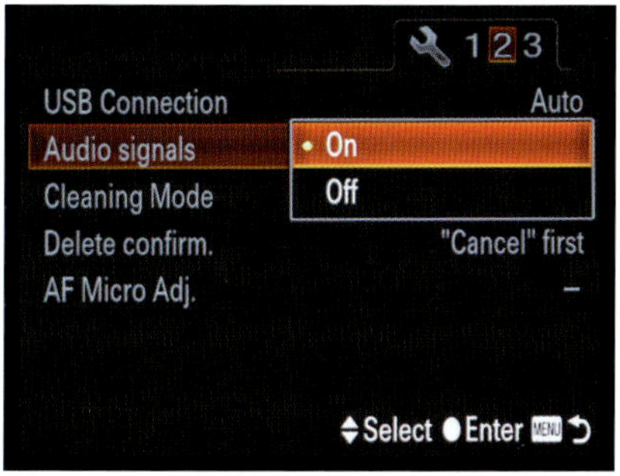

› Audio signals

Your A77 will make various sounds to confirm when certain functions are activated (when the focus is locked, for example). If you prefer a quieter approach to your photography, these audio signals can be turned **Off** with this option.

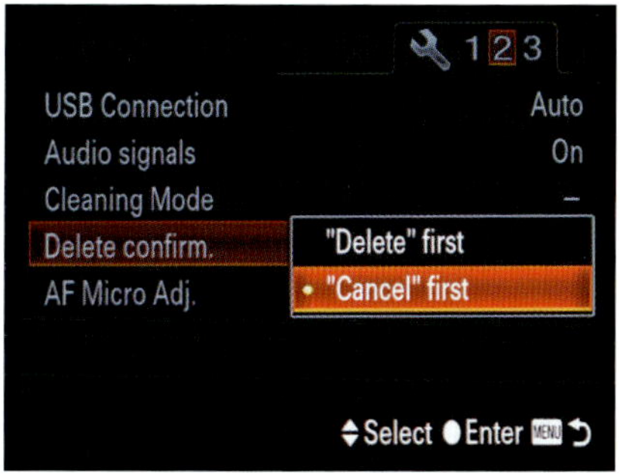

› Delete confirm.

The A77 really doesn't want you to delete your images. When you press **Delete**,

Cancel is initially highlighted on the confirmation screen, so you have to press ▲ to highlight **Delete** and then press ● before the image is deleted. Set this option to **"Delete" first** so that Delete is highlighted immediately and you can save a few seconds for every image you delete.

› AF Micro Adj.

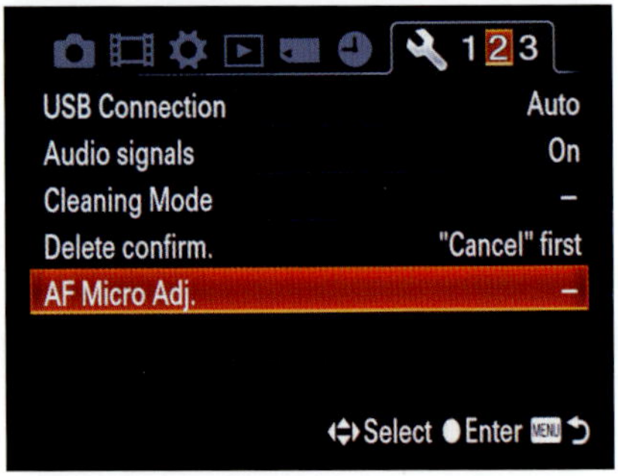

In most shooting situations, critical focusing is relatively unimportant, but there are times when focusing has to be exactly right, at which point the flaws in AF become apparent. There are two potential problems.

The first, known as "backfocus," occurs when the AF system focuses slightly behind the intended focus point. The second, known as "front focus," occurs when the AF system focuses slightly forward of the intended focus point.

AF Micro Adj. allows you to correct this problem for up to 30 lenses, so that each time you fit a fixed lens, back- or front focus problems are automatically compensated for.

The difficulty with adjusting the AF is knowing how much adjustment to make. Fortunately there are tools available that will help enormously. The first is free and can be viewed at *photo.net/learn/focustest*. The second, called LensAlign, is a commercial solution created by Michael Tapes Design (*www.michaeltapesdesign.com*).

Adjusting AF

1) Highlight **AF Micro Adj**. and press ●.

2) Press ● and set **AF Adjustment Setting** to **On**.

3) Highlight the amount and use ▲ to select a negative adjustment value (moving the focus forward), and ▼ to select a positive adjustment value (moving the focus backward). Each step equals 0.5mm, so the adjustment is very fine. The maximum adjustment is ±20, which equals 1cm of adjustment.

4) Press ● to return to the main Setup 2 menu.

> ***Notes:***
> Whenever a non-adjusted lens is fitted, the AF Micro Adj. amount is set to ±0.
>
> To erase all adjustments highlight Clear, press ●, highlight Enter, and press ● once more.

» SETUP MENU 3

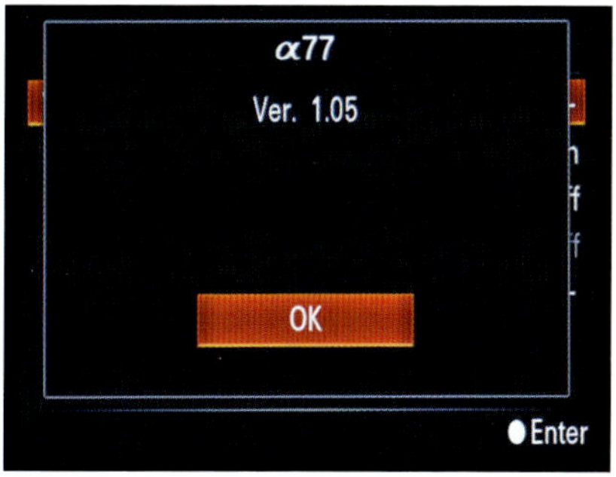

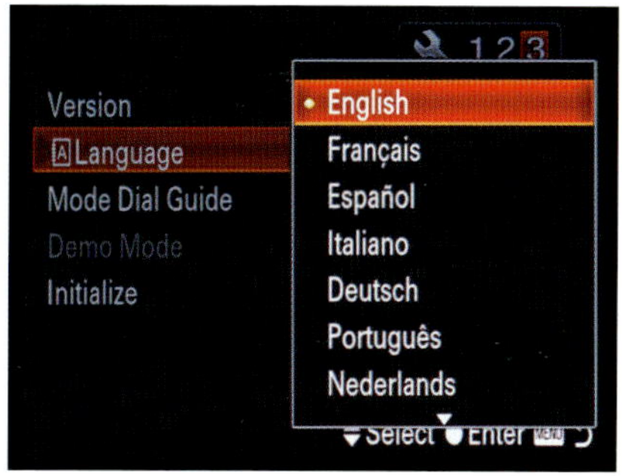

› Version

Your A77 is essentially a mini-computer, and like all computers it requires software to run. On digital cameras this is known as the firmware. Every so often Sony will issue firmware updates for the A77 to improve its functionality. The version number is the firmware update that is currently installed.

Sony announces updates on its web site, via news forums, or by email if you registered your camera online. Full instructions on how to update your camera will be included with the firmware update.

At the time of writing, the current firmware upgrade is version 1.05. This update fixed the slight time lag experienced when the camera was first switched on and when moving between menu screens. The camera functionality was also improved with an increase in the number of lenses profiled by the **Lens Compensation** function, and enhanced AF accuracy.

› Language

The A77 can display menu and shooting options in the following languages: English, French, Spanish, Italian, German, Portuguese, Dutch, Russian, Swedish, Danish, Norwegian, Finnish, Polish, Czech, Hungarian, Greek, and Turkish. Simply choose which one you prefer.

Tip

If you have a new Mac computer that uses a 64-bit kernel, Sony's firmware update software won't run: it only works using a 32-bit kernel. To switch temporarily, boot your Mac while holding down the 3 and 2 keys. This will boot it into 32-bit mode. When you next start your computer it will revert to 64-bit mode automatically.

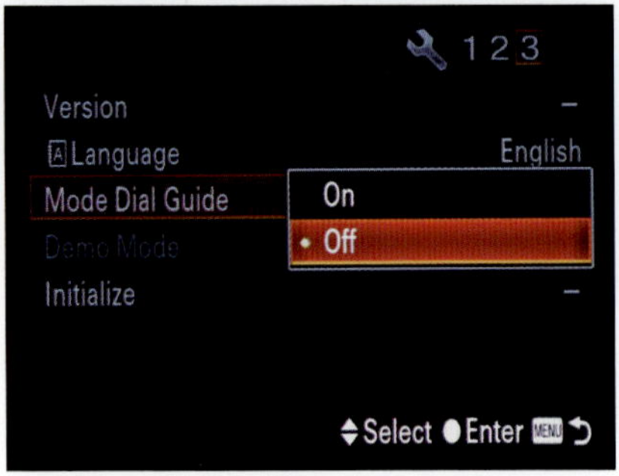

› Mode Dial Guide

As you turn the mode dial on your A77 a brief description of the selected mode is displayed. Once you feel you know your way around the camera, set this option to **Off** to help make the operation of your camera slightly faster.

› Demo Mode

Demo Mode is a slightly odd option that will play movies recorded on the memory card if the camera is left inactive for a short period of time (and if not set to power off). However, it's unlikely that you'll be able to set this option as it is permanently grayed out.

FIND A VIEW *(opposite)*
It's all too easy to shoot a conventional view of a familiar subject, but try to look for unusual juxtapositions and viewpoints.

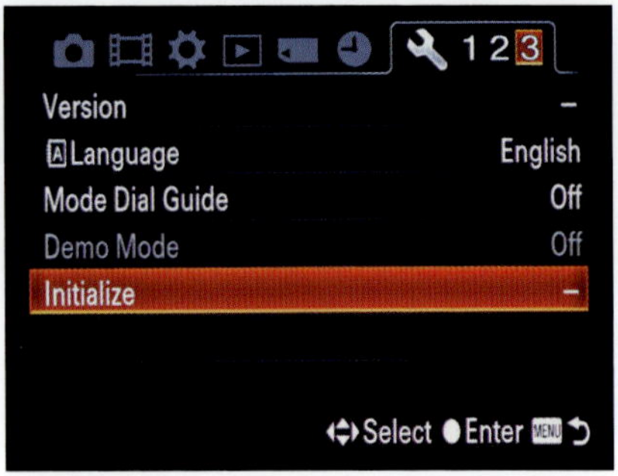

› Initialize

As the A77 is so customizable, it's possible to get to the point that you can't remember how the camera's functions are set. The **Initialize** option allows you to reset your A77 back to its original factory-settings.

Selecting **Reset Default** completely resets your A77, while **Rec mode reset** only resets functions related to still image and movie shooting. **Custom reset** only restores the ✲ Custom menus.

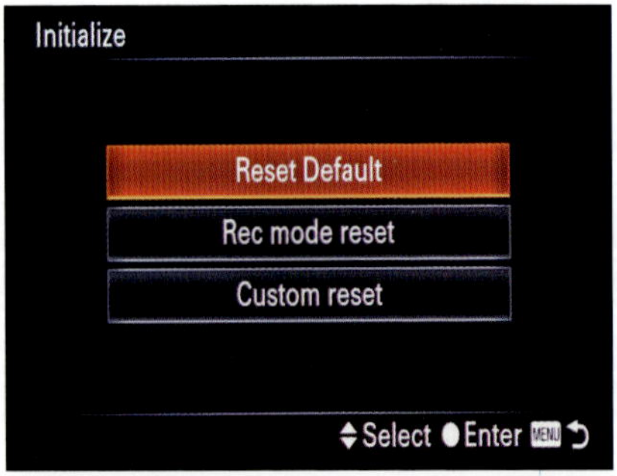

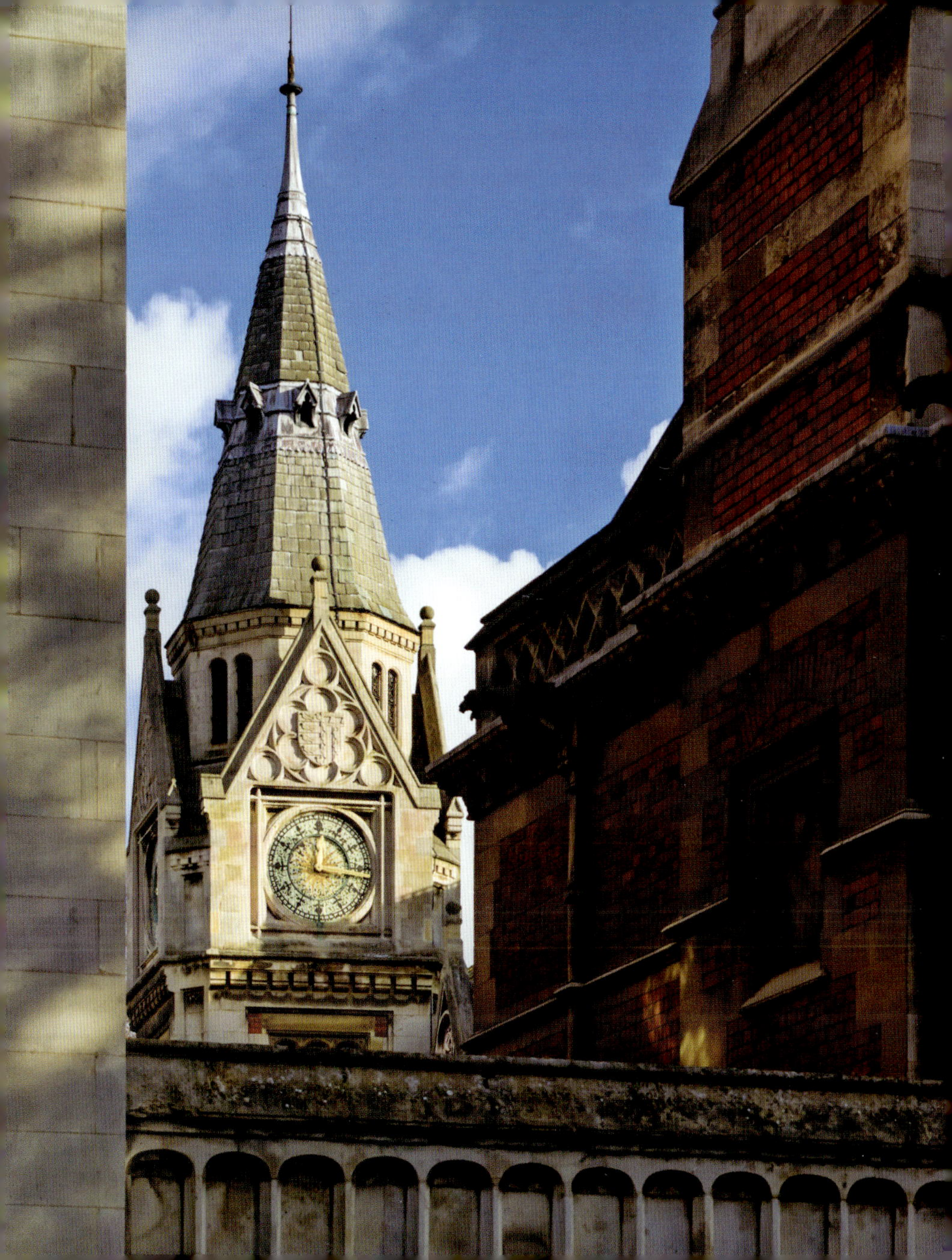

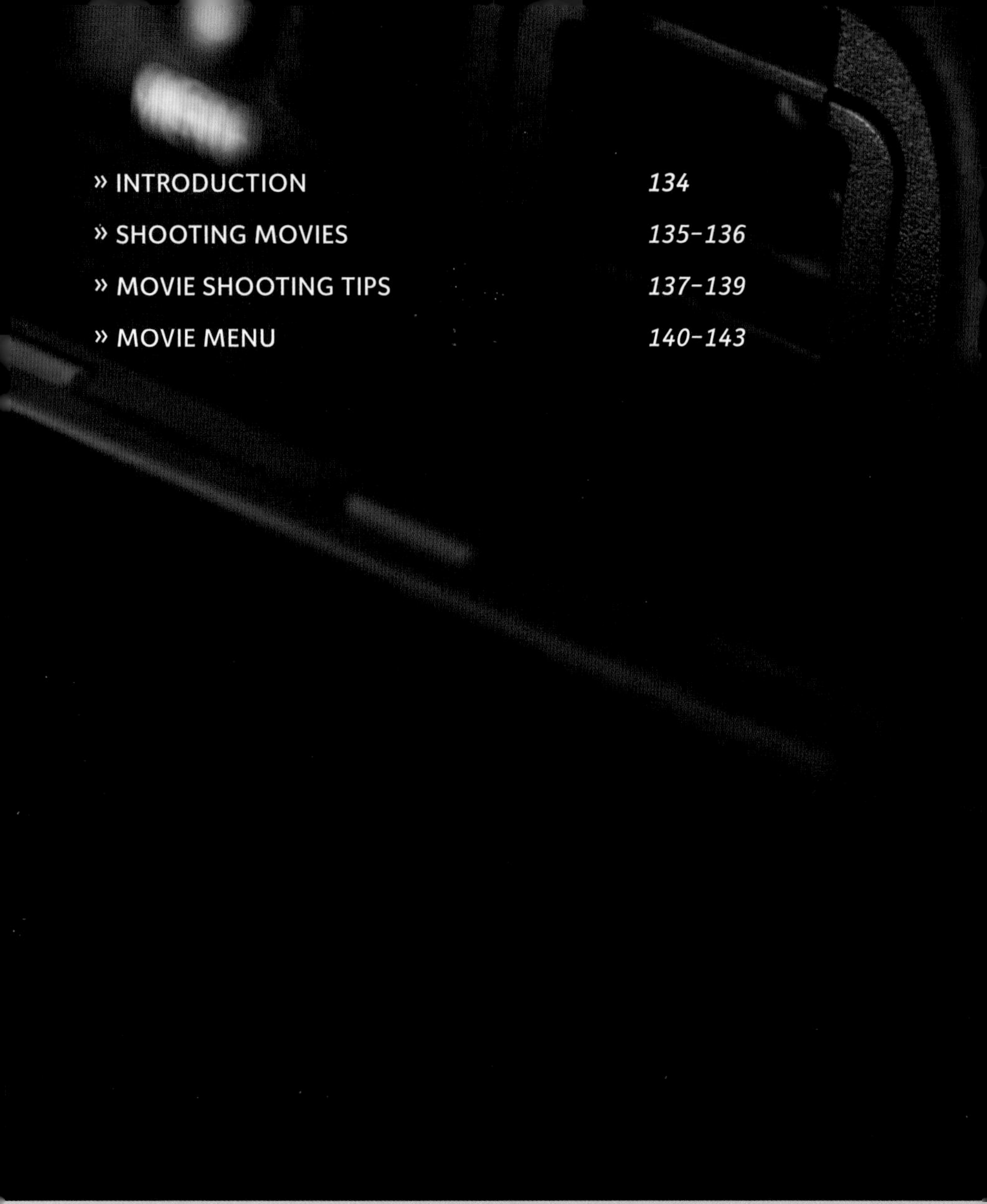

Chapter 3
MOVIES

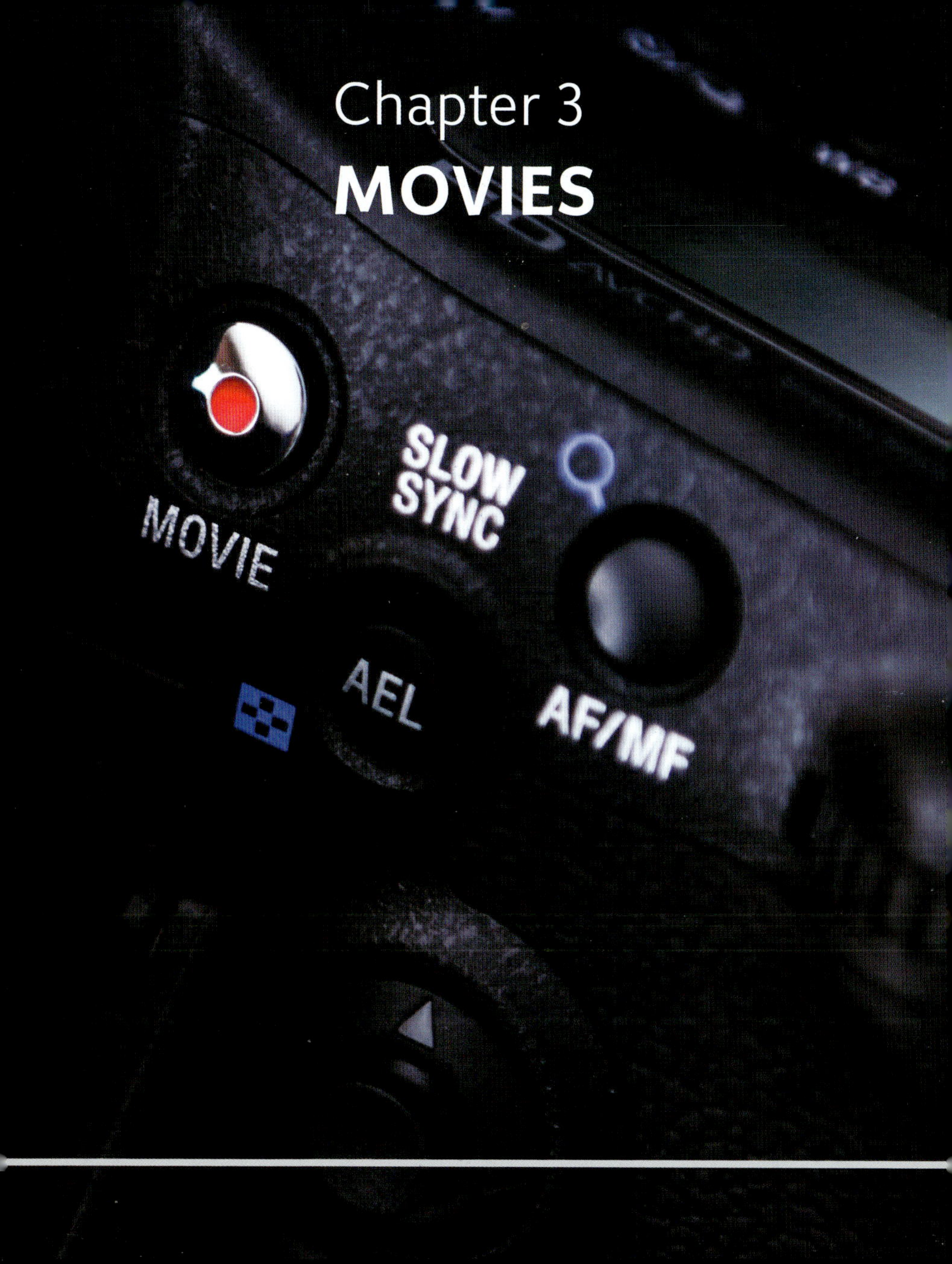

3 MOVIES

Sony wasn't the first camera manufacturer to release an interchangeable-lens camera that could shoot movies, but the company has more than caught up with the competition with the A77.

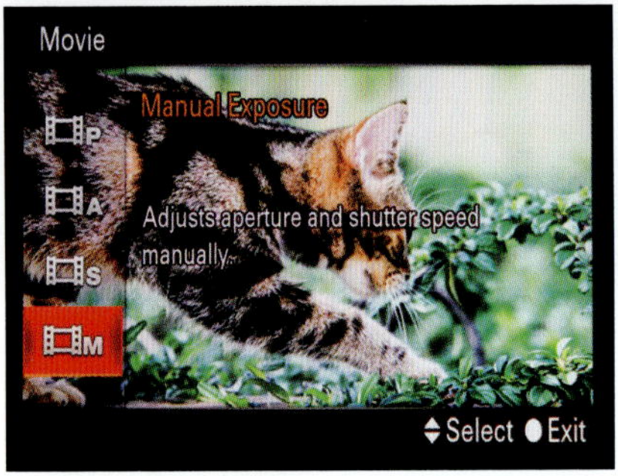

The A77 has a dedicated button that can be used to start and end movie recording, regardless of where the mode dial is positioned. This makes it quick and easy to shoot video at a moment's notice. However, setting the mode dial to gives you greater control of how the movie is recorded.

A77 movies are shot using an aspect ratio of 16:9, which is the same aspect ratio as a High Definition television (the default aspect ratio of still-image shooting is 3:2, the aspect ratio of the A77's sensor). When you press the movie record button in any mode other than , the display switches from 3:2 to 16:9, so if you have composed your movie for 3:2 you will lose a significant area at the top and bottom of the frame.

Another point to note is that the full area of the A77's sensor is not used for movie recording. This has an effect on the angle of view of a lens. The crop factor of a lens is normally 1.5 when shooting stills. When shooting movies the (horizontal) crop factor is closer to 1.86. This is most noticeable if you're shooting with a wide-angle lens as it will no longer appear as wide as it does when shooting still images. As an example, a 24mm lens used when shooting stills has the same angle of view as a 30mm lens when shooting movies.

When you switch the mode dial to the viewfinder alters before you begin shooting a movie, making composition far easier. The one drawback to working in mode is that you can't shoot still images, as the shutter-release button is effectively disabled.

Tip

If you set **Grid Line** *on 2 to any option other than* **Off** *there are tiny crosshairs in the corners of the frame that show you the area of the image used when shooting movies.*

» SHOOTING MOVIES

If you press the movie record button while the A77's mode dial is set to one of the still shooting modes, the viewfinder changes to show the area used during movie capture; the camera focuses; and movie recording begins.

The following settings chosen for still shooting, before pressing the movie record button, are used for recording your movie: AF area, Creative Style, D-Range optimizer, exposure compensation, Face Detection, ISO, Lens Compensation (Shading, Chromatic Aberration, and Distortion), metering mode, Picture Effect, Object Tracking, and white balance. As the movie is recording you can change ISO, AF area, and Object Tracking by pressing Fn, and exposure compensation by pressing ☒.

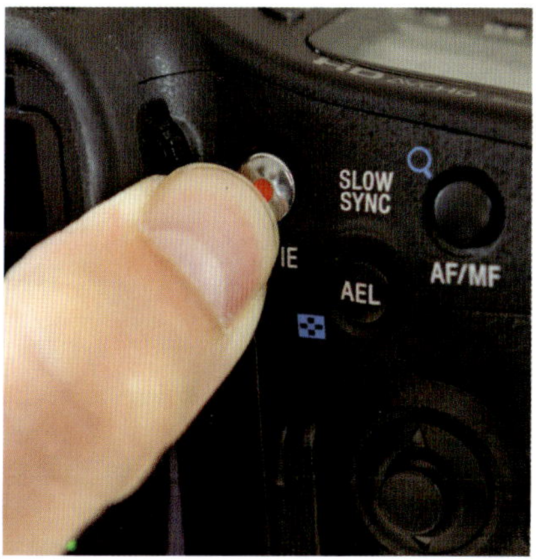

The ISO range available is ISO 100–1600 (if the value set in still shooting mode is lower or higher, the A77 will switch temporarily to ISO 100 or ISO 1600 respectively).

The A77 will automatically adjust focus and exposure during movie shooting, though you can switch to MF and/or adjust the exposure using exposure compensation and altering the ISO.

Once you're ready to stop recording, press the movie button again. The A77 will stop recording, although there may be a slight delay before you can use your camera again as the final few seconds of the movie are written to your memory card. The screen reverts to the standard display and your A77 is a still image camera again.

> ***Note:***
> Your A77 can get very hot during movie recording. If [▲] is displayed on screen, turn the camera off and allow it to cool down.

Movie recording in 🎞 mode

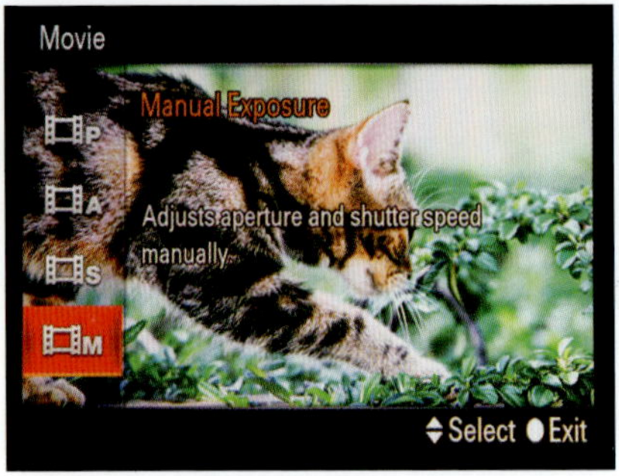

If you turn the mode dial to 🎞, more options are available to you in terms of controlling the exposure settings for your movies. However, you need to have your A77 set to MF in order to be able to use them all. Set to AF, only Program Auto is available, which sets the exposure automatically and works essentially the same way as movie shooting described on the previous page.

It's only when you switch to MF that the other three movie shooting options are available: Aperture Priority, Shutter Priority, and Manual. In practice these work exactly the same as their still shooting counterparts. With Aperture Priority, you set the aperture used for movie recording and the camera sets the shutter speed; in Shutter Priority you set the shutter speed and the camera decides on the aperture; and with Manual you control both aperture and shutter speed (and so have maximum control over the exposure).

It may seem odd that you need to switch to MF in order to have control over the exposure in this way, but there's a very practical reason for this. Autofocus requires light, and the more light there is, the more accurate the AF will be. For this reason Program Auto movie shooting defaults to as wide an aperture as possible to maintain accurate focus during movie shooting, whereas with manual focus you're given greater control of exposure and are able to use any exposure setting your wish.

> **Tip**
>
> *Use Focus Peaking as an aid to accurate focusing when focusing manually and shooting movies.*

SETTING MOVIE MODE »

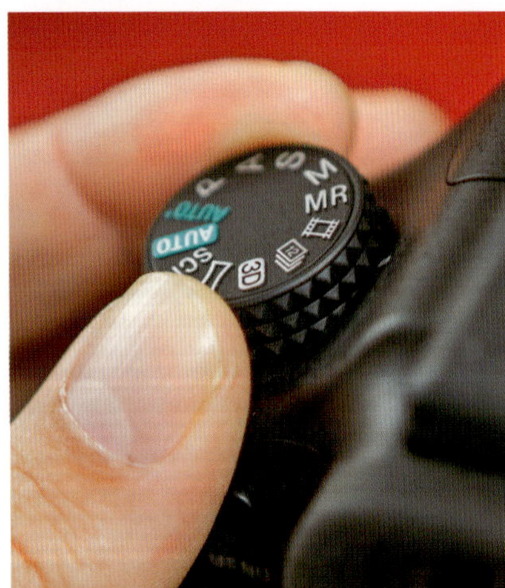

» MOVIE SHOOTING TIPS

Exposure

One of the major benefits of using a camera with a large sensor to record video is the chance to use lenses with large maximum apertures, which can provide you with a shallow depth of field for a cinematic look. This is one of the exciting aspects of the A77's movie Aperture Priority mode.

However, with a shallow depth of field, accurate focusing is a must, and Hollywood cinematographers use tape measures to guarantee the focus is accurate. Although there's no need to be quite so obsessive, it's still important to be as careful as possible when setting up a shot, and the longer the lens you use, the more accurate you will need to be. If your subject is a person, focus on their eyes and try to persuade them not to move around too much while you are recording.

The shutter speed you choose will have an impact on the look of your movie as well. A movie is shot at a certain frame rate, and your A77 allows you to choose between 60, 30, or 24 frames per second (North America/Japan) or 50 or 25 frames per second (Europe).

The shutter speed does not have to match the frame rate, so you could for instance use a shutter speed of 1/400 sec. However, using such a fast shutter speed will produce very staccato movie footage that has a stroboscopic feel to it. It can be very effective visually when shooting action sequences, but it is not comfortable to watch for any period of time.

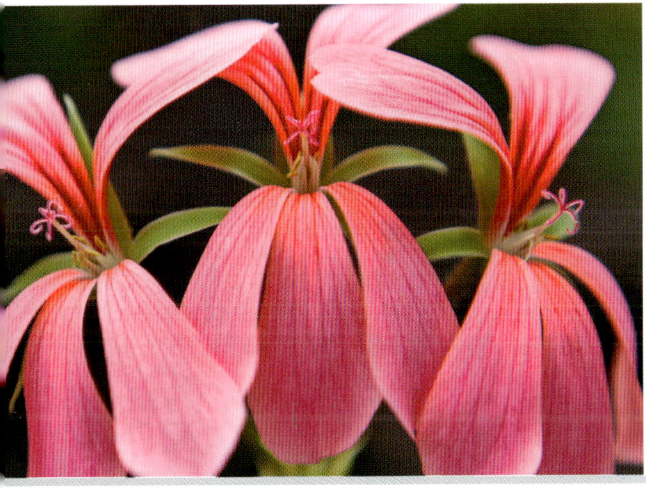

DEPTH OF FIELD «
Creating movies with a restricted depth of field is far easier with a camera such as the A77 than it is with a conventional camcorder.

The human eye actually prefers to see some motion blur when watching movie footage, so the ideal shutter speed to use is one that is twice the frame rate. So, when shooting at 24 fps use a shutter speed of 1/50 sec. (the nearest shutter speed value to the ideal), for example. Shooting at a lower shutter speed than the frame rate of the movie will produce smeary footage, particularly if there is a lot of movement.

Movement

Movies require you to constantly move the camera, right? After all it's implicit in the term itself. However, too much movement can be a bad thing. There's nothing worse than watching footage where the picture sways and bobs around randomly (in fact, this can make your audience feel nauseous). Instead, make the movement smooth and slow if the camera has to move.

Using a tripod when making movies is even more import than when shooting still images. Tripods are necessary to avoid random "jiggles" caused by handholding a camera, but tripod heads designed for photography aren't necessarily that effective for video work: a dedicated video head will allow you to make smoother movements as you pan your camera. Fast zooming can also be very off-putting, and can be difficult to achieve smoothly, so if you want to zoom, do it slowly and don't zoom over an extreme focal length range.

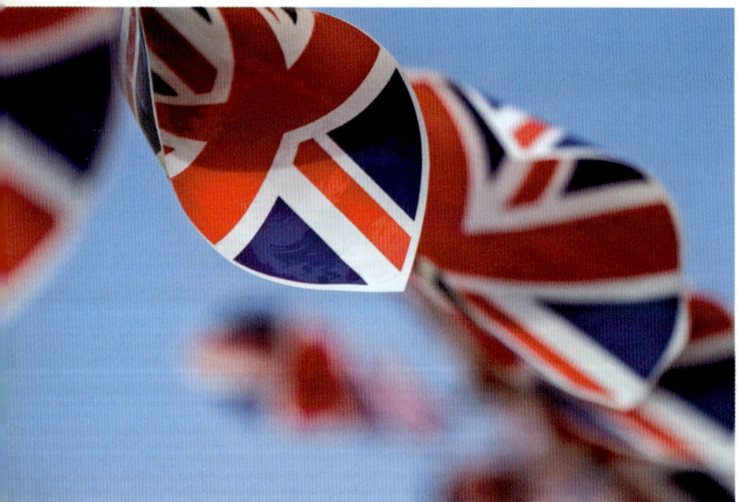

MOVEMENT «
Fast movement can look disconcertingly "choppy" when a fast shutter speed is used to shoot movies.

Composition and viewpoint

Composition is just as important when shooting movies as it is with still images, and using the A77's **Grid Line** function to set up your shots before you begin recording is a good idea if you want to keep your horizon level. This is another good reason to use a tripod. If you're recording people, use a long lens, and frame your shots to fully capture their facial expressions.

Viewpoint is important too. If you're recording children, get down to their level for a more natural perspective, and no matter what the subject is, be prepared to stop recording to set up a different composition of the scene. Switching from a wide-angle view of a scene (which is good for establishing context) to a close-up (to show detail) is an effective way of drawing your viewers into your movie.

Story

A good movie should have a structure that holds a viewer's interest, regardless of whether it's a Hollywood blockbuster or your vacation. A linear structure, where the narrative starts at a definite beginning, and progresses to the middle, before reaching a conclusion is the easiest structure, but whatever structure you decide to use, it's vitally important to determine what you intend to do before you begin shooting.

Professional movie makers will use storyboards as an aid to outlining the story's structure and this is a method of working that is well worth copying. Stick figures will suffice if you aren't great at drawing.

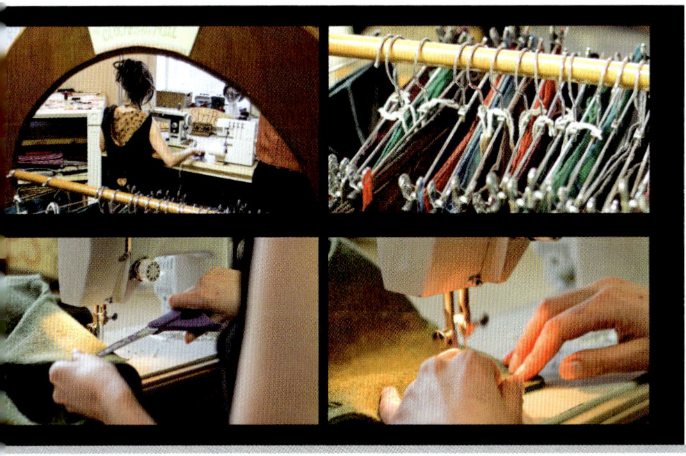

TELL A STORY «
It is a good idea to think about the flow of your movie's narrative when planning a sequence of shots.

» MOVIE MENU

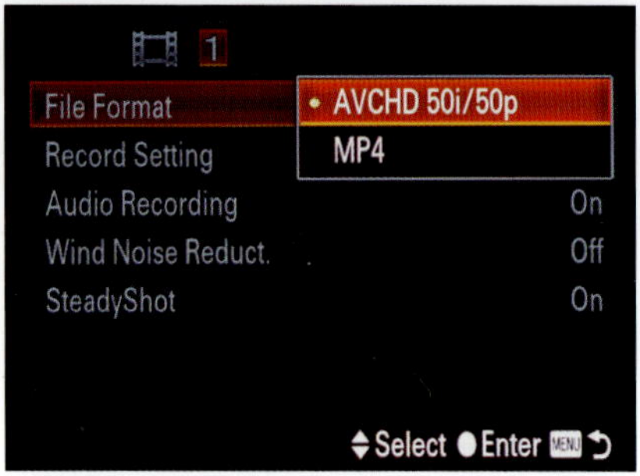

File Format

The HDTV standard supports resolutions of 1280 x 720 pixels, 1366 x 768 pixels, and 1920 x 1080 pixels, with the latter figure being the resolution that your A77 is capable of shooting at. The HDTV standard allows for a variation in the frame rate too, so countries that use the 50Hz system (mainly Europe) typically have HDTVs with frame rates of 25 or 50fps, while 60Hz systems (chiefly North America and Japan) support 24, 30, or 60fps. Finally, an HDTV can either be progressive or interlaced. Progressive systems draw each line of pixels down the screen in sequence over the course of a frame, before returning to the top for the next frame. Interlace systems draw all the odd lines first, before drawing all the even lines.

When the specifications of a particular HDTV are described, the factors above are shortened into a string of numbers and letters, so a 1080i60 HDTV set would have a resolution of 1920 x 1080 pixels and use interlace scanning at a frame rate of 60fps (meaning it is likely to be a North American television set).

The options found under **File Format** will depend on the region you bought your camera from. If it's from a 50Hz region you'll see **AVCHD 50i/50p** and **MP4**; if you bought your camera from a 60Hz region you'll see **AVHCD 60i/60p** and **MP4**.

AVHCD and MP4 refer to the file format used when saving the video. AVHCD is a professional-grade file format developed by Panasonic and Sony, and is used on many high-end video cameras. MP4 is an older video file format and is generally more compatible with video-editing software and online video resources such as YouTube. Which one of these formats you use will be largely down to what you want to do with your movies later on. An AVHCD movie file will be high resolution with an image quality suitable for use on Blu-ray players, but it will need to be converted to another format for more general use.

Record Setting

When you shoot a movie, the video and sound information is compressed. The amount of compression will affect the quality of the final movie and how much storage space is required on a hard drive

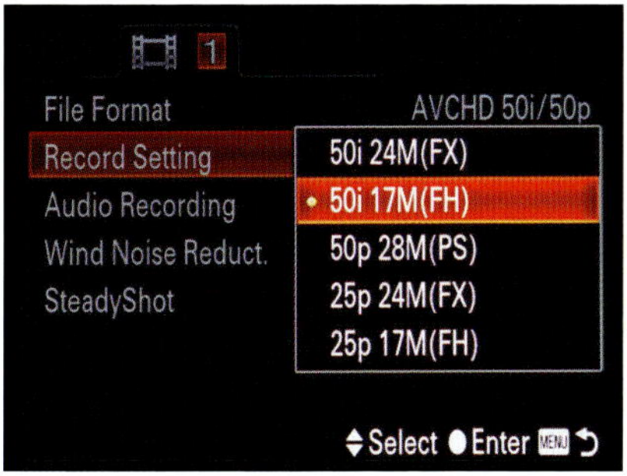

or memory card. If the compression is too high, the image quality will be seriously compromised, but the movie file will be smaller. Use too low a compression and you'll have wonderful image quality, but you may not have the storage capacity to shoot more than a few minutes or even seconds of footage.

The A77 allows you to set the bit rate of your footage. This is essentially how much data is used for every second of footage, and is determined by the compression: the higher the bit rate, the lower the compression rate. The bit rate is measured in Mbps (Megabits per second), and as a comparison, DVD is able to cope with movie files compressed to 18 Mbps, while Blu-Ray handles movie files compressed to 48 Mbps.

AVHCD

File format	Average bit-rate	Description
60i 24M(FX) 50i 24M(FX)	24 Mbps	Records high-quality, low-compression movies at 1920 x 1080 pixels. Can be used for making Blu-ray movies, but is not suitable for DVD.
60i 17M(FH) 50i 17M(FH)	17 Mbps	Records lower quality, higher-compressed movies at 1920 x 1080 pixels.
60p 28M(PS) 50p 28M(PS)	28 Mbps	Highest quality images for lowest compression at 1920 x 1080 pixels. Needs to be re-encoded to be usable for Blu-ray.
24p 24M(FX) 25p 24M(FX)	24 Mbps	Records high-quality, low-compression movies at 1920 x 1080 pixels. Can be used for making Blu-ray movies, but is not suitable for DVD.
24p 17M(FH) 25p 17M(FH)	17 Mbps	Records lower quality, higher-compressed movies at 1920 x 1080 pixels.

MP4		
File format	**Average bit-rate**	**Description**
1440 x 1080 12M	12 Mbps	Records movies at 1440 x 1080 pixels.
VGA 3M	3 Mbps	Records movies at 640 x 480 pixels. Suitable for web use or streaming over a network.

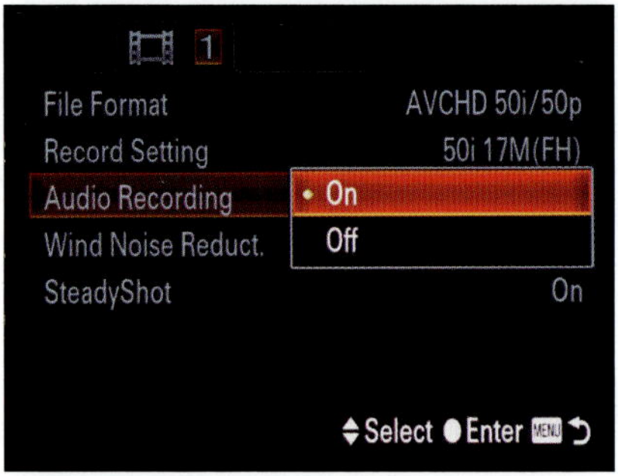

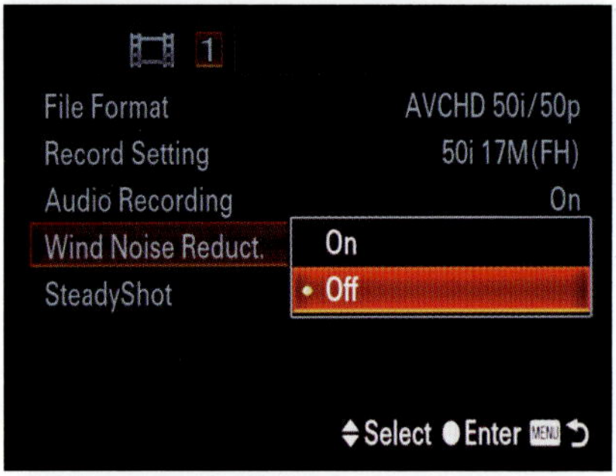

Audio Recording

If you want to take the silent movie approach to film making you can switch **Audio Recording** to **Off**. In many respects this is no bad thing: the A77 has built-in stereo microphones on the top of the camera, but built-in microphones are not ideal unless your subject is relatively close to the camera, and they can also suffer from wind noise. If you don't have access to a suitable external microphone it's often better to record a soundtrack later to mix with the video. This will involve a lot of work—particularly if dialog is needed—but the resulting movie will be far more polished and professional.

Wind Noise Reduct.

Wind noise can be distracting on a movie soundtrack. External microphones can be fitted with covers and baffles that help to reduce the noise of wind on a movie soundtrack, but this is harder to do with a built-in microphone.

When switched **On**, **Wind Noise Reduct**. electronically filters out the bass noises associated with wind. It works reasonably well, as long as there aren't other, more vital, noises that in the same register. Switch **Wind Noise Reduct. Off** if there is no wind where you are shooting.

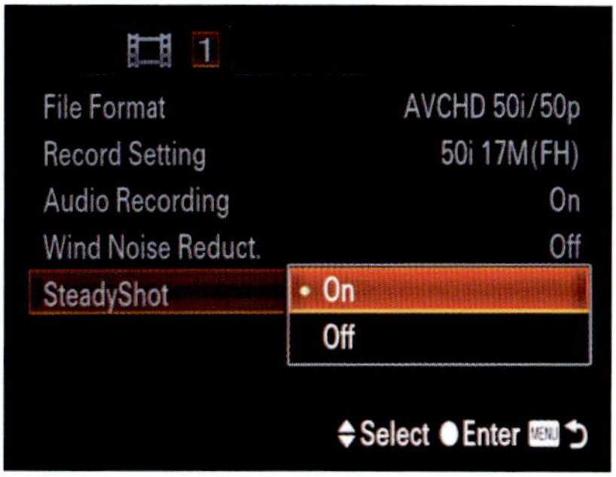

SteadyShot

SteadyShot can be activated or deactivated separately for still image and movie shooting, but the stabilization system works in the same way for both.

EQUIPMENT »

You can begin shooting movies with just your A77, but if you want to go further, Sony sells additional equipment that will make video making easier. Pictured here is the CLM-V55 external monitor (which connects to the A77's HDMI socket), a bracket, and the ECM-CG50 external microphone.

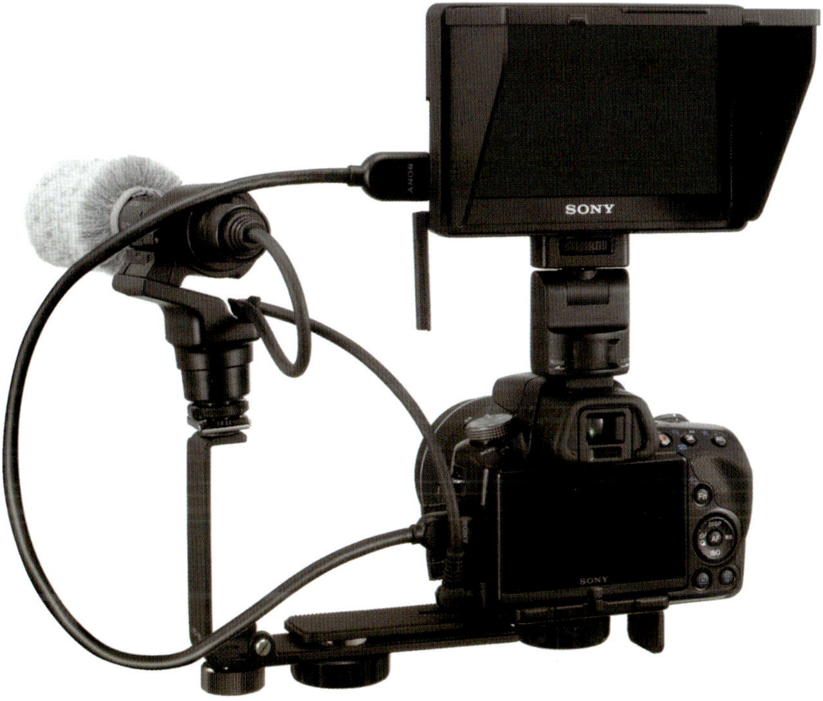

Chapter 4
LENSES

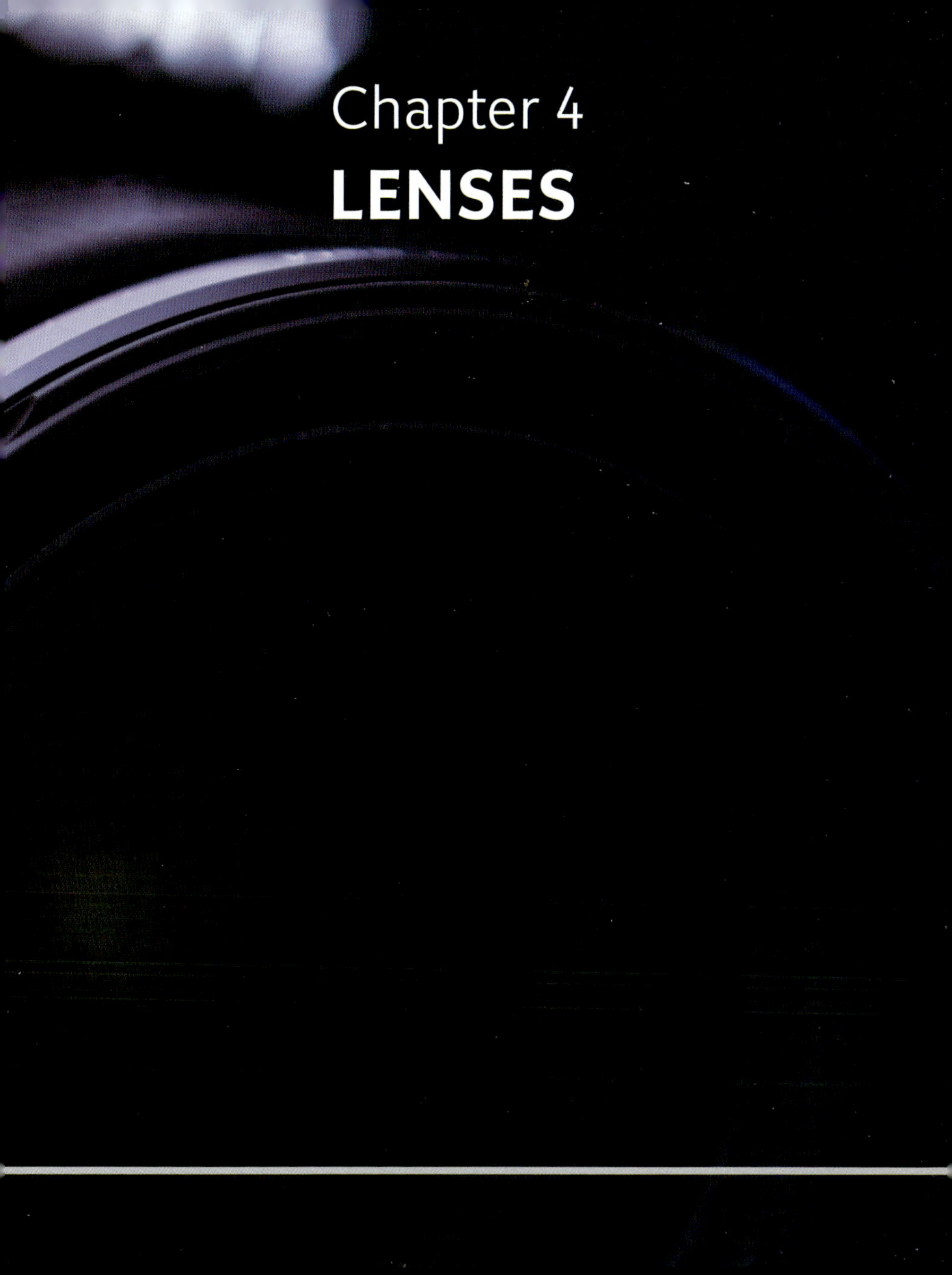

4 LENSES

When Sony bought the rights to Konica Minolta's camera system it inherited a lens range that was developed in the 1980s. In the intervening years Sony has introduced new lenses designed specifically for digital cameras. The upshot of this is that there is now an extensive choice of lenses, both new and pre-owned, that can be fitted to your A77.

There are currently 36 different lenses produced by Sony. The range encompasses consumer zoom lenses and professional grade zooms, prime and macro lenses, as well as a few interesting types unique to Sony, such as the auto-focusing 500mm mirror lens.

The lens range is in continual development, and at the time of writing Sony has announced a hand-built 600mm lens for the discerning photographer with very deep pockets.

Of course, you don't have to use Sony-branded lenses with your A77. Third-party manufacturers such as Sigma and Tamron also support the A-mount system, and lenses from these manufacturers are often equal to Sony's offerings in terms of performance. There is also a huge array of pre-owned Konica Minolta lenses that can be found readily in camera stores and on the Internet.

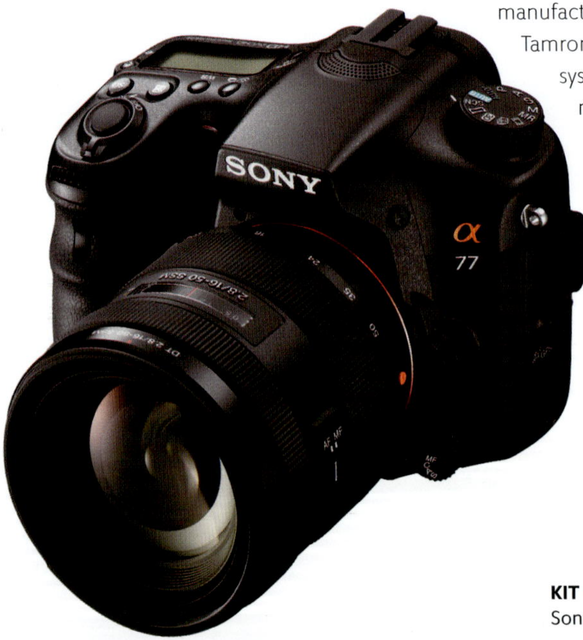

KIT LENS «
Sony A77 with 16–50mm "kit" lens.

» LENS TECHNOLOGY

Looking at Sony's expanding lens line-up it is very easy to become overwhelmed by the acronyms, esoteric terms, and strings of numbers that describe the various functions of a lens. The following is a short guide to the Sony lens range and the technologies used in its construction:

Anomalous Dispersion (AD) glass

All lenses suffer to a certain extent from chromatic aberration. AD glass has a low refractive index and is designed to keep chromatic aberration to a minimum.

Aspheric elements

Light passing through the central area of a lens cannot always be focused at precisely the same distance as light passing through the edge. This can cause uneven image sharpness. Lenses with aspheric elements are optimized to focus light evenly across the image.

Carl Zeiss

Lenses designed and manufactured by Carl Zeiss for Sony's A-mount are regarded as the very best in the range, with superb build quality and exceptional optics. This quality comes at a price though, as Carl Zeiss lenses are expensive, particularly in comparison to similar lenses in Sony's DT range. Unique to Carl Zeiss is the T* coating on the optical surfaces of its lenses, which allows higher light transmission, and minimizes flare and ghosting.

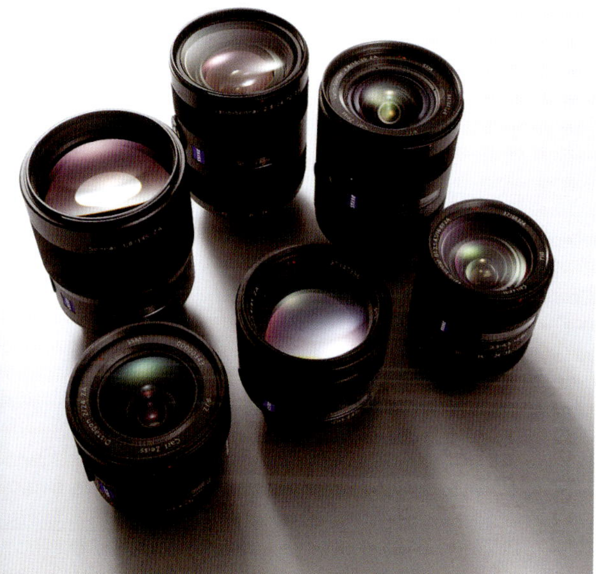

CARL ZEISS «
The current range of Carl Zeiss lenses.

4

Circular aperture

A lens aperture is made up of a number of blades that form a polygonal shape. Out-of-focus highlight areas in an image roughly take on this shape. A lens with a larger number of aperture blades—producing more aesthetically pleasing circular out-of-focus highlight shapes—is generally preferable to a lens with fewer aperture blades.

Direct Manual Focus (DMF)

A lens with DMF allows you to manually make fine adjustments to focus after the camera has locked focus using the AF system. This is particularly useful when shooting portraits or macro subjects when accurate focus is critical.

Digital Technology (DT)

Lenses designated as DT are designed specifically for APS-C sensor cameras such as the A77. To date, this means that they are compatible with every A-mount camera produced by Sony with the exception of the full-frame A900 and A850 cameras (with a third full-frame camera confirmed for release late 2012).

If you plan to upgrade to a full-frame camera at some point it may be sensible to avoid DT lenses, but this does mean foregoing ultra-wide lenses for your A77, such as Sony's 11–18mm DT lens.

Typically, DT lenses are the least expensive in the Sony range. This often means that cheaper materials are used in their construction. DT zoom lenses also restrict you to a relatively small maximum aperture. Most of Sony's DT lenses use SAM or SSM technology.

E-mount

The E-mount is a new lens system, introduced by Sony for its NEX camera models. E-mount lenses are not compatible with Sony's DSLR and SLT cameras, but it is possible to use A-mount lenses on NEX cameras with Sony's LA-EA1 and LA-EA2 lens adapters.

Floating focusing

A lens with a floating focusing mechanism has one or more optical elements that move independently of the other elements as the lens is focused. This system is

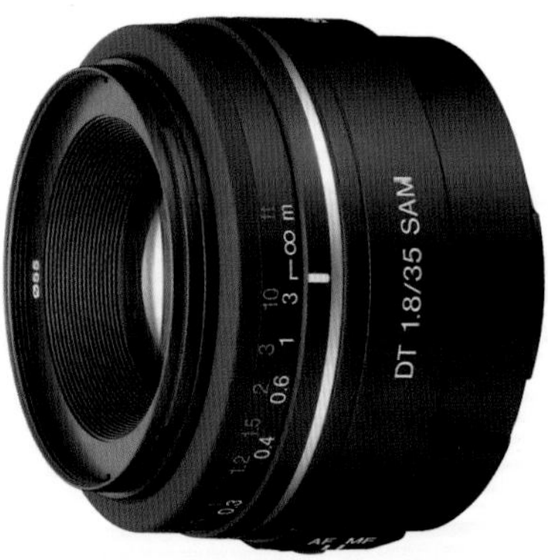

DT LENS «
Sony 35mm DT lens.

typically used on wideangle lenses to reduce chromatic aberration, particularly when the lens is used at its closest focus.

Focus hold

The focus hold button can be used to temporarily disable AF without the need to switch it off using the main switch on the camera or lens.

Focus range limiter

This system is mainly found on macro lenses to limit the AF to a narrow range of focusing distances, rather than allowing it to hunt across the entire focus distance range.

G lenses

Sony's G lenses rival those of Carl Zeiss for build and optical quality and are regarded as the company's "professional" range. G-series lenses tend to have larger maximum apertures than "consumer" lenses and are therefore heavier and larger. The G in the name stands for "Gold"—the concept and name introduced originally by Konica Minolta.

Internal focus (IF)

A lens with internal focus is able to focus without rotating the front lens element. This is achieved by moving an internal lens element group (or groups). A lens without IF can be frustrating when using filters that require precise alignment for their effect, especially polarizing filters. IF is also of benefit when shooting macro subjects; as the front element of lens does not extend outward during focusing, it is less likely to disturb (or even touch) your subject as it focuses.

Konica Minolta

As stated previously, it's possible to use Konica Minolta lenses on the A77. Some current Sony lenses are essentially rebranded Konica Minolta lenses, but there are also some lens types no longer used by Sony: the High Speed (HS) lens series, for example, as well as Konica Minolta's xi series.

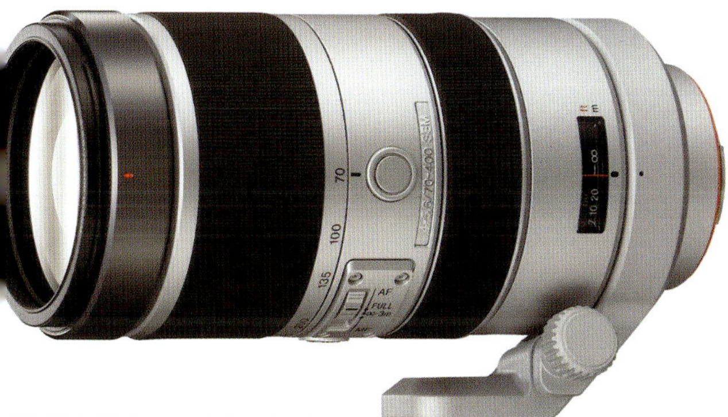

G LENS «
Sony 70–400mm G-series lens.

Reflex lenses

The longer the focal length of a lens, the longer and heavier it will be. Reflex lenses (also known as a mirror or catadioptric lens) are far smaller, lighter, and cheaper than an equivalent conventional lens. This is achieved by the use of a series of mirrors to focus light instead of a lens. Sony currently produces a 500mm reflex lens (product code SAL-500F80), which is the only lens of its type—across all brands—that supports AF.

There are a few compromises that need to be accepted when using reflex lenses. Unlike a standard lens, a reflex lens has a fixed aperture, which on the Sony 500mm lens is of f/8. This reduces the efficiency of the AF system in all but the brightest conditions, and obviously gives no control over depth of field. Another quirk of reflex lenses is the distinctive donut-shaped out-of-focus highlights, which can look distinctly odd when they are dominant in an image.

SAM and SSM

SAM is short for Smooth Autofocus Motor, and SSM stands for Supersonic-Wave Motor. Prior to the introduction of SAM and SSM lenses, a motor housed in the camera body drove AF, but a SAM/SSM lens has a built-in AF drive. Although the A77 features an AF motor inside the body, so it is backward compatible with non-SAM/SSM lenses, SAM/SSM lenses offer a faster, smoother, and quieter AF experience.

Tripod collar

Tripod collars wrap around long, heavy lenses, allowing you to fix the lens (rather than the camera) to a tripod. This is beneficial in several ways. Firstly, it reduces the strain on the camera's lens mount. Secondly, it shifts the center of gravity closer to the center of the camera/lens combination, making the setup more stable and less prone to movement during exposure.

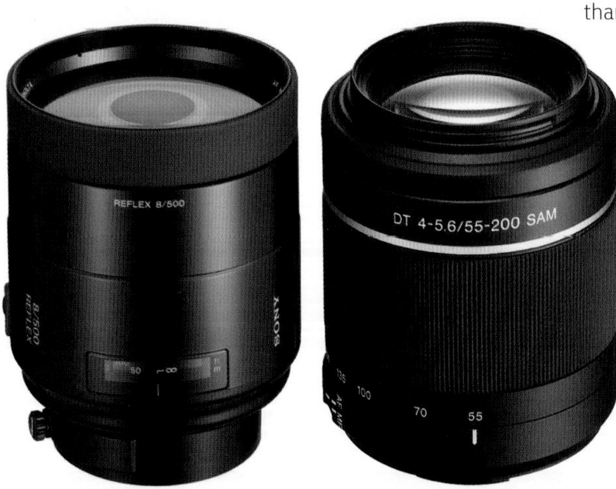

REFLEX AND SAM LENSES «
Sony 500mm reflex lens *(far left)* and Sony 55–200mm DT lens with SAM *(left)*.

» LENS PROPERTIES

Focal length

The dictionary definition of focal length is the distance in millimeters from the optical center of the lens to the focal plane when a subject at infinity is in focus (the A77's sensor lies on the focal plane, shown by the ⊖ mark on the top plate of the camera). Practically, the focal length of a lens determines the magnification at which distant objects are recorded. The smaller the focal length of a lens, the less distant objects are magnified and the smaller they will appear in the image. The longer the focal length of a lens, the greater the magnification and the larger they will appear.

It is important to understand that the focal length of a lens never changes: a focal length of 50mm is always 50mm, regardless of the camera it is mounted to. What will change, however, is the angle of view of the lens depending on the size of the sensor. Lenses either have a fixed focal length—commonly referred to as a "prime" lens—or have a variable focal length, known as a zoom lens.

Angle of view

The angle (or field) of view of a lens is the angular extent of the image projected by the lens and recorded by the sensor in the camera. The angle of view is expressed in degrees (°) and can refer to either the horizontal, vertical, or diagonal coverage of the lens. Typically, if you see one angle of view figure it will refer to the diagonal. The angle of view is dependant on the focal length of a lens and the size of the sensor that records the image projected by the lens.

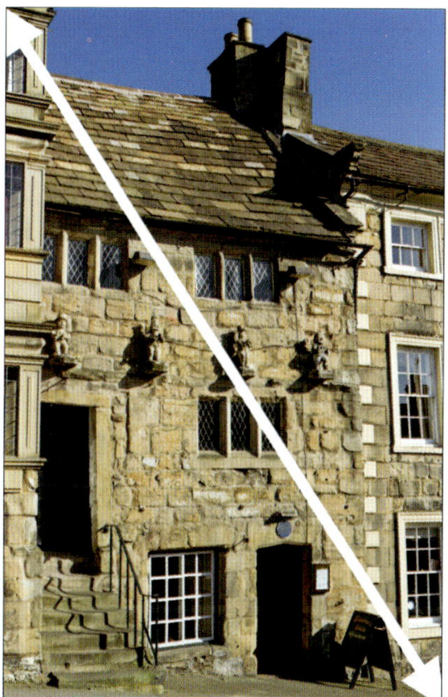

DIAGONAL «

This image was shot with a 35mm lens, which has a diagonal angle of view (indicated) of 44° when mounted on the A77.

4

Crop factor

Sony uses two different sized sensors for its range of interchangeable lens cameras. The first, and largest, sensor type is based on the dimensions of the 35mm film format (or "full-frame"), while the second is based on the dimensions of the APS-C film format. APS-C is the type of sensor that is used in the A77 and as it is smaller than 35mm/full-frame, it causes the angle of view of a lens to be reduced.

The crop factor is a figure that tells you how much the angle of view is reduced between the two formats, and with the Sony A77 the crop factor is 1.5x. This means that while a 50mm lens has an angle of view of 48° on a full-frame camera, it will have a more restricted angle of view of 32° (48/1.5) when mounted on the A77. As this suggests, a lens will appear to have a longer focal length when fitted to the A77 than when fitted to a full-frame camera. This isn't strictly true (the focal length isn't actually changed), but it's reasonable to think that way and many manufacturers use the term "35mm equivalent" to describe lenses for just this reason. For example, the

CROPPED
The main image was shot on a full-frame camera using a 28mm focal length. If a 28mm focal length was used on the A77, the angle of view would be reduced—only the section within the red box would be recorded.

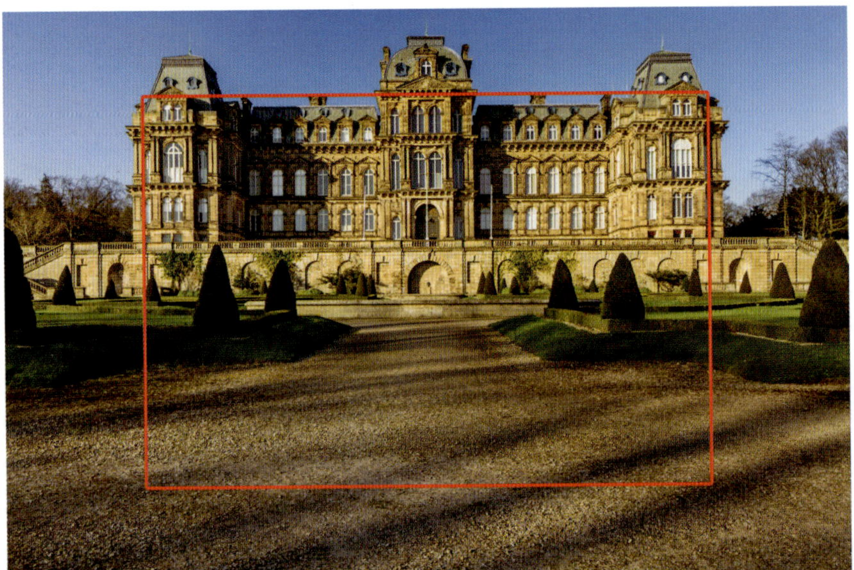

16–50mm kit lens for the A77 is equivalent to a 24–75mm lens fitted to a full-frame camera in terms of its angle of view.

Perspective

In photography, perspective describes the spatial relationships of elements within an image. Elements can appear to be far apart within an image, or apparently stacked together; the effects of a wideangle and telephoto lens respectively.

An important aspect of photography is the choice of lens that creates the most pleasing perspective for your subject and its surroundings. A good example is portraiture. A wideangle lens is a good choice if you want to shoot a portrait of a person in the context of their surroundings, but a simple head-and-shoulders shot would involve getting in very close to your subject. The perspective from such a short distance is not ideal, as it will result in a distorted image. A better solution would be to use a longer lens, which would allow you to step back from your subject and create a more natural perspective.

PERSPECTIVE »

The change in perspective isn't due to the lens you use; it is caused by your position relative to the subject. The image on the left was taken from within a few feet of the subject using a 24mm focal length, while the image on the right was taken from a greater distance using a 70mm focal length.

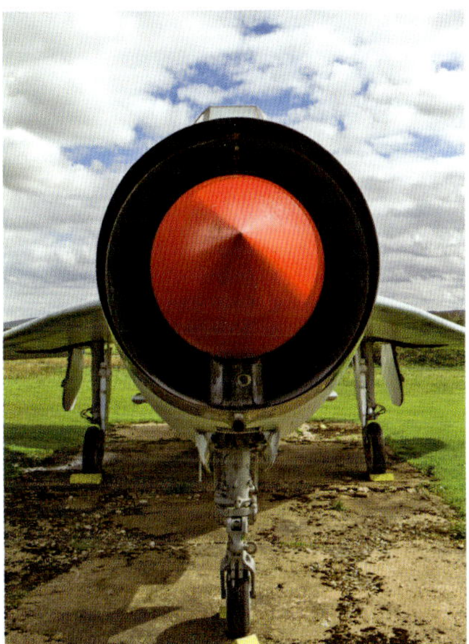

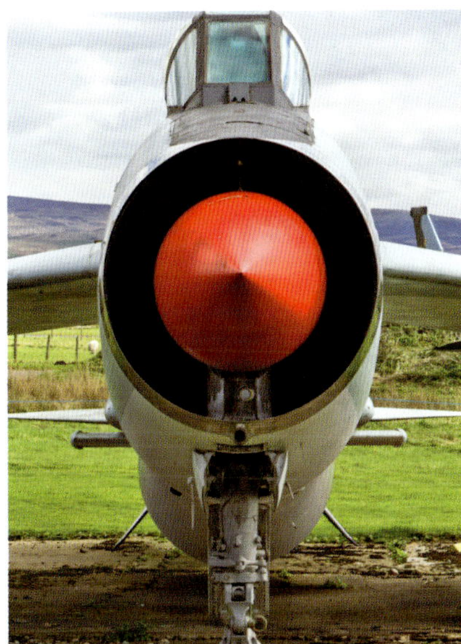

Standard lenses

A standard (or "normal") lens is one that creates an image with a field of view and perspective similar to that seen by the human eye. This is usually achieved with a lens that has a focal length equal to the diagonal size of the sensor.

On full-frame cameras this is usually regarded as a 50mm lens (though 43mm is actually closer to the mark) and on the A77—with its APS-C size sensor—a standard lens is closer to 28mm. The kit lenses that are supplied with the A77 happily include this focal length, although Sony also sells 28mm prime lenses that could be used as an alternative.

KIT LENS »

The 18–55mm and 16–50mm kit lenses both cover the A77's "standard" focal length of 28mm.

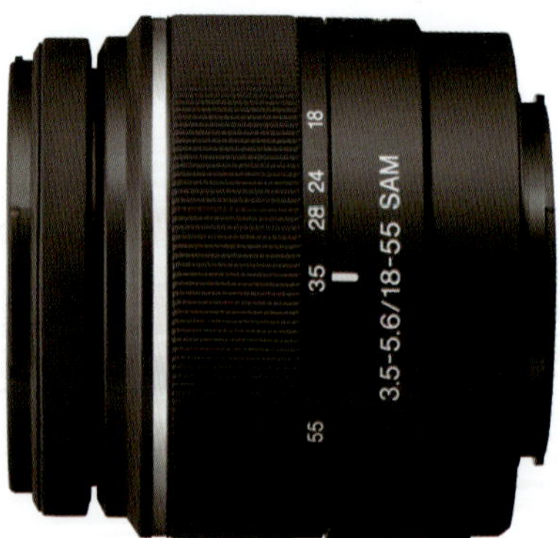

Wideangle lenses

A wideangle lens is a lens with an angle of view that is wider than a standard lens. On the A77 this means a lens with a focal length of less than 28mm. The wider a lens, the more unnatural the perspective of an image will look, with the distance between elements in a scene appearing to increase.

The most extreme example of a wideangle lens is a fisheye lens. Fisheye lenses typically have an angle of view approaching 180°—essentially the entire view in front of the camera. The images from fisheye lenses are distinctly odd to look at, with few straight lines to be seen. Sony produce one fisheye lens—the SAL-16F28—although the A77's crop factor means that the angle of coverage is reduced to 110°. Less extreme is the SAL-1118 DT lens, an 11–18mm super wideangle lens for the A77 that comes close to matching the extreme angle of view of a fisheye lens.

Tip

A 50mm lens on an A77 has an angle of view closer to a 75mm lens on a full-frame camera. This turns a 50mm lens on an A77 into an excellent portrait lens.

Because of the visual qualities of a wideangle lens they don't make good close-up portrait lenses, but they are commonly used by landscape photographers to help convey a sense of space or when working close to a subject to emphasize the subject in relation to its surroundings. Another use for a wideangle lens is when shooting in a location where there may be little space to work, such as an interior.

Telephoto lenses

Strictly speaking, a telephoto lens is one that uses special optical elements enabling the physical length of the lens to be shorter than the focal length. However, the term telephoto is now mainly used to describe a lens with a long focal length, and this is the way the term is used here. Telephoto lenses will magnify a distant subject, reducing the need to get close to it, and yet still allowing you to fill the frame. Telephoto lenses are popular with photojournalists, sports, and wildlife photographers, as they allow the photographer to maintain a discreet distance between themselves and their subject to avoid either disturbing it or alerting it to the photographer's presence.

SPACE »
With an 11mm focal length, huge swathes of a landscape can be captured.

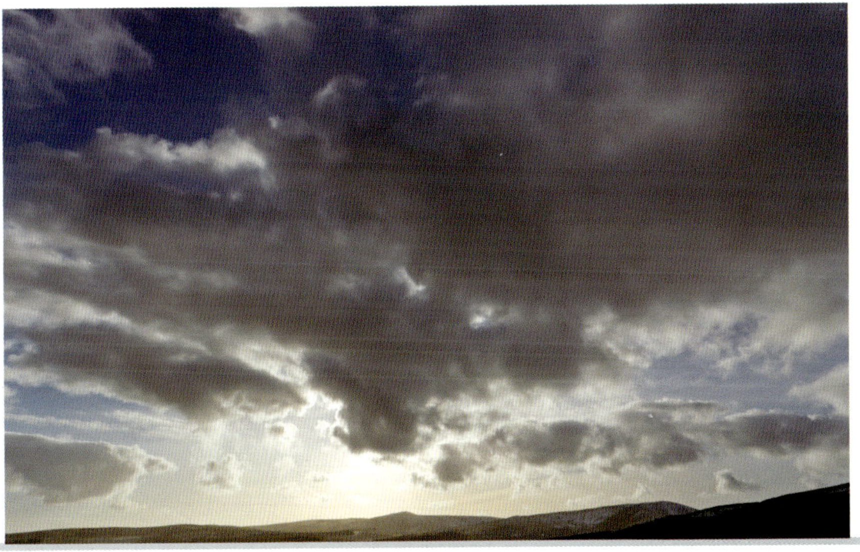

For more general use, a mild telephoto makes a good lens for portrait photography. This is partly because moving back from the subject creates a more flattering perspective, but it is also because it's less intimidating for the subject when the camera is further away.

Longer telephoto lenses are often bulky and difficult to handhold successfully, and as they have a high magnification, any movement of the lens will be exaggerated. The A77's SteadyShot function will help to some degree, but the only way of guaranteeing sharp images is to use a tripod. Some of Sony's longer telephoto lenses have their own mount-collars for added stability when attached to a tripod.

Prime lenses vs. zooms

A prime lens has a fixed focal length, such as 28mm, 50mm, or 200mm. This is opposed to a zoom lens, which has a variable focal length, such as the A77's 16–50mm kit lens. The main drawback with prime lenses is that you need lots of them if you want to cover a range of focal lengths, and obviously the more lenses you have in an equipment bag, the heavier it will get. You'll also need to change lenses more frequently, and there's always the chance that the wrong lens is fitted to your camera just as that once-in-a-lifetime photographic moment presents itself.

It's perhaps not surprising then that primes are often overlooked in favor of zoom lenses: it would be possible to own just one wide-ranging "superzoom" and never need to buy another lens. However, prime lenses do have some advantages over zooms. For a start, they tend to have superior optical quality (although zooms are starting to catch up in this respect) and also generally have larger maximum apertures, making them ideal for low-light work or for minimizing depth of field. While it's possible to buy zoom lenses with large maximum apertures, these tend to be both heavy and expensive.

Sony produces a number of prime lenses for the A mount, ranging from a 16mm wideangle to the specialist 500mm reflex lens.

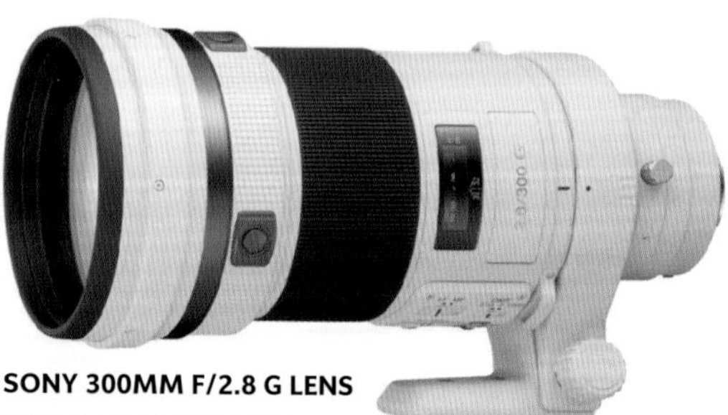

SONY 300MM F/2.8 G LENS

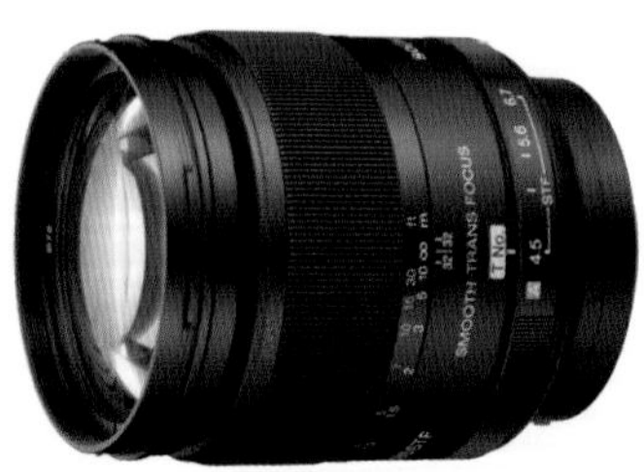

SONY 135MM F/2.8 G LENS

» TELECONVERTERS

Teleconverters fit between a camera body and a lens to increase the focal length of the lens by a given factor. This is achieved through the use of lens elements within the teleconverter. Sony currently produces two teleconverters for the A-mount. The first, a 1.4x model, increases a lens's focal length by a factor of 1.4, while the second, a 2x model, increases the focal length by a factor of 2.

Teleconverters are a useful way to increase the range of a lens collection at a relatively low cost, but they do involve an element of compromise. As a teleconverter adds complexity to a lens system image quality is inevitably degraded, and using a teleconverter also makes a lens "slower": the 1.4x teleconverter reduces the amount of light reaching the sensor by one stop and the 2x by two stops.

Notes:

Only selected Sony lenses work with the teleconverters: 70–200mm f/2.8G, 300mm f/2.8, 135mm f/2.8 STF, and 70–400mm F4-5.6 G SSM. The latter two also become MF only.

The smaller the maximum aperture of your lens, the less likely that the A77's AF will work effectively (if indeed it will work at all).

Teleconverter	Sony product code	Specifications	Dimensions: (diameter x length)	Weight
1.4x	SAL-14TC	Lens group elements: 4-5	64 x 20mm	170g
2x	SAL-20TC	Lens group elements: 5-6	64 x 43.5mm	200g

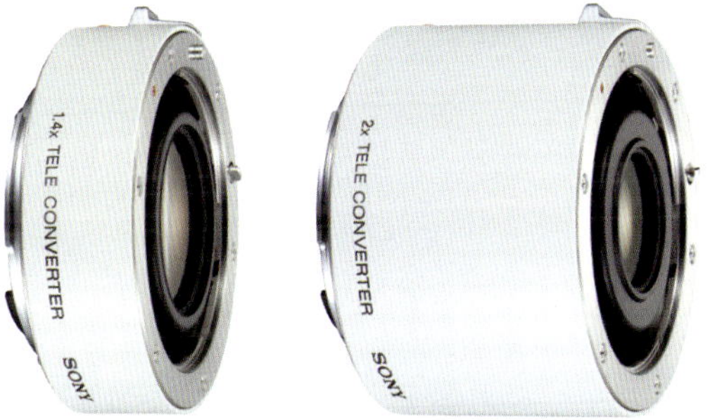

TELECONVERTERS «
Sony's SAL-14TC *(left)* and SAL-20TC *(right)*.

SONY LENSES	Sony product code	35mm equivalent focal length	Angle of view
Zoom			
11–18mm f/4.5–5.6 DT	SAL-1118	16.5–27	104–76
16–35mm f/2.8 Carl Zeiss Vario-Sonnar T*	SAL-1635Z	24–53	83–44
16–50mm f/2.8 SSM	SAL-1650	24–75	83–32
16–80mm f/3.5–4.5 DT Zeiss Vario-Sonnar T*	SAL-1680Z	24–120	83–20
16–105mm f/3.5–5.6 DT	SAL-16105	24–157.5	83–15
18–55mm f/3.5–5.6 DT SAM	SAL-1855	27–82.5	76–29
18–200mm f/3.5–6.3 DT	SAL-18200	27–300	76–8
18–250mm f/3.5–6.3 DT	SAL-18250	27–375	76–6.3
24–70mm f/2.8 ZA Carl Zeiss Vario Sonnar T*	SAL-2470Z	36–105	61–23
28–75mm f/2.8 SAM	SAL-2875	42–112.5	54–21
55–200mm f/4–5.6 DT SAM	SAL-55200-2	82.5–300	29–8
70–200mm f/2.8 G	SAL-70200G	105–300	23–8
70–300mm f/4.5–5.6 G	SAL-70300G	105–450	23–5.2
70–400mm f/4–5.6 G	SAL-70400G	105–600	23–4
75–300mm f/4.5–5.6	SAL-75300	112.5–450	21–5.2
Macro			
30mm f/2.8 Macro DT	SAL-30M28	45	50
50mm f/2.8 Macro	SAL-50M28	75	32
100mm f/2.8 Macro	SAL-100M28	150	16
Prime			
16mm f/2.8 Fisheye	SAL-16F28	24	110
20mm f/2.8	SAL-20F28	30	70
24mm f/2.0 Carl Zeiss Distagon T*	SAL-24F20Z	36	61
28mm f/2.8	SAL-28F28	42	54
35mm f/1.8 SAM	SAL-35F18	52.5	44
35mm f/1.4 G	SAL-35F14G	52.5	44
50mm f/1.4	SAL-50F14	75	32
50mm f/1.8 SAM	SAL-50F18	75	32
85mm f/2.8 SAM	SAL-85F28	127.5	19
85mm f/1.4 Carl Zeiss Planar T*	SAL-85F14Z	127.5	19
135mm f/1.8 Carl Zeiss Sonnar T*	SAL-135F18Z	202.5	12
135mm f/2.8 (T4.5) STF	SAL-135F28	202.5	12
300mm f/2.8 G	SAL-300F28G	450	5.2
500mm f/4 G SSM	SAL-500F40G	750	3.1
500mm f/8 Reflex	SAL-500F80	750	3.1

inimum ocus distance neters)	Minimum aperture	Magnification ratio	Filter thread size (mm)	Dimensions (max diam. x length; mm)	Weight (g)
.25	22–29	1:8	77	83 x 80.5	360
.28	22	1:4.2	77	83 x 114	900
	22	1:5	72	81 x 88	577
.35	22–29	1:4.2	62	72 x 83	445
.4	22–36	1:4.3	62	72 x 83	470
.25	22–36	1:2.9	55	69.5 x 69	210
.45	22–40	1:3.7	62	73 x 85.5	405
.45	22–40	1:3.4	62	75 x 86	440
34	22	1:4	77	83 x 111	955
.38	32	1:4.5	67	77.5 x 94	565
.95	32–45	1:3.4	55	71.5 x 85	305
.2	32	1:4.7	77	87 x 195.5	1340
.2	22–29	1:4	62	82.5 x 135.5	760
.5	22–32	1:3.7	77	94.5 x 196	1490
.5	32–38	1:4	55	71 x 122	460
.129	22	1:1	49	70 x 45	150
.2	32	1:1	55	71.5 x 60	295
.35	32	1:1	55	75 x 98.5	505
.2	22	1:6.6	(integrated)	75 x 66.5	400
.25	22	1:7.7	72	78 x 53.5	285
.19	22	1:3.4	72	78 x 76	555
3	22	1:7.7	49	65.5 x 42.5	185
.23	22	1:4	55	70 x 52	170
.3	22	1:5	55	69 x 76	510
.45	22	1:6.6	55	65.5 x 43	220
.34	22	1:5	49	70 x 45	170
.6	22	1:5	55	70 x 52	175
.85	22	1:7.7	72	81.5 x 72.5	560
.72	22	1:4	77	88.5 x 115	1050
.87	31	1:4	72	80 x 99	730
.0	32	1:55	(dedicated)	122 x 242.5	2310
	32	1:77	(dedicated)	140 x 367.5	3460
	8	1:7.7	55	89 x 118	665

» SIGMA LENSES

Sigma manufactures lenses for most popular camera systems, including Sony's. Sigma's A-mount range actually exceeds Sony's in number and many of the lenses are very highly regarded. As a result, there is a Sigma lens to suit every photographer's needs, from fisheyes to an enormous f/4.5 500mm telephoto lens.

However, Sigma does not license the firmware built into all Sony lenses and this can lead to problems: some Sigma lenses have been found not to focus correctly—if at all—on the A77 and other SLT cameras. This issue only affects the camera when it's set to AF (and does not affect non-SLT A-mount cameras). Fortunately, Sigma will update the firmware of affected lenses free of charge. For full details you will need to contact your nearest Sigma service center, but the problem should not affect lenses manufactured after the release of the A77.

Affected lenses

4.5mm F2.8 EX DC Circular Fisheye HSM
10mm F2.8 EX DC Fisheye HSM
10–20mm F3.5 EX DC HSM
17–50mm F2.8 EX DC OS HSM
17–70mm F2.8–4 DC Macro HSM
17–70mm F2.8–4 DC Macro OS HSM
18–50mm F2.8–4.5 DC OS HSM
18–125mm F3.8–5.6 DC HSM
18–250mm F3.5–6.3 DC OS HSM
24–70mm F2.8 IF EX DG HSM
50mm F1.4 EX DG HSM
50–200mm F4–5.6 DC HSM
50–500mm F4.5–6.3 DG OS HSM APO
70–200mm F2.8 EX DG OS HSM APO
85mm F1.4 EX DG HSM
120–400mm F4.5–5.6 DG OS HSM APO
150–500mm F5–6.3 DG OS HSM APO

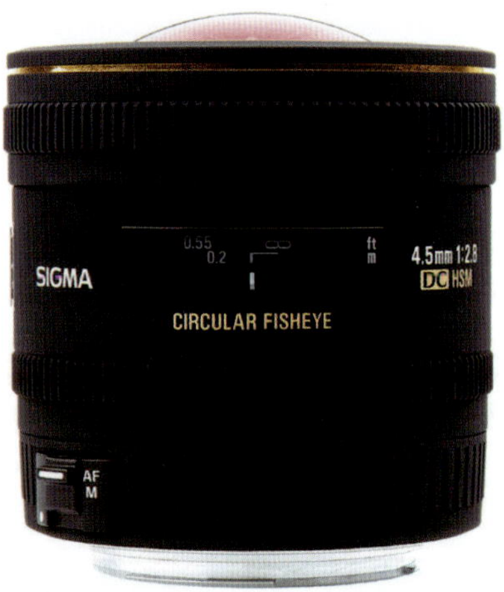

SIGMA 4.5MM »
Sigma's A-mount fisheye lens.

» WIDEANGLE

Architectural subjects will benefit from keeping the camera as close to parallel to the subject as possible. The closer you are to your subject, the wider the lens will need to be to keep the entire subject within the frame. However, this will mean that the perspective will look decidely unnatural.

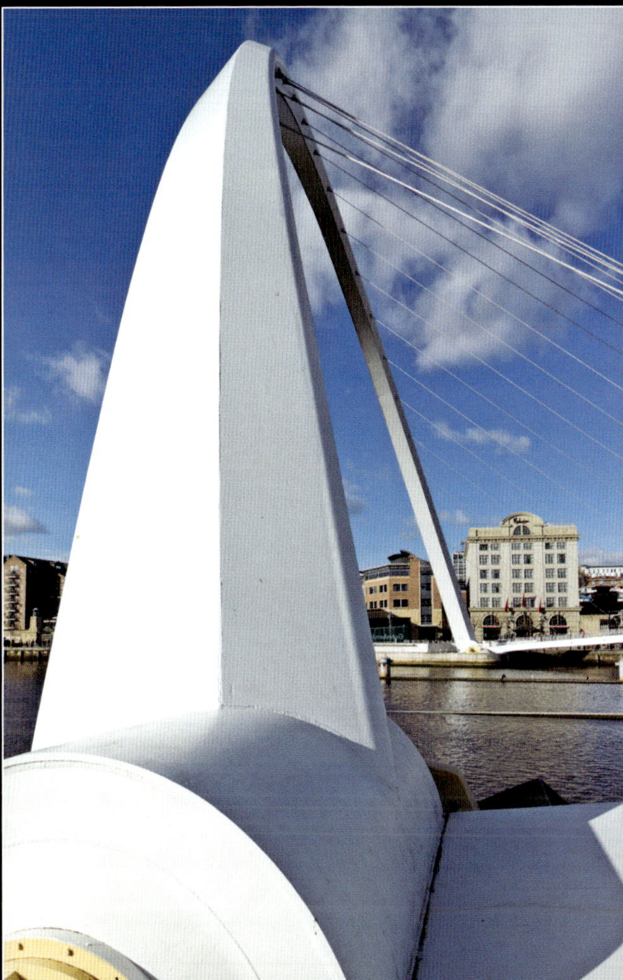

Settings

- *Lens:* 11–18mm (at 13mm)
- *Aperture:* f/8
- *Shutter speed:* 1/160 sec.
- *ISO:* 100

» TELEPHOTO

This image shows the "stacking" of elements in an image, which is typical of a telephoto lens. This is due to the perspective created by shooting further back from the subject. Contrast this shot to the image on page 161, which was shot close up with a wideangle lens.

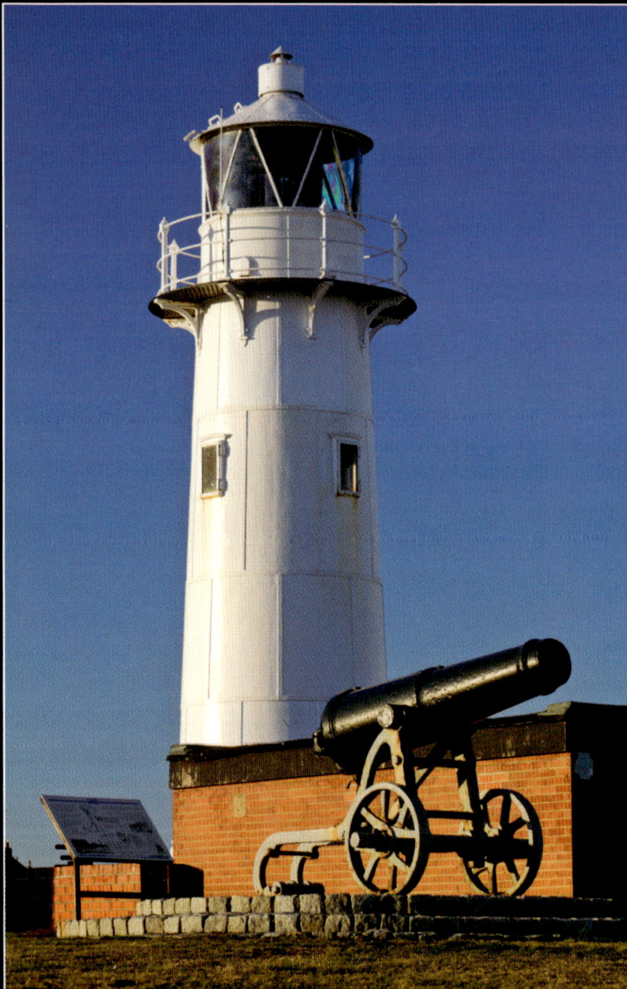

Settings

- *Lens:* 70–200mm (at 75mm)
- *Aperture:* f/9
- *Shutter speed:* 1/60 sec.
- *ISO:* 100

» ZOOM

Zoom lenses are the ideal companion on days out, as it's easier to react to events with just one lens that can be adjusted to suit the subject. This shot of a moving tram was one of a sequence that started at the longest end of the zoom and finished at the widest focal length setting.

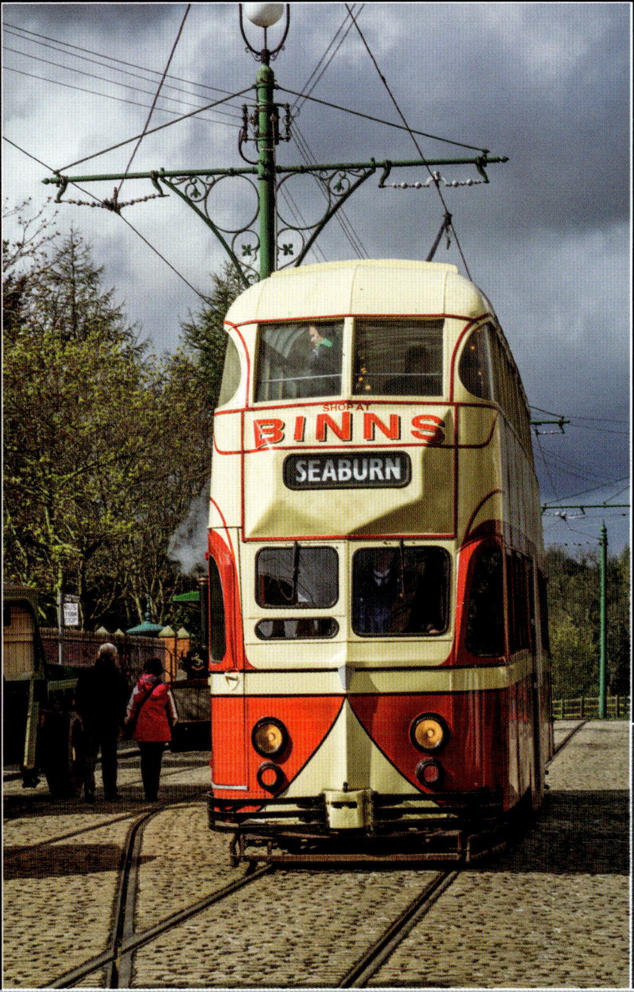

Settings

- *Lens:* 24-70mm (at 70mm)
- *Aperture:* f/8
- *Shutter speed:* 1/500 sec.
- *ISO:* 100

Chapter 5
FLASH

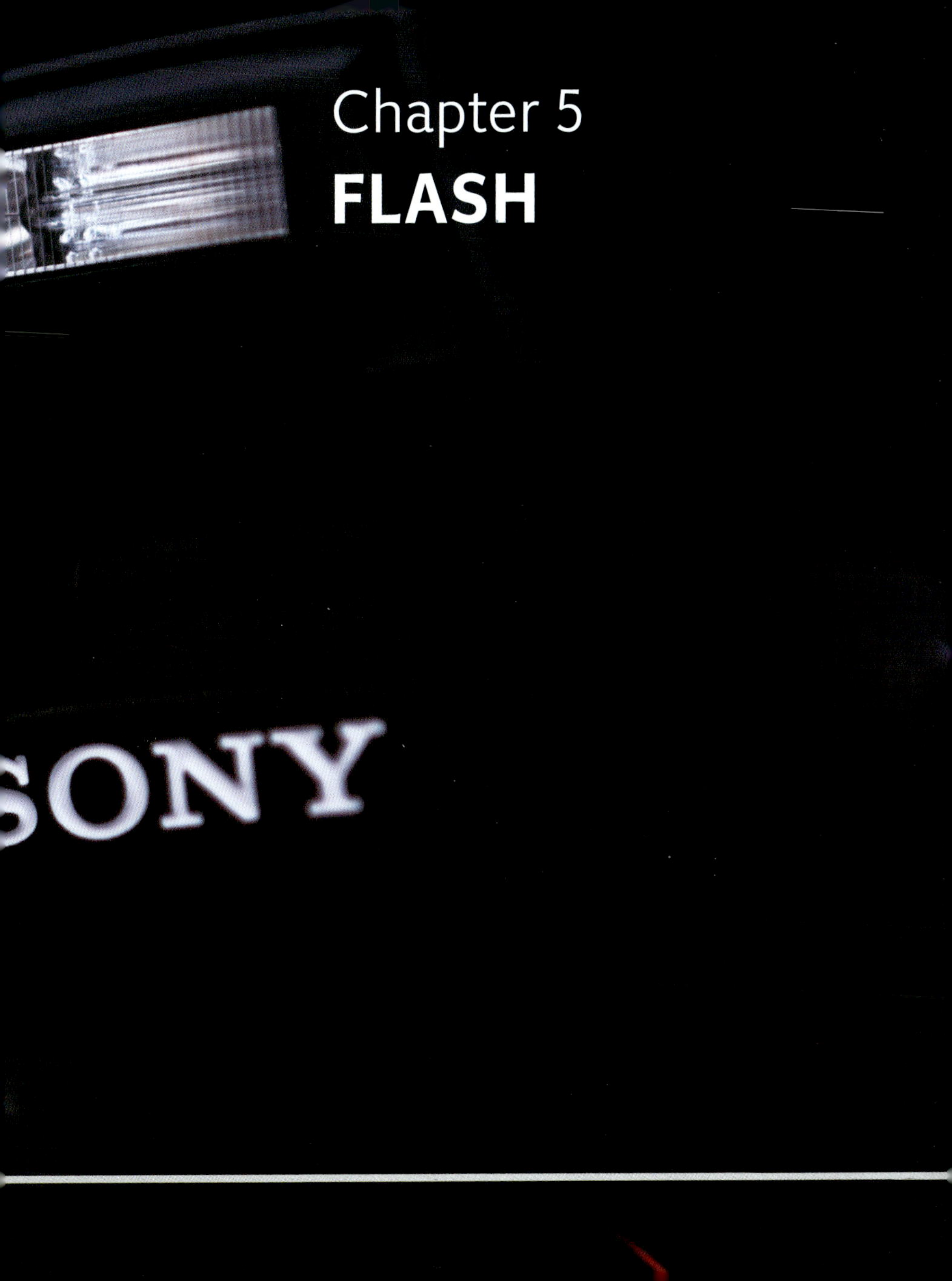

5 FLASH

To make a photographic image requires light. When the ambient light level needs a helping hand, the A77 can use its own built-in flash or one fitted to the hotshoe to help make an exposure.

› Guide numbers

The power of a flash—the amount of light it can produce when fired—is shown as a numerical value known as a guide number (or GN). The GN is a good way to quickly compare different flash units, and it also allows you to calculate the flash unit's range in either meters or feet. The higher the ISO used, the greater the range of the flash (and therefore the larger the GN), so to avoid confusion manufacturers use ISO 100 as a standard value when quoting the GN of a flash unit.

The GN can be used to determine the aperture value needed to correctly expose a subject at a given distance, or calculate the effective range of the flash at a chosen aperture. The formula to calculate both is respectively:

GN/distance=aperture
GN/aperture=distance

The A77's built-in flash has a GN of 39ft/12m. At an aperture setting of f/8, and with the camera set to ISO 100, this means the effective flash distance is 4.9ft/1.5m. When the ISO on the camera is doubled, the effective flash distance is multiplied 1.4 times, so at ISO 200 (and still at an aperture of f/8), the effective flash distance will be increased to 6.1ft/2.1m.

› Shutter speed and aperture

The shutter speed you use when shooting with flash has no effect on the flash exposure: only the ISO setting and aperture you use will affect the range of the flash. If you switched your flash to manual—with the output set to full power—you could control the effective distance of the flash by opening and closing the aperture or by increasing or decreasing the ISO. If your subject is further than the effective flash distance for the aperture you've used, the subject will be underexposed. If the subject is closer than the effective flash distance, it will be overexposed, unless you close the aperture or lower the ISO to reduce the effective distance of the flash (you could also reduce the power output of the flash if it allows you to).

Although the shutter speed does not need to be thought about when using flash—at least in terms of the exposure—every camera has a sync speed, which is the fastest shutter speed available when shooting with flash. The sync speed of the A77 is 1/250 sec., but the camera has a further trick up its sleeve. External flashes such the HVL-F58AM can be used as "hi-speed" flashes, which allows the use of faster shutter speeds than 1/250 sec. This is achieved by "pulsing" the flash very quickly. The drawback is that the effective range of the flash is greatly reduced, although you may find that this is a small price to pay in return for being able to use flash as a fill-in light in bright conditions.

Note:
The built-in flash does not have a hi-speed mode.

LIGHTING THE WAY
Flash can be used as a main light or, as in this image, as a fill light to solve problems with high contrast.

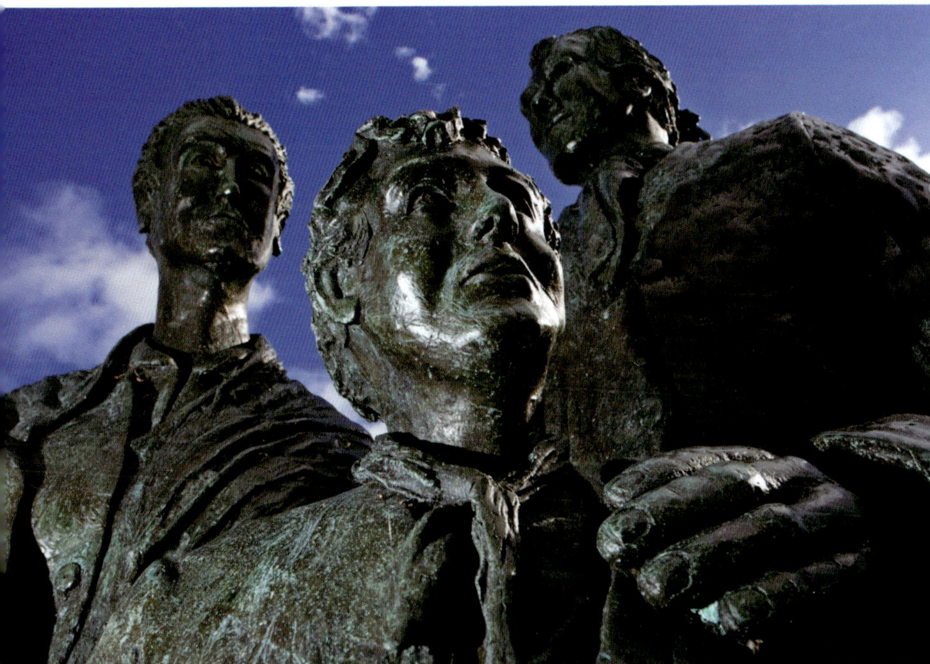

5

» BUILT-IN FLASH

The A77 is equipped with a built-in flash, which fixed in position directly above the lens axis. In the AUTO, AUTO+, and **SCN** modes the flash will pop up automatically if required when the shutter-release button is lightly pressed down halfway. This will happen if the A77 decides that the light levels are too low or if your subject is backlit. The built-in flash can be raised manually in the **P**, **A**, **S**, **M**, MR, and 12 modes by pressing the flash release button.

The built-in flash is effective with lenses with a focal length of 16mm or higher. If you use the flash with a wider lens, you run the risk of the flash coverage dropping off on either side of the image. In common with external flash units that are fixed to a camera, the built-in flash will light your subject frontally, which can be harsh and unflattering, and can flatten form.

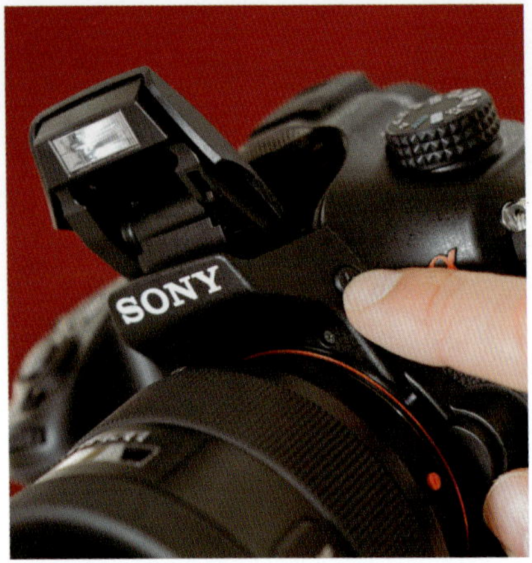

Note:
The built-in flash is deactivated automatically when shooting in movie, 3D, and panorama modes.

BUILT-IN FLASH SETTINGS

SYMBOL	MODE	RESULT
Flash Off symbol	Flash Off	Flash completely disabled
AUTO	Autoflash	Flash fires as required, depending on ambient lighting conditions
Flash symbol	Fill-flash	Flash fires every time the shutter-release button is pressed
REAR	Rear Sync.	Flash fires at the end of the exposure
WL	Wireless	Fires an external off-camera flash remotely

However, having the option to use flash is better than not having it, and the built-in flash can be very useful as a fill-in light.

> ***Note:***
> If the ⚡● flash indicator on the LCD is blinking, the flash is charging and the shutter-release button will not be operable. Once the ⚡● indicator is lit, the flash is charged and the photograph can be taken.

FILL-IN FLASH »
Fill-in flash is invaluable if your subject is not as well lit as the background.

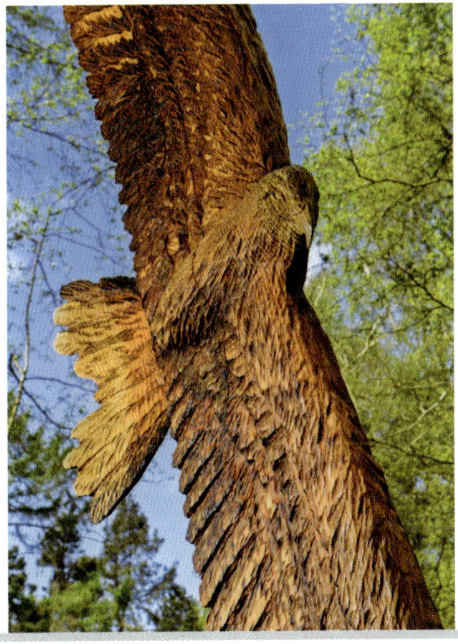

› Controlling and using the built-in flash

The functions of the built-in flash are controlled via the Fn screen. The functions that are available are dependent on the selected shooting mode.

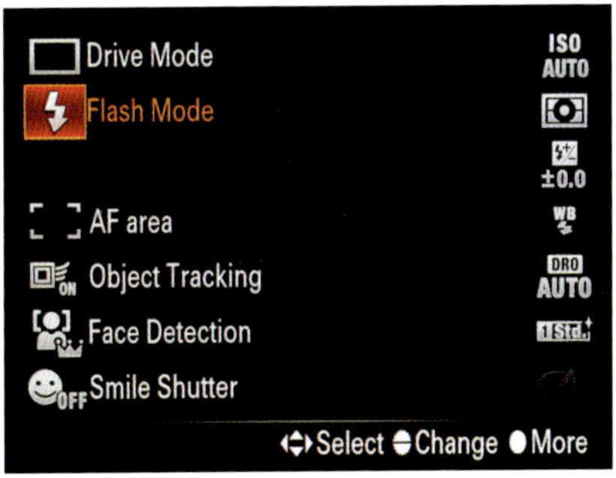

1) Press **Fn**.

2) Highlight **Flash mode** using the multi-selector and press ●.

3) Highlight the desired flash function using ▲/▼ and press ● to confirm. The A77 will return to shooting mode.

4) Press the ⚡ release button to raise the flash if necessary.

5) Compose and then press the shutter-release button to take the shot.

6) If the built-in flash is no longer required, push the flash lightly, but firmly back down into the camera body until it clicks into place.

5

› AUTO Autoflash and Fill-flash

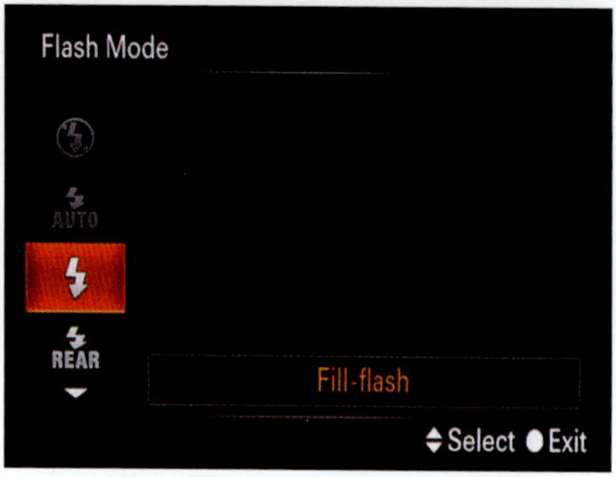

The usual meaning of fill-flash (or fill-in flash) is when flash is used to illuminate areas of shadow in high-contrast scenes, such as when a subject is backlit by a bright light source. The greater the contrast between the shadows and the rear light source, the more powerful the flash needs to be. However, Sony uses the term fill-flash to specify that the flash will always fire, whether it needs to or not, every time the shutter-release button is pressed. The flash is only fired when the A77 deems necessary with the flash set to AUTO Autoflash.

Fill-flash (in the non-Sony sense of the term) is a useful technique to master. Backlighting is aesthetically pleasing when shooting portraits, as your subject's hair will be "rim lit" by the backlight and he or she won't be squinting, which would be more likely if they were facing the bright light source. The key to successful fill-flash is using the right amount of flash so that the contrast is lowered and the overall exposure

FILLING IN
Fill-in flash is invaluable when the background is more brightly lit than your subject.

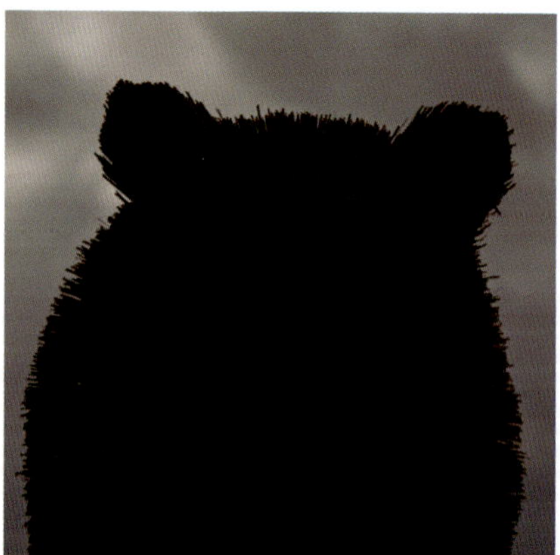

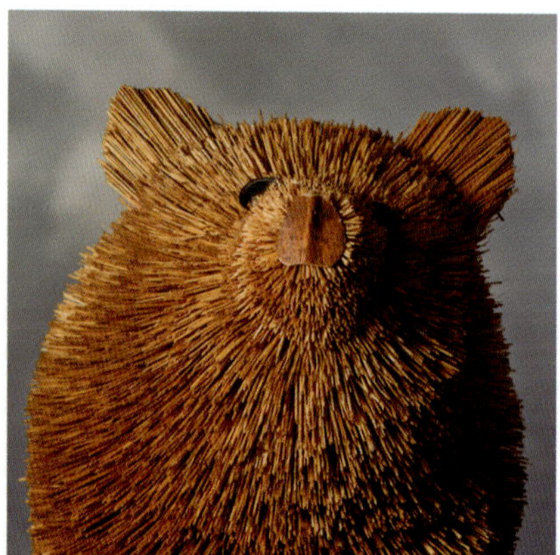

is more even, but not so much that the backlighting is overpowered. The flash-to-subject distance is one way of controlling the effect of the flash, but a slightly more consistent way to work is to adjust the power of the flash using ⚡± and judging the results in playback. Generally, a negative flash compensation value is more effective than a positive one when it comes to employing fill-flash.

› ⚡REAR Rear sync

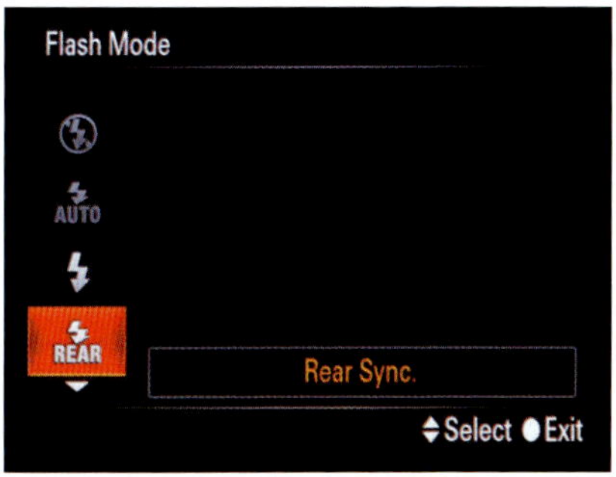

How your flash synchronizes with the opening and closing of the shutter will affect the look of an image. The A77 offers two ways to alter the flash synchronization.

> ***Note:***
> ⚡REAR is only available in **P**, **A**, **S**, **M**, and [12] modes.

By default, the A77 uses front-curtain sync, which means that the flash is fired the moment the first (or front) curtain begins to rise, at the start of the exposure. You can also set the flash to fire when the rear curtain begins to rise, at the end of the exposure, and this is shown as **Rear Sync**. on the flash mode menu.

You may well now be shrugging your shoulders at this odd option, and usually it makes no differences to your images whether you set the camera to front or rear sync. However, if you're using slow sync flash (flash with a slow shutter speed) and your subject moves across the image frame during the exposure then your choice is far more important.

Using front curtain sync, the subject's movement will be frozen by the flash at the start of the exposure. As the subject continues to move during the long exposure, any movement subsequent to the flash firing will be recorded as a blurred trail that will appear in front of the subject in the final image.

Using rear sync, the subject will move across the frame during the ambient light exposure, creating blurred movement, and will not be lit (and "frozen") by the flash until the end of the exposure. In this way, the movement before the flash is recorded as a trail behind the subject, which looks far more natural.

› Wireless flash

Your A77 can be set to fire a compatible flash wirelessly. This is achieved by using the light from the built-in flash as a trigger, and it means that you will have more control over the direction of the main (off-camera) flash light and how it illuminates your subject. The only slight drawback is that the off-camera flash has to be able to "see" your A77 to be triggered successfully. Wireless flash is available in **P**, **A**, **S**, **M** and [12] modes.

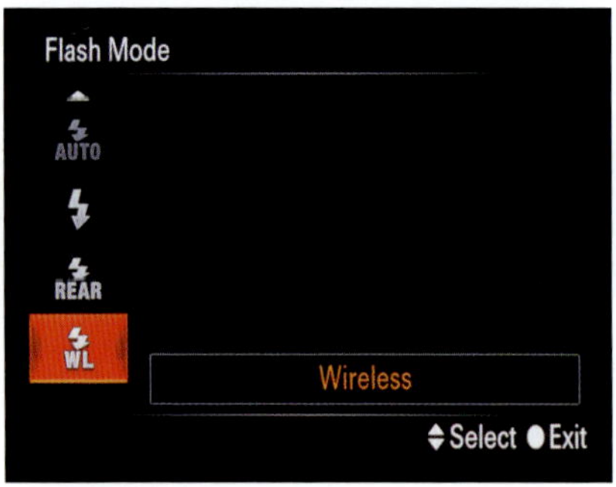

Setting wireless flash

1) Make sure that both the camera and flash are switched off.

2) Slide the wireless compatible flash into the A77's hotshoe.

3) Switch the camera and flash on.

4) Press **Fn** and select **Flash mode** and then WL. Remove the flash from the hotshoe and press the flash button to activate the built-in flash.

5) If you test fire the flash, use the AEL button to lock the exposure.

6) Turn off the wireless flash via the **Fn** menu once wireless flash shooting has finished.

> ***Notes:***
> If the built-in flash is used without an external flash when the A77 is set to wireless mode, you will get inaccurate flash exposures.
>
> The AEL button should be set to **AEL Hold** when wireless flash is used.

› Slow sync

When you shoot with flash, either the built-in unit or one fitted externally, the A77 will default to a relatively fast shutter speed to minimize the risk of camera shake. However, this can mean that the background is underexposed, particularly if the ambient light levels are low.

Slow sync forces the camera to use a shutter speed that will correctly expose the background, leaving the flash to illuminate the foreground. To use slow sync flash, hold down the AEL/ button as you press the shutter-release button to make the exposure. ✱ will be displayed on LCD and EVF to confirm that slow sync has been selected.

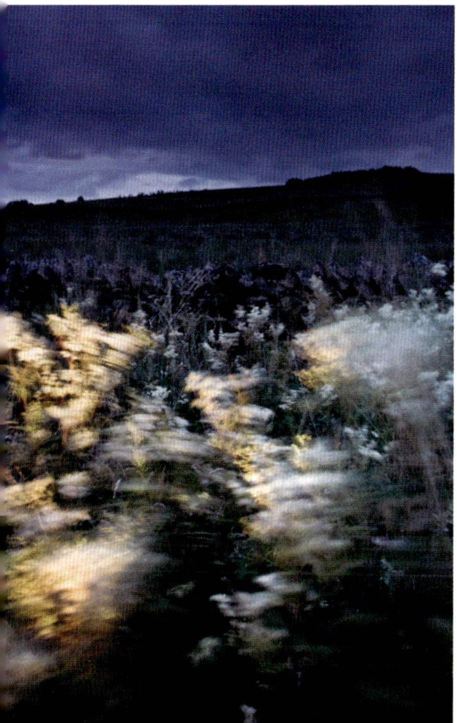

Notes:
Slow sync is not possible when using the **S** and **M** shooting modes.

If Func. of **AEL** button on the ⚙ **3** menu is not set to **AEL Hold**, slow sync cannot be used unless **AEL Hold** has been assigned to either the **ISO** button or AF/MF button on the ⚙ 3 menu **ISO Button** or **AF/MF button** options respectively.

SLOW SYNC FLASH «
Off-camera slow sync flash was used for this outdoor scene to illuminate the foreground, while still allowing the background to be exposed correctly.

Flash exposure should be straightforward. However, the A77 offers three methods of determining the correct flash exposure and one method for overriding automatic exposure if necessary.

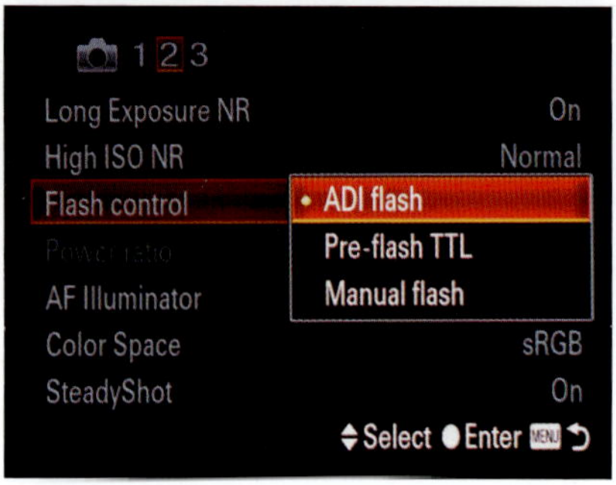

› Flash control

The **Flash control** options can be found on the 2 menu.

ADI flash

ADI (Advanced Distance Integration) flash uses the focus distance information from an ADI compatible lens (if fitted) and combines this information with metering information taken from a pre-exposure flash burst. ADI is potentially very accurate. However, it is less effective when the flash-to-subject distance cannot be determined, such as when wireless flash is used or when the light from the flash is bounced using a reflector.

Pre-flash TTL (Through the Lens)

This method uses metering information taken from a pre-exposure flash burst only. Subjects with unusually high or low reflectivity can fool Pre-flash TTL into underexposing or overexposing respectively.

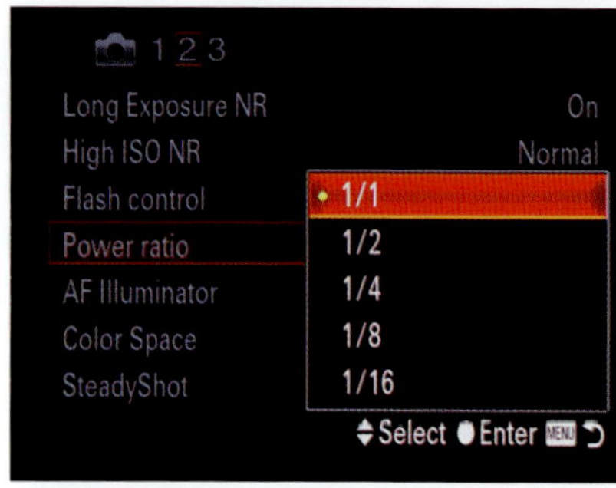

Manual flash

Fires a set amount of light regardless of the exposure required. The amount of light can be adjusted by altering the **Power ratio** on the 2 menu. A power ratio of 1/1 fires the flash at maximum, 1/2 has half the power output, 1/4 a quarter, and so on.

Notes:

Flash compensation is not available in the AUTO, **AUTO+**, Sweep Panorama, 3D Sweep Panorama, or **SCN** modes.

Although you are adjusting the power output of the flash, you can't increase the power of the flash beyond its effective range for a particular ISO and aperture setting.

› Manual exposure

Use the grid below to gauge the maximum effective distance for the built-in flash when it is used at different ISO sensitivities and aperture values.

Aperture	f/2.8	f/4	f/5.6	f/8	f/11	f/16
ISO						
100	14.0ft 4.3 m	9.8ft 3.0m	7.0ft 2.1m	4.9ft 1.5m	3.6ft 1.1m	2.5ft 0.8m
200	19.7ft 6.0m	13.8ft 4.2m	9.8ft 3.0m	6.9ft 2.1m	5.0ft 1.5m	3.4ft 1.1m
400	27.5ft 8.4m	19.3ft 5.9m	13.8ft 4.2m	9.6ft 2.9m	7.0ft 2.1m	4.8ft 1.5m
800	38.5ft 11.8m	27.0ft 8.2m	19.3ft 5.9m	13.5ft 4.1m	9.8ft 3.0m	6.7ft 2.1m
1600	53.9ft 16.5m	37.7ft 11.5m	27.0ft 8.2m	18.9ft 5.8m	13.7ft 4.2m	9.4ft 2.9m

Adjusting flash exposure

1) With the flash raised press Fn and highlight **Flash Comp**. Press ●.

2) If the flash has overexposed your subject use ◀ to reduce the power of the flash by up to three stops in increments of a third of a stop.

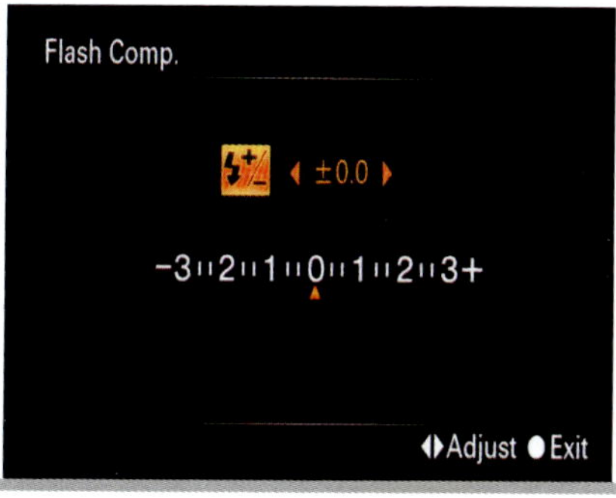

3) If the flash has underexposed your subject, use ▶ to increase the power of the flash by up to three stops in ⅓-stop increments.

4) Press ● or lightly down on the shutter-release button to confirm the new setting and return to shooting mode.

5) After creating the photograph reset flash compensation back to 0.

Although using flash should be trouble-free there are certain situations that may require either you or your A77 to intervene.

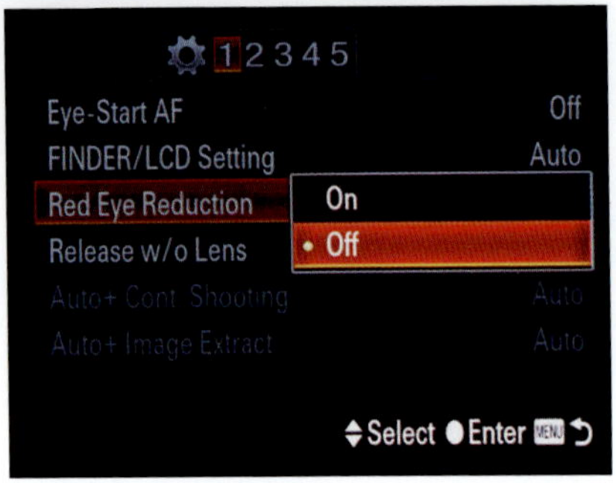

› Red Eye Reduction

The phenomenon of red eye is one of the most common problems experienced when shooting portraits with flash. It occurs when the light from a flash bounces off the back of your subject's eye(s), and, in doing so, picks up the color of the blood vessels. Red eye is particularly problematic when the flash is close to the camera lens, as it is with the A77's built-in flash.

Your A77 can be set to reduce the risk of red eye, which it attempts to do by pulsing light from the flash prior to the main exposure. This causes the pupils of your subject's eyes to contract, which minimizes the amount of light that enters the eye.

Enabling red eye reduction

1) Press **MENU** and select ⚙ 1.

2) Set **Red Eye Reduction** to **On**.

› Flash and Live View

Having a Live View display with a continuously updated histogram is of real benefit when determining the correct exposure for an image. However, the Live View histogram is not accurate with flash, as the final exposure is only determined when the flash is fired as you press the shutter-release button. When using flash, be prepared to view the histogram for an image in Playback and then reshoot, adjusting flash exposure if necessary.

Notes:

Red eye can also be tackled in post-production by using Sony's PMB software.

If your subject is likely to be distracted or disturbed by the pulsing of light before exposure set the A77's **Red Eye Reduction** to **Off.**

» EXTERNAL FLASH UNITS

Adding an external flash will extend the possibilities of your image making, since it will offer greater lighting power than the A77's built-in flash.

› Accessory shoe

Sony uses a unique external flash mounting system, different to the ISO 518 standard used by virtually all other camera manufacturers. Although this limits the range of third-party flashes that can be fitted to the A77, the connection system is very stable and the attached flash is less likely to become detached from the camera. If you want to use a third-party flash it has to be designed specifically for the Sony system or be attached via an adapter.

Attaching an external flash

1) Ensure that both the camera and the flash are switched off.

2) Push the mounting foot of the flash firmly onto the A77's accessory shoe. The flash will be locked into place automatically.

3) Switch on the camera and flash unit.

4) On the camera, set the white balance setting to flash or automatic.

5) To remove the flash unit, press the mounting foot release button on the flash unit and pull it back off the camera.

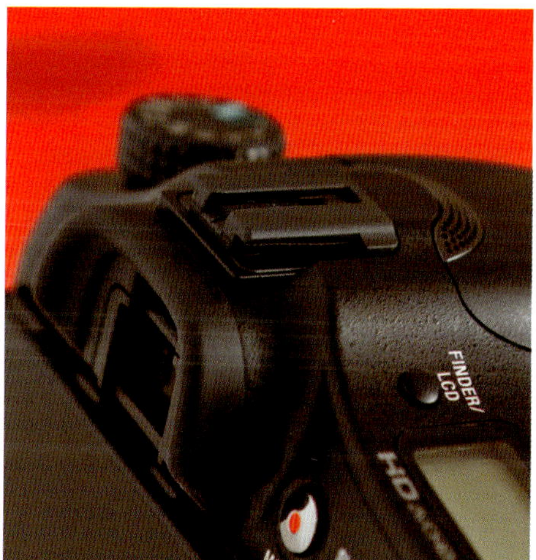

Note:
Sony refers to the flash mount as an "accessory shoe," although the mount is also often known as a hotshoe. A hotshoe has electrical contacts to activate a flash (or other device such as a radio transmitter). This is in contrast to a "cold shoe," such as those found on some lighting stands, which has no electrical contacts and is designed simply to hold a flash.

› Flash sync terminal

If your flash has a flash sync terminal you can use this to connect it to your A77. Flash sync cables are readily available and can be bought in a variety of lengths. The terminal on your external flash must have the opposite polarity to your A77.

The flash exposure will not be determined automatically by your A77 when the flash sync terminal is used, so you will need to set the correct aperture or adjust the power output of your flash to obtain the right exposure. Alternatively, some flashes have a sensor, known as a thyristor, which cuts off the light from the flash once the correct exposure has been achieved. This facility is usually activated by setting the flash to Auto (or similar), and while it is generally reliable, it can be affected by the reflectivity of your subject. When connecting a flash via a sync cable, it is important not to use a shutter speed faster than 1/250 sec. (the A77's flash sync speed), as this will result in uneven exposure across the image.

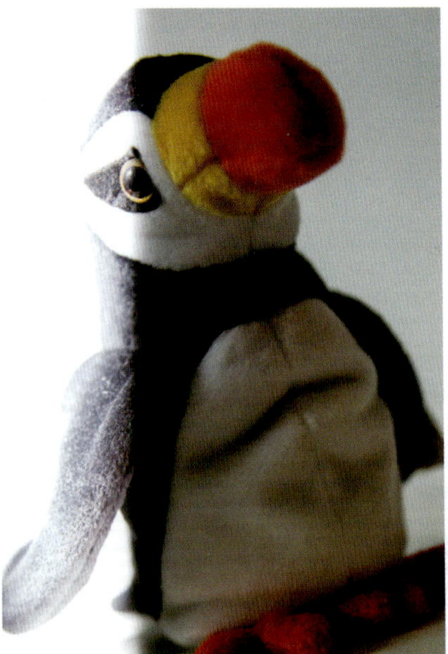

Using the flash sync terminal

1) Make sure that both the camera and the flash are switched off.

2) Open the cover of the ⚡ sync terminal on your A77 and plug in the flash sync cable.

3) Plug the other end of the cable into the flash.

4) Switch the camera and flash unit on.

> ***Notes:***
> Only use a flash with a sync voltage of 400 volts or less.
>
> The ⚡ indicator will not be displayed when a flash is connected to the A77 using a sync cable.

FLASH SYNC «
Using a shutter speed faster than 1/250 sec. will lead to uneven flash exposure across the frame.

› FLASH ACCESSORIES

Sony produces a number of accessories that can be used with its external flash units to increase their creative potential.

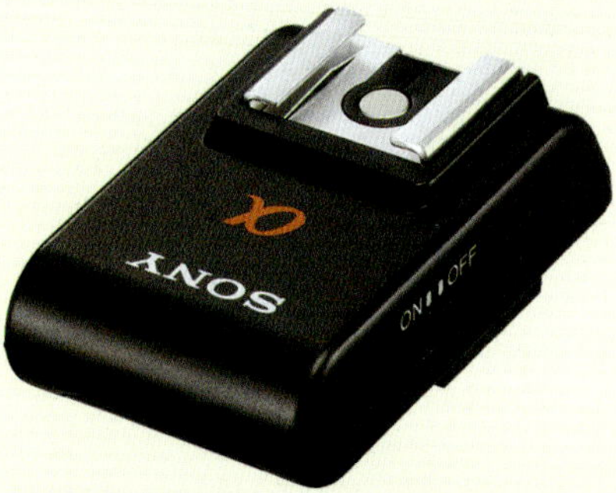

FA-HS1AM HOTSHOE ADAPTER

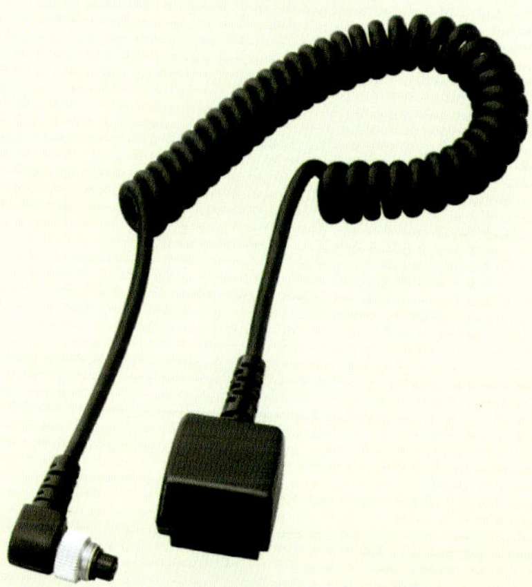

FA-CC1AM OFF-CAMERA FLASH CABLE

Off-camera flash cable (FA-CC1AM)
A 60 inch (1.5m) extension cable that enables you to take your flash off-camera for less direct lighting.

Extension cable for flash (FA-EC1AM)
Doubles the length of the off-camera flash cable FA-CC1AM (to 120in/3m).

Multi-flash cable (FA-MC1AM)
The FA-MC1AM is a connecting cable for use in multi-flash lighting setups, allowing you to trigger three flashes simultaneously.

Hotshoe adapter (FA-HS1AM)
Converts the proprietary Sony hotshoe for compatibility with third-party flashes that use the ISO 518 hotshoe standard.

External battery adapter (FA-EB1AM)
The FA-EB1AM is an additional power supply for the HVL-F56AM that reduces flash recycling times.

Triple connector (FA-TC1AM)
Allows the connection of up to three additional flash units to the A77, using additional FA-EC1AM extension cables. No longer available new.

› EXTERNAL FLASH UNITS: HVL-F20AM

This is an affordable, compact flash unit with a guide number of 20 (meters), offering an immediate improvement over the A77's built-in flash. The clever, lightweight design allows it to be folded down neatly and left mounted on the camera when not in use. Despite its diminutive size, the HVL-F20AM supports Sony's ADI system of flash exposure metering, and it also offers intelligent white balance adjustment, based on the camera's own color temperature information and settings.

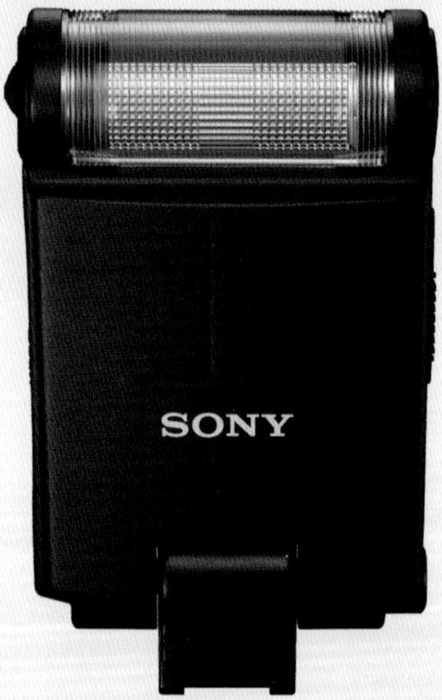

Guide number (GN)
20m @ ISO 100 with 35mm lens

Flash coverage
18mm (Standard mode)
35mm (Tele mode)

Continuous flash
Not supported

Wireless TTL
No

Tilt/swivel
75° vertical (using bounce switch)

Recycling time
0.1–5 sec. (alkaline batteries)
0.1–4 sec. (Ni-MH batteries)

Approximate number of flashes per set of batteries
590 (alkaline batteries)
150 (Ni-MH batteries)

Dimensions (w x h x d)
2½ x 3¾ x 1in (62 x 94 x 24mm)

Weight
3.5oz (98g) without batteries

Included accessories
Soft carry case, user manual

› EXTERNAL FLASH UNITS: HVL-F43AM

This midrange flash is ideal if you need a well-specified flash, but don't use flash enough to justify the top-of-range HVL-F58AM. The HVL-F43AM shares many of the same features as its larger sibling in a smaller, lighter, but less powerful package. Shared features include wireless flash, high-speed sync, and multi-flash functions. The HVL-F43AM has a wide tilt and swivel range, which is useful for bounce flash.

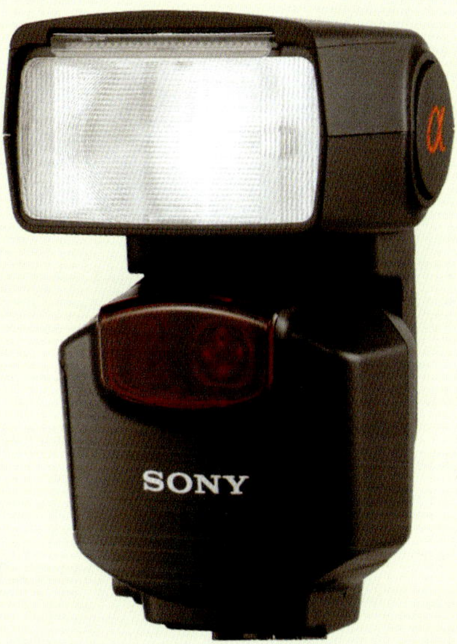

Guide number (GN)
43m @ ISO 100 with 105mm lens

Flash coverage
24–105mm
(15mm with built-in wide panel)

Continuous flash
40 flashes at 10 flashes per second

Wireless TTL
Yes

Tilt/swivel
150° up; 8° down; 90° left and right

Recycling time
0.1–2.9 sec. (alkaline batteries)
0.1–2.2 sec. (Ni-MH batteries)

Approximate number of flashes per set of batteries
200 (alkaline batteries)
250 (Ni-MH batteries)

Dimensions (w x h x d)
3 x 8⅛ x 3½in (75 x 129 x 87mm)

Weight
12oz (340g) without batteries

Included accessories
Mini stand for wireless shooting, soft carry case, user manual

› EXTERNAL FLASH UNITS: HVL-F58AM

The HVL-F58AM is Sony's flagship flash unit. It is the largest, heaviest, and most powerful of Sony's flashes. Naturally, this also makes it the most expensive. The flash uses the ADI metering system for accurate exposures as well as offering TTL. The flash head can be pivoted on both the horizontal and vertical axes, allowing fine control over the direction of the flash. Hi-speed flash is also available across the full shutter speed range of the A77.

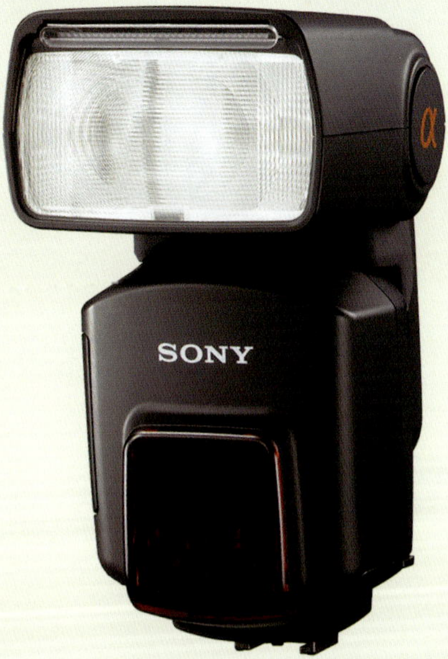

Guide number (GN)
58m @ ISO 100 with 105mm lens

Flash coverage
24–105mm
(16mm with built-in wide panel)

Continuous flash
0 flashes at 5 flashes per second

Wireless TTL
Yes

Tilt/swivel
150° up; 10° down; 90° left and right

Recycling time
0.1–5 sec. (alkaline batteries)
0.1–3 sec. (Ni-MH batteries)

Approximate number of flashes per set of batteries
100 (alkaline batteries)
200 (Ni-MH batteries)

Dimensions (w x h x d)
3⅛ x 5⅞ x 4¼in (77 x 147 x 106mm)

Weight
15.6oz (440g) without batteries

Included accessories
Mini stand for wireless shooting, soft carry case, user manual

» OTHER ACCESSORIES

Flash diffusers

Flash is a point light source, which means the light is hard, with sharply defined shadows. A flash diffuser, fitted over the flash head, spreads the light from the flash to make it softer.

There is a variety of different types of flash diffuser commonly available. The simplest are roughly the size of the flash head and are made of translucent plastic. Fitting them to the flash head will soften the light, but only to a degree—taping translucent tissue paper to the flash head will have a similar effect.

More effective are diffusers that spread the light from the flash over a greater surface area. These types of diffuser can either be clipped onto the flash itself, or, in the case of brollies, the flash is fired into or through them. These types of diffuser are invariably far bigger than the flash itself. This can make them cumbersome to use, but despite this they are very effective at softening the light from a flash. As a guide, the bigger the diffuser, the softer the light it will create.

BROLLY DIFFUSER »

Flash brackets

In conjunction with an FA-CC1AM extension cable, a flash bracket will allow you to mount your flash to the side of your A77. This moves the flash away from the lens axis, reducing the risk of red eye. Flash brackets are particularly useful when you need to handhold your camera but want to control the position of the flash without resorting to lighting stands.

> **Tip**
>
> *A flash diffuser, in combination with the flash's bounce head, will allow you to soften the light further. However, a lot of light will be lost in the process, so your subject will need to be very close to the flash.*

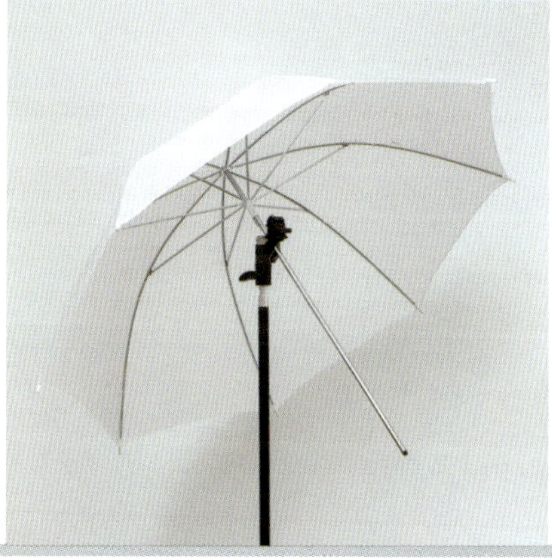

5 » BOUNCE FLASH

Another way to reduce the hardness of the light from your external flash is to reflect, or "bounce" the light from another surface onto your subject. Bouncing flash in this way spreads it across a larger area, softening it. For this technique to work, you will need a flash with a head that can be angled upward or sideways. The most common surface to bounce flash from is a ceiling, although a wall or reflector board could also be used. This technique is easier to get right with more powerful flashes. The light reaching your subject is inevitably weaker than if the flash were used directly, which is partly because the light from the flash is traveling further to reach your subject, and partly because the surface you bounce the light from will absorb some of that light. Another thing to note is that the light from the flash will be tinted by the color of the surface from which you bounce it, so try to use a neutral colored surface if you want to avoid unwelcome color casts.

BOUNCED FLASH
The photo below left was shot with direct flash, while the photo below right was shot with the flash head angled upward, with the light bounced from a white reflector board.

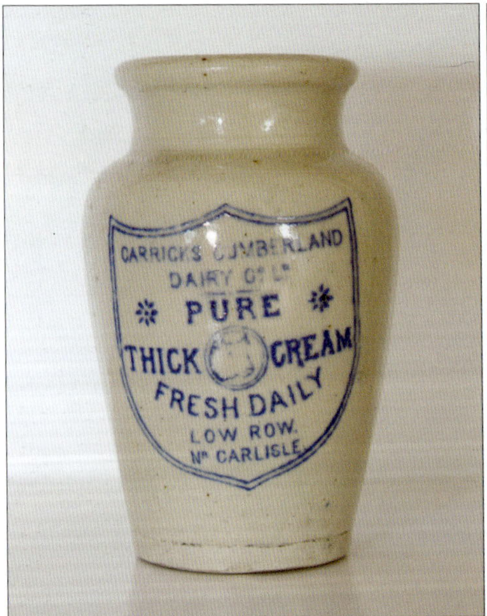

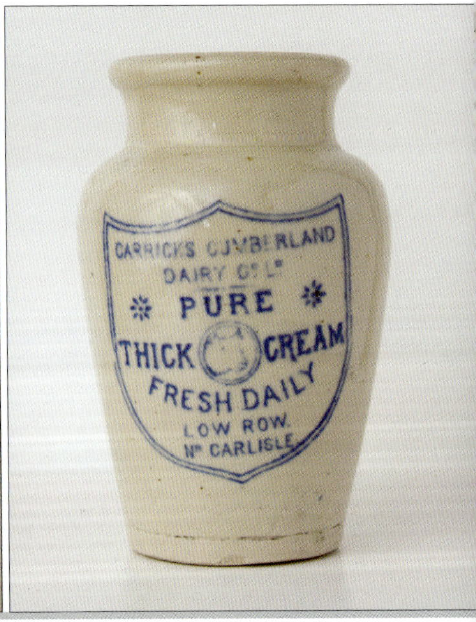

» WIRELESS

Using wireless flash enables you to position the flash so that it lights your subject in the most sympathetic way. For this shot I had the flash to the right of the A77 to light the lens board of this film camera. When the flash was mounted on the camera's hotshoe the lighting was far less pleasing.

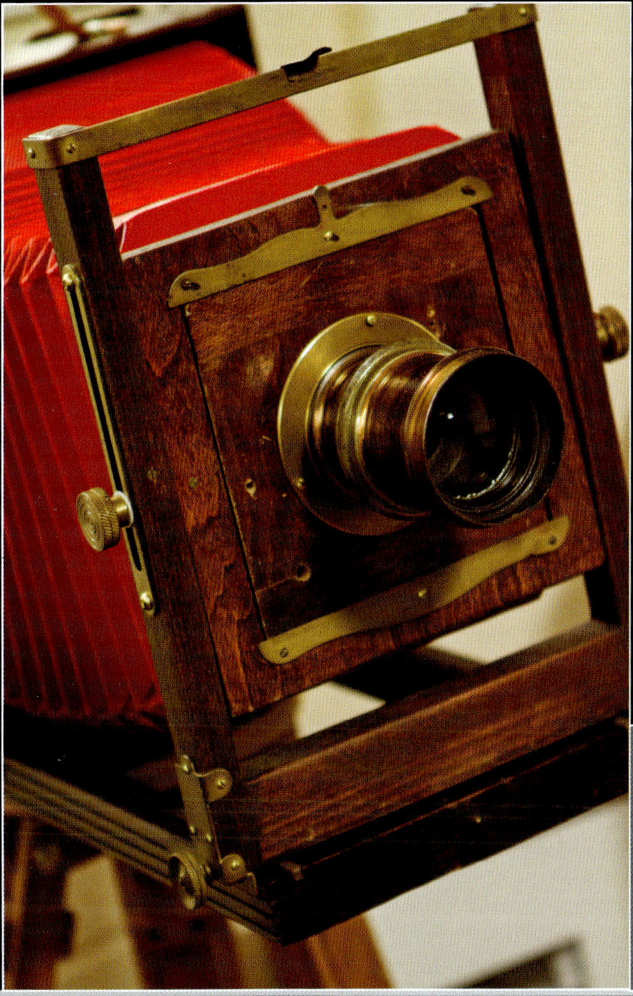

Settings

- *Lens:* 24–70mm (at 70mm)
- *Aperture:* f/2.8
- *Shutter Speed:* 1/30 sec.
- *ISO:* 100

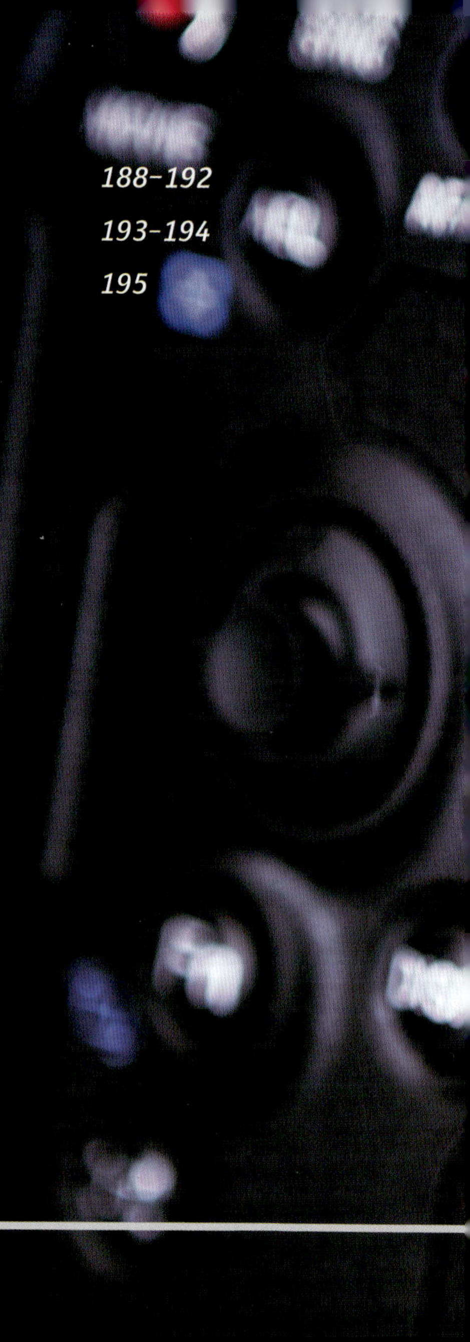

Chapter 6
ACCESSORIES

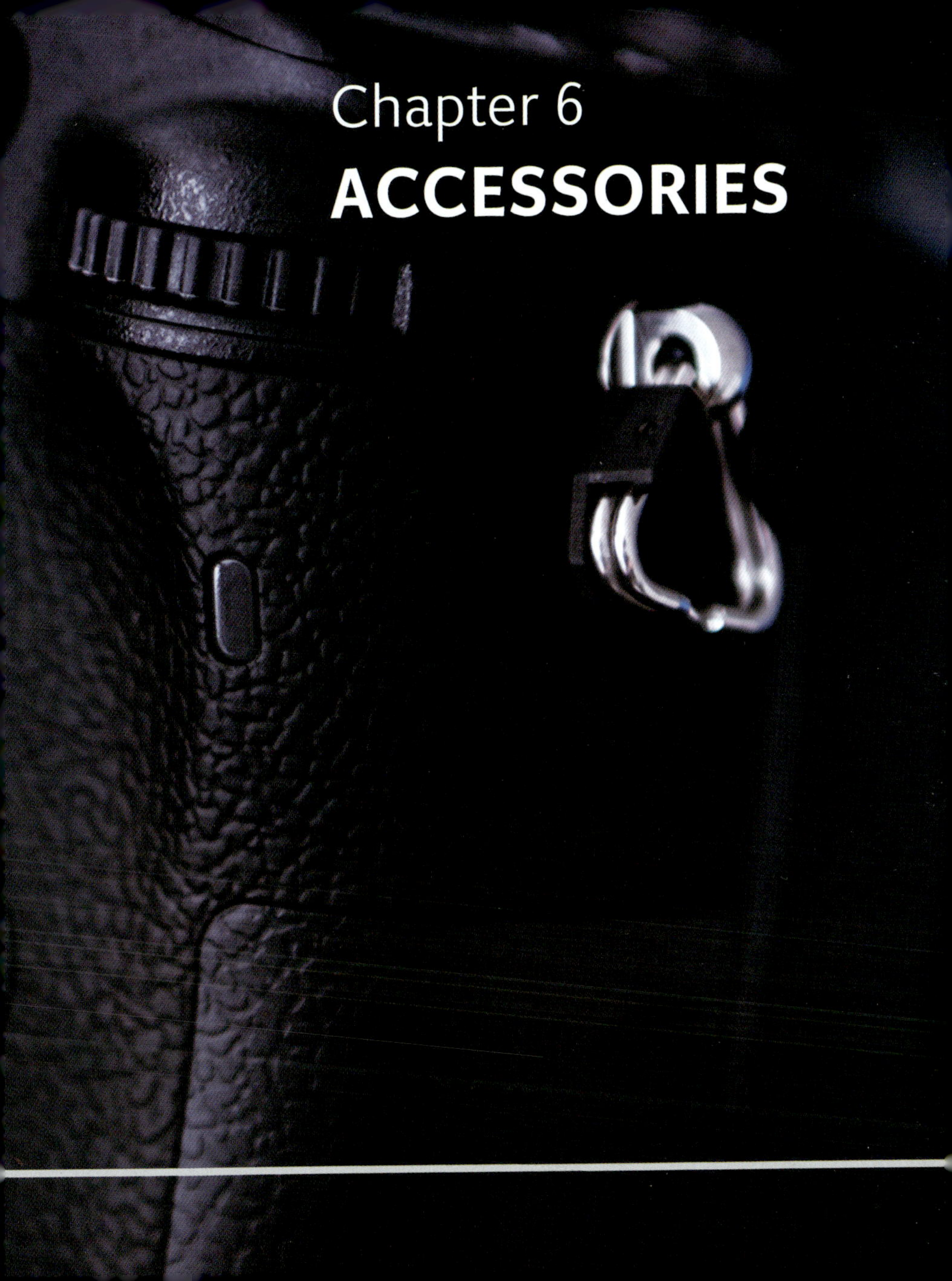

6 ACCESSORIES

There is a bewildering range of accessories compatible with the A77. Some of them are useful and will help to improve your image-making creativity, while others are... well, "less useful," and often get used once and then put away and forgotten. The key to navigating your way through the choices is to critically assess how you work and decide where an accessory would make your photographic life easier.

» FILTERS

A filter is a piece of glass, gelatin, or optical resin that affects the light hitting the camera sensor in some subtle (or not so subtle) way.

Filters are commonly available in two forms, either round and threaded, so they can be screwed to the front of a lens, or square/rectangular and designed to fit into a slotted holder that is attached to the lens.

Round filters are usually made of high-quality optical glass with a metal or heavy-duty plastic surround. If you intend only ever using one lens they are ideal, but if you buy another lens you may find that it has a different thread size requiring you to buy another set of filters. One way round this is to buy a large filter—82mm diameter, for example—and then buy adapter rings so that it can be fitted onto every lens in your collection.

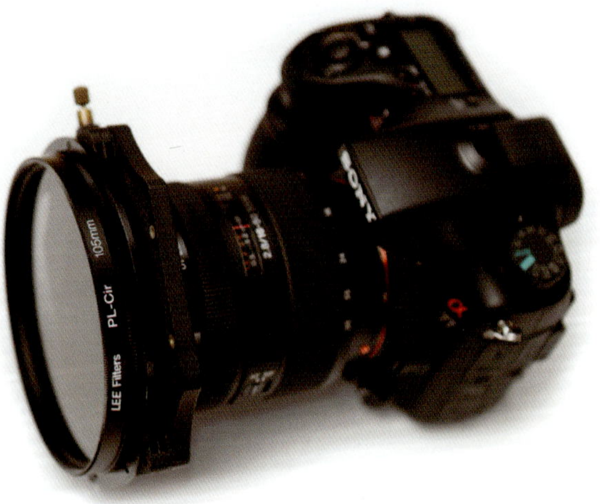

FINAL CUT EXPRESS «
An A77 fitted with a Lee Filters holder and polarizing filter.

Filters designed to fit into a holder are typically made of optical resin or gelatin. There are several manufacturers of filter holder systems such as Cokin, Lee Filters, and Kood. Inexpensive adapter rings allow you to use the filter holder (and the filters) on every lens you own, although the filters are generally more expensive than round, screw-in filters. Unless you have a suitably large holder and filters, the holder can also encroach into the corners of shots taken with wideangle lenses.

› UV and skylight filters

UV and skylight filters absorb ultraviolet light, which is typically found at high altitude and on hazy days, and can create a blue cast in an image. Skylight filters have a slightly pink tint to them, helping to warm up the image (although this may be counteracted by the A77's AWB facility), while UV filters are more neutral. Neither of these filters affects exposure, so they are often used to protect the front elements of lenses from damage.

Note:
Some lenses require drop-in filters. This type of filter is relatively uncommon and is "dropped" into a compartment in the lens rather than attached to a filter thread on the front of the lens.

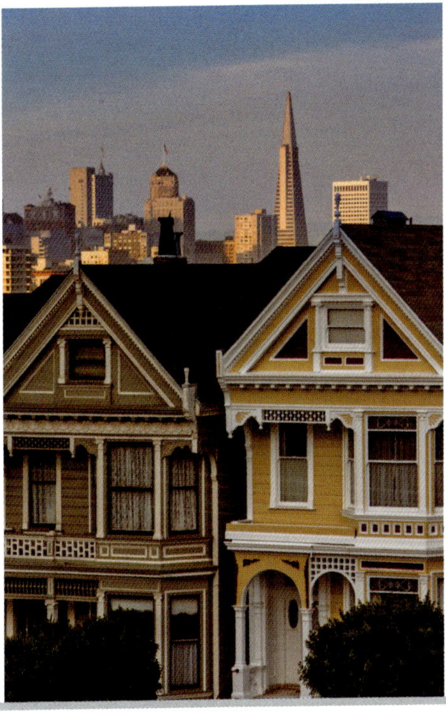

BALANCE «
Even with techniques such as HDR, there's still a place for filters such as the 2-stop graduated ND filter that was used here to balance the exposure between the foreground and background.

› Polarizing filter

When light is reflected from a non-metallic surface it is scattered in all directions, causing glare and a reduction in color saturation. This scattered light has been "polarized." A polarizing filter, or polarizer cuts out this polarized light, restoring saturation and reducing glare. Polarizers are made of glass and mounted in a holder that can be rotated through 360°, allowing you to vary the strength of the effect by rotating the holder.

The classic use for a polarizer is to deepen blue sky, causing clouds to stand out more brilliantly. This effect works best when the filter is at 90 degrees to the sun, and diminishes away from this angle until, at a 180 degree angle, a polarizer has no effect. The height of the sun will also determine how strongly the polarizing filter appears to work.

Another use for a polarizer is to control the amount of light reflected from non-metallic surfaces, such as water, shiny paint, and even the leaves of trees. The effect is noticeable even on overcast days and not just when the sun is shining.

As a polarizer is slightly opaque, it will reduce the amount of light reaching the sensor. The A77's exposure meter will automatically compensate for this unless you're shooting in AUTO, in which case the exposure compensation must be set manually. The amount of compensation required will vary, but 2 stops is a good starting point.

> **Tip**
>
> *Polarizing filters are available as either linear or circular, but this has nothing to do with the shape. For technical reasons linear polarizers are only really suitable for MF lenses—you should buy only the circular type for use with the A77.*

BLUE »
The use of a polarizer has deepened the blue of the sky as well as reducing glare from the glass roof of this building.

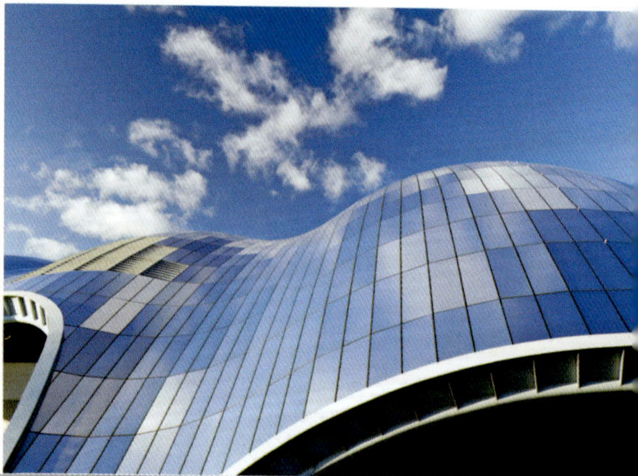

› Neutral density filters

Although the A77's ISO can be set to ISO 50, there are good reasons not to do this. Using a neutral density, or ND filter can help you achieve the same effect without a reduction in dynamic range. ND filters are at their most useful in bright light, when you want to use a slow shutter speed or wide aperture, and in the simplest sense they act like sunglasses for your camera, cutting down the amount of light reaching the sensor and allowing you to use a greater range of exposure settings.

As the name suggests, ND filters are neutral in color, so do not add a color tint to the image. They also come in a variety of strengths from 1 stop to 5 stops and are generally available either as a round screw-in type or square to fit a filter holder.

A recent innovation is the 10-stop ND filter. This type of filter looks opaque to the eye and can extend shutter speeds to several seconds or even minutes depending on the ambient light level. Because of their thickness they aren't strictly speaking neutral and do tint images (often quite strongly), and in low light conditions the AF system of the A77 can struggle. It's therefore advisable to focus and then lock focus before fitting the filter.

Note:
A polarizer can be used as an alternative to an ND filter as it will reduce exposures by approximately 2 stops when it is set to give its strongest effect.

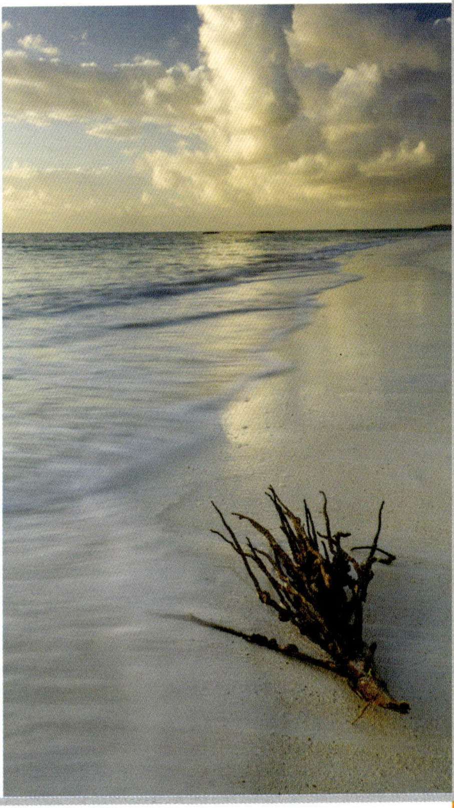

WAVE POWER »
The way that moving water is captured is affected by shutter speed. ND filters will help extend shutter speeds for a more ethereal effect.

› Graduated ND filters

Graduated ND filters are related to ND filters, but a graduated ND is divided into two: the bottom half of the filter is clear and the top half has a semi-opaque ND coating. The transition from clear to semi-opaque can be soft, hard, or very hard, and graduated ND filters are available in different strengths, such as 1 stop, 2 stop, and 3 stop.

Graduated ND filters are used when the exposure of one half of a scene differs significantly from the other half, making a single exposure impossible without losing detail in one area. It's probably fair to say that landscape photographers benefit most from graduated ND filters, and they are most often used to balance the brightness levels between the bright sky and darker foreground. The greater the difference between the two halves of an image, the stronger the graduated ND filter would need to be.

Graduated ND filters are available in screw-in form, but they are more useful when used with a filter holder, as they can be moved up and down (or rotated) and positioned most precisely.

DARK SKY
This scene benefited from the use of a graduated ND filter. Unlike the church tower, the path wasn't lit by direct light. This caused an exposure problem that was resolved by using a 2-stop graduated ND filter, so the filter covered the area indicated in red in the picture below right.

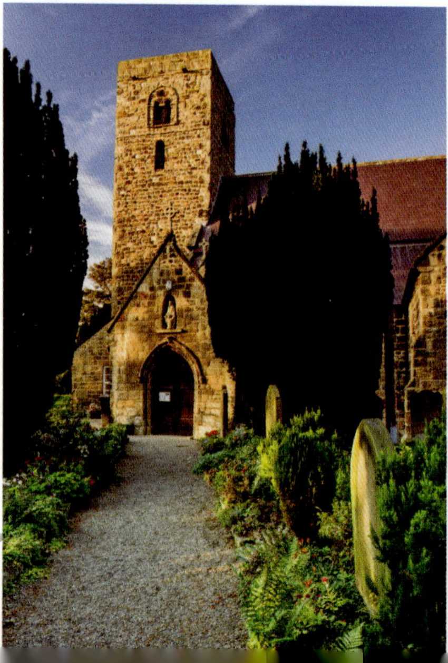

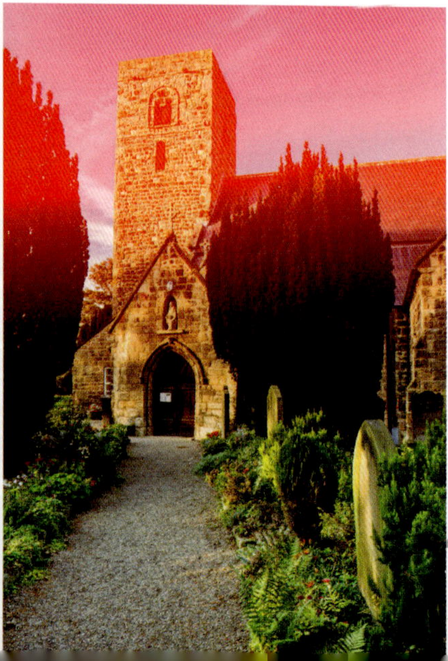

» SONY ACCESSORIES

Sony makes a wide range of accessories that are compatible with the A77.

Battery (NP-FM500H)
Running out of power before the end of a photography session is frustrating, so it makes sense to carry a spare, fully charged battery. It is more likely to be needed in cold conditions, as low temperatures reduce a battery's charged state more quickly.

AC adapter (AC-PW10AM)
If you work indoors, the AC-PW10AM AC adapter is the ideal way to power your camera without relying on batteries.

Screen protector (PCK-LM3AM)
Although the A77's LCD screen is reasonably scratch proof (and can be folded away for protection), this protective sheet fits over the screen to offer complete peace of mind.

Shotgun microphone (CG50)
When plugged into the A77's microphone jack this external mic gives you more control over sound recording when you are shooting movies.

Vertical control grip (C77AM)
Shooting with the A77 held vertically is relatively straightforward, but it can be more awkward than shooting horizontally. The C77AM vertical grip attaches to the bottom of your camera, and includes many controls such as a shutter-release button and four-way controller, to make vertical shooting far easier. The grip can also hold two NP-FM500H batteries for extended shooting time.

Angle finder (FDA-A1AM)
The Sony FDA-A1AM Angle finder slots on to the eyepiece of the A77, allowing you to look through it from above or from the side. The finder also features a 2x magnifier to allow more accurate manual focusing. An angle finder may seem like an expensive luxury when you have a tilting LCD screen, but it's highly recommended if you regularly shoot macro images and need to check critical focus.

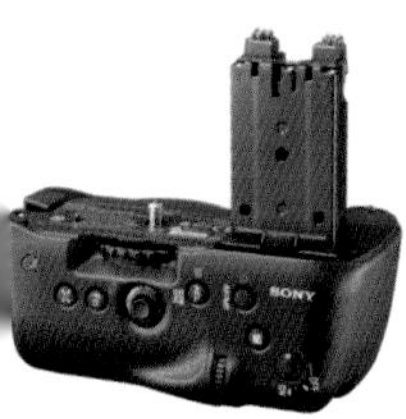

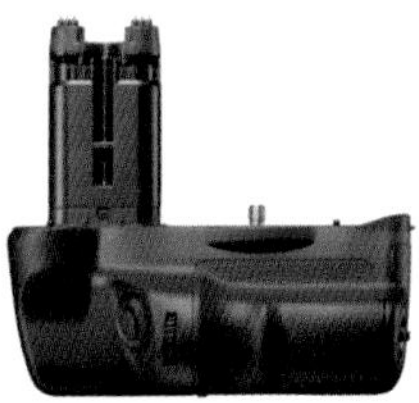

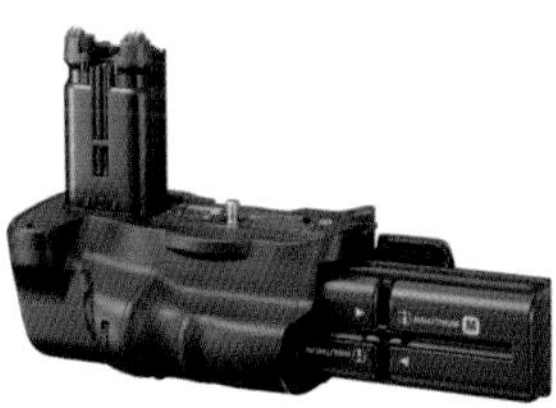

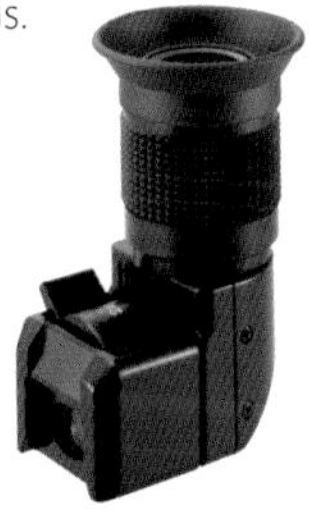

Magnifiers (FDA-ME1AM/FDA-M1AM.AE)

The FDA-ME1AM and FDA-M1AM.AE fit onto the A77's eyepiece, increasing the magnification by 1.15x and 2.3x respectively.

Remote commanders (RM-S1AM/ RM-L1AM/RMT-DSLR1)

Sony produces two types of remote commander for the A77. The RM-S1AM and RM-L1AM are both cable types that fit into the remote terminal connection on the side of the A77: the cable lengths are 20 inches (50cm) and 16½ feet (5m) respectively. The RMT-DSLR1 is a wireless remote commander that can be used to fire the shutter as well as control playback on your A77 when it is connected to a printer or TV.

SONY FILTER CHART

Type	Sony product code	Filter thread size
Multi-coated protection	VF-49MPAM	49mm
Multi-coated protection	VF-55MPAM	55mm
Multi-coated protection	VF-62MPAM	62mm
Multi-coated protection	VF-67MPAM	67mm
Multi-coated protection	VF-72MPAM	72mm
Multi-coated protection	VF-77MPAM	77mm
Circular polarizer	VF-49CPAM	49mm
Circular polarizer	VF-55CPAM	55mm
Circular polarizer	VF-62CPAM	62mm
Circular polarizer	VF-67CPAM	67mm
Circular polarizer	VF-72CPAM	72mm
Circular polarizer	VF-77CPAM	77mm
Neutral density	VF-49NDAM	49mm
Neutral density	VF-55NDAM	55mm
Neutral density	VF-62NDAM	62mm
Neutral density	VF-67NDAM	67mm
Neutral density	VF-72NDAM	72mm
Neutral density	VF-77NDAM	77mm

» SUPPORTING THE CAMERA

Combine the A77's high ISO ability with SteadyShot and you'd think that the camera could be handheld in any shooting situation. However, there are times when there is no alternative to using a tripod or other form of camera support.

› Tripods

Tripods can be cumbersome and awkward to set up, but they are also invaluable when light levels are low and shutter speeds are lasting several seconds, rather than fractions of seconds.

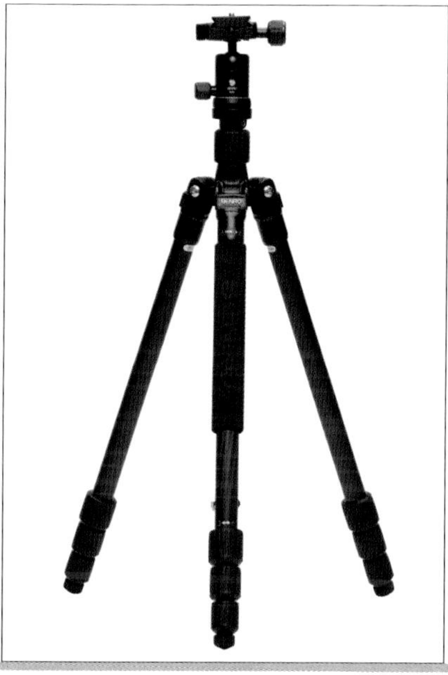

When choosing a tripod, buy one that you're prepared to carry, but which is still large and heavy enough to be stable when the A77 and your heaviest lens is attached.

A tripod that brings the camera to eye-level without the use of the center column is ideal, but a tripod of this size will almost invariably be large, heavy, and probably expensive. Materials such as carbon fiber make tripods lighter for any given size compared to a metal type, but again this is more expensive.

A good tripod will come without a head, allowing you to choose the type you want to fit. For still shooting, a ball-head offers the best weight-to-strength ratio, but they can be fiddly to use. A three-way head is a good compromise. A geared head will give you the most control but they are usually much heavier than either the ball or three-way head.

Shooting video requires a different type of tripod head. It is possible to buy dedicated video heads, which are designed for smooth pans. These generally don't allow the camera to be tilted vertically, so are less useful for still photography.

BENRO CARBON FIBER TRIPOD «
C0681TB Travel Angel.

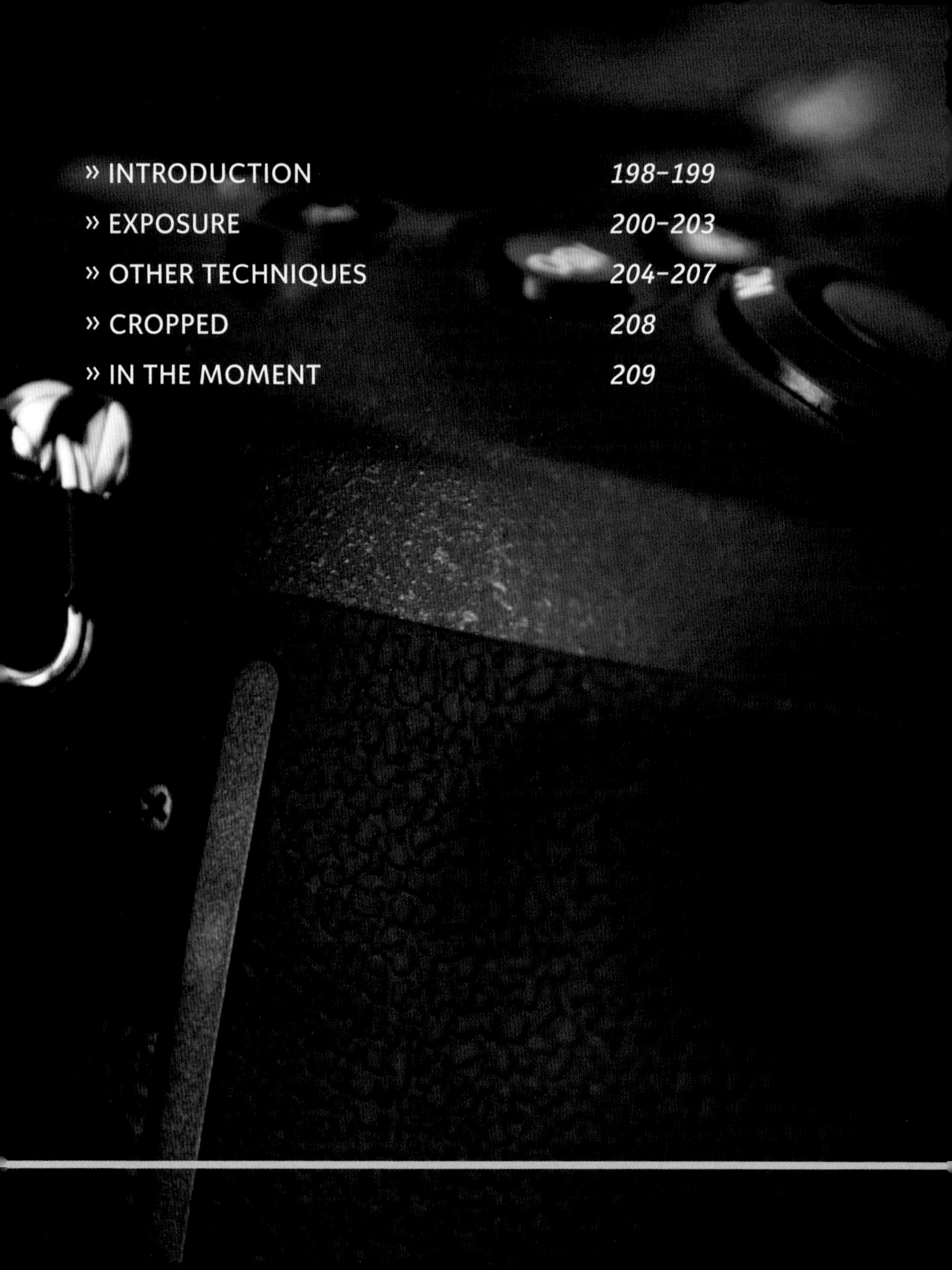

Chapter 7

IN THE FIELD

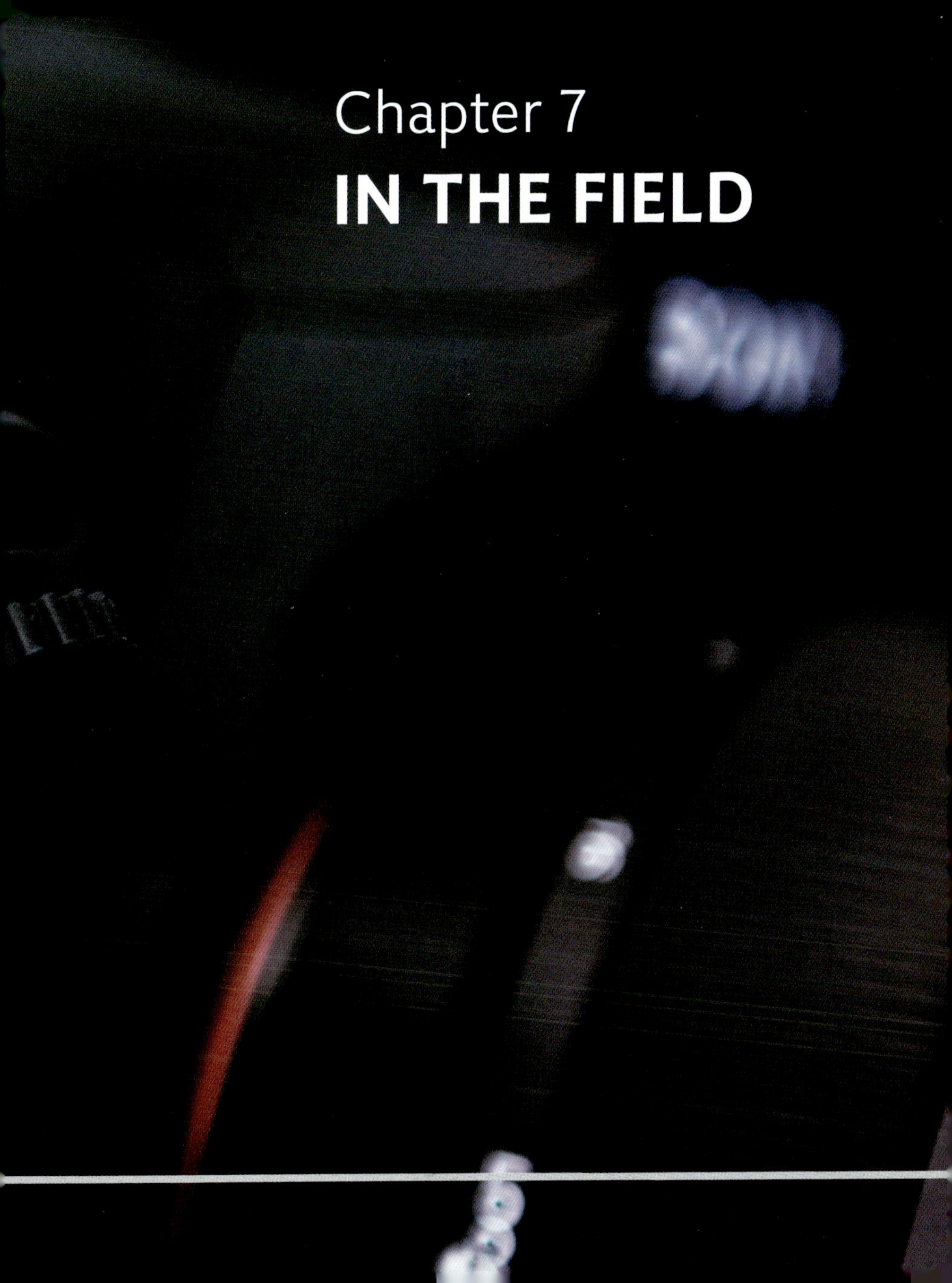

7 IN THE FIELD

It's tempting to switch your A77 to "automatic" and take a machine-gun approach to photography. While there is nothing wrong with this approach, it is not the best way to get creative fulfilment from your camera.

› Caring for your A77

Your A77 is a robust camera, but that doesn't mean you should be careless with it. If you're out in the rain, keep your camera covered when not in use. If it gets wet, wipe it dry as best you can before covering it up again. Once you're back indoors, check the camera thoroughly, and dry it again if necessary.

You should also check the lens to make sure there is no moisture on the lens surface, and take special care near salt water. Salt is very destructive to electronic components and metal generally, so dry your camera immediately if it is splashed with salt water and wipe it down again when you get home.

The maximum operating temperature of the A77 is 104°F (40°C). Do not use the camera in temperatures hotter than this, and if possible try to keep it in cool shade when not in use. The warmer the ambient temperature, the less time your camera will operate in movie shooting mode.

Cold brings its own set of problems, and in extremely cold conditions lubricants in the camera can freeze. Even in less extreme temperatures, your camera's batteries will become far less efficient when they're cold and a new battery that is fully charged will not last as long as it would in warm conditions. If you have a spare battery, keep it warm by placing it in a pocket inside your jacket.

When you return indoors, allow your camera to slowly return to room temperature and check that condensation hasn't built up on the lens or LCD. Keeping a big packet of silica gel in your camera bag will help to stop excessive moisture building up.

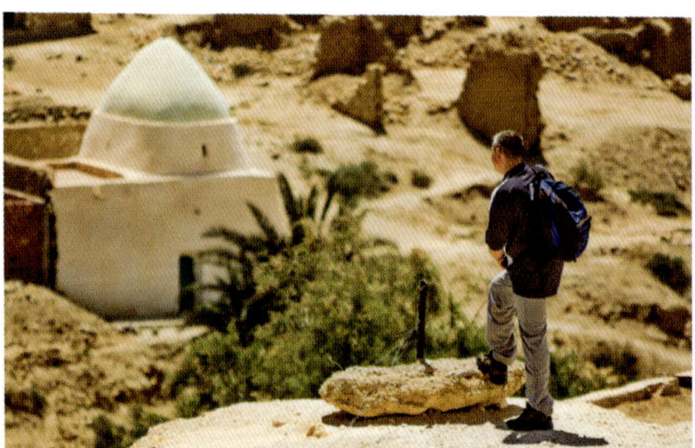

HEAT «

Stay in the shade as much as possible when working in hot locations. This will protect you, as well as your camera.

› Dust

Sand and dust are the bane of a photographer's life. Dust on the lens can contribute to flare and create unsightly spots on your photos if it sticks to the digital sensor or the A77's translucent mirror. If you're out shooting in these conditions, keep your A77 inside a bag when it is not in use. When changing lenses do so as quickly as possible, using your body to shield the camera from any breeze. If dust or sand is on your lens use a blower and avoid touching the lens surface.

Dust in an image is seen as fuzzy blobs and specks, usually most prominent in areas of even tone, such as sky. The A77 has a cleaning mode that shakes the sensor to remove dust, and running the cleaning mode every so often may be all that you need to do to keep your sensor clean (one of the advantages of the SLT design is that the mirror protects the sensor from dust). If you do need to clean the sensor manually, refer to the manual that came with your A77 for details.

The smaller the aperture you use—and therefore the greater the depth of field—the greater the likelihood that dust will show in your image. This is particularly true if there are spots of dust on the mirror. This is a good reason not to always shoot at minimum aperture.

Cleaning the sensor

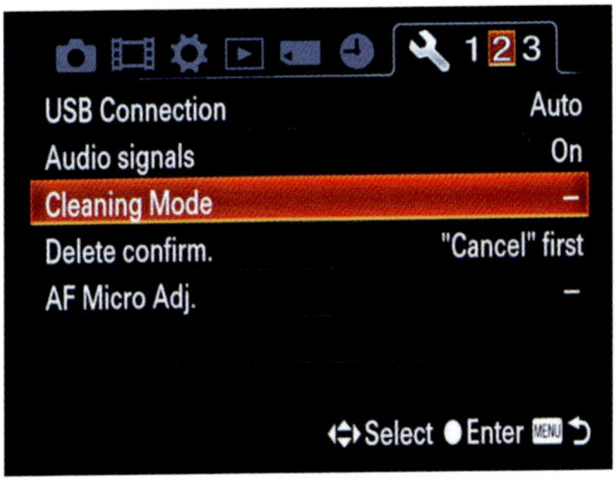

1) Press **MENU** and then navigate to Setup 2.

2) Highlight **Cleaning Mode** and press ●.

3) Scroll to **Enter** and press ● again.

4) Your A77 will make a brief buzzing noise and then display a message asking you to turn the power off. Switch the camera off and then on again.

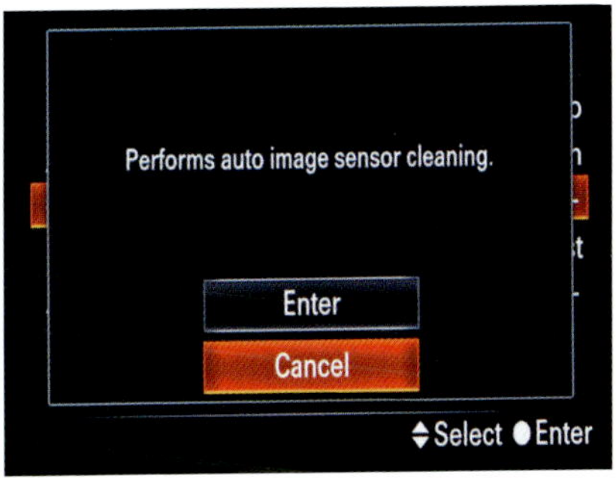

Understanding how your camera meters a scene is the key to consistent results.

› Metering

The exposure meter in your A77 is a reflective meter, so called because it measures the light reflected from the scene. Exposure meters work by assuming that all the tones in the scene average out to a mid-gray, which means that camera meters work best with "average" scenes. Grass and rock (if they are exposed correctly and converted to black and white) generally equate to mid-gray.

The problem with assuming that a scene is averagely reflective is that not every scene is: if a scene is lighter than average (sand or snow, for example), the meter will underexpose to drag the lighter tonal range back to mid-gray. The opposite is true if the scene is darker than average: the meter will overexpose, again to drag the overall (dark) tonal range back to mid-gray. To achieve the correct exposure in these situations it is therefore often necessary to apply exposure compensation, as outlined previously.

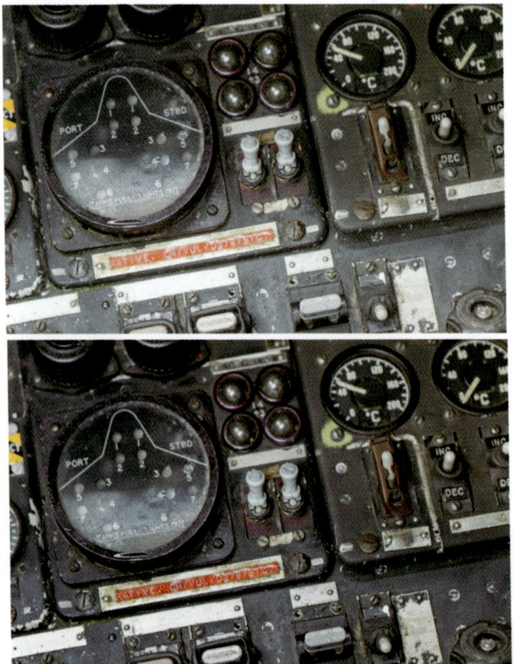

BACK TO BLACK «
This control panel was dominated by dark tones, resulting in slight overexposure (top). By applying -1 stop exposure compensation I was able to place the tonal range exactly where I wanted it (bottom).

› Histograms

On the A77 a "live" histogram can be displayed before exposure and then another histogram called up when you review an image. A histogram is a graph showing the distribution of tones, and it is a very quick and precise way of assessing whether an image is correctly exposed or not. It is far more precise than using the LCD screen or EVF to judge exposure, and with practice it's possible to interpret the information on the histogram in such a way that you can precisely fine tune the exposure of your images if necessary.

The left half of a histogram shows the range of tones in an image that are darker than mid-gray, with black at the extreme left edge. The right half of the histogram shows the tones in an image that are lighter than mid-gray with white at the extreme right edge. The vertical axis of the histogram shows the number of pixels in an image of a particular tone.

If a histogram is skewed to the left, this may be an indication that the image is underexposed; if skewed to the right, it may be overexposed. If a histogram is squashed against either the left or right edge of the histogram it has been "clipped," which means there are areas of pure black or pure white pixels in the image respectively. Clipped areas contain no usable image data.

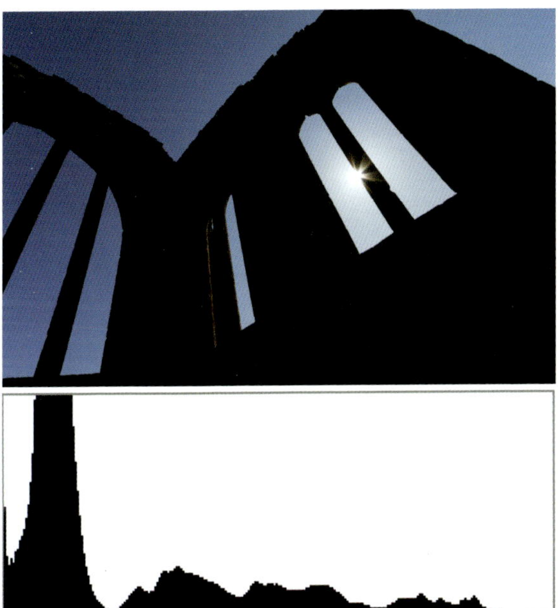

ASSESSING «
With practice it becomes easy to see how the histogram corresponds to the tones in an image.

› Exposing to the right

The digital sensor in your A77 captures more usable data for the brighter areas of an image than it does for the darker areas. This means that if you deliberately underexpose an image you are losing a lot of potentially useful image data that can be used in post-production. "Exposing to the right" (ETTR) helps to maximize the usable image data, providing you with greater scope for adjustment in post-processing. This technique is best suited to shooting Raw images.

ETTR involves exposing an image so that the histogram is skewed to the right, but without clipping the highlights. This often means ignoring the exposure set by the camera and applying positive exposure compensation. When it is reviewed, the image will look decidedly washed-out and lacking in contrast, but this is OK: adjustments to exposure and contrast can be made in Image Data Converter (or another Raw converter of your choice) to optimize the image.

Before you expose to the right, it's a good idea to set the Creative Style to Neutral. This is because the histogram on the LCD that you see in playback is not generated directly from the Raw file, but from a JPEG that is created using the selected Creative Style. Using Creative Styles such as Clear, Deep, or Light will cause the histogram to skew in a way that means it won't provide you with an accurate representation of the Raw data.

> ***Note:***
> Some high-contrast scenes won't allow you much leeway to shoot ETTR.

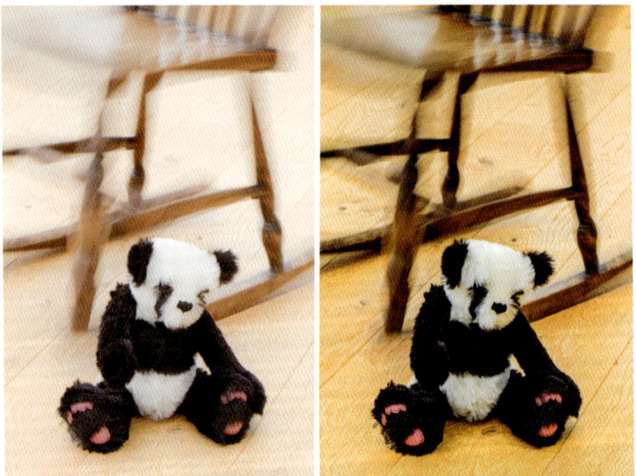

ETTR «
On the left is an ETTR image. It's lacking contrast, but the shadow areas are noise free. The image on the right has been corrected by reducing the exposure and boosting the contrast in post-production.

› White balance and histograms

The A77 displays four histograms in playback. The first is a luminance histogram, which shows the brightness levels across the image as if the image were composed entirely of shades of gray. The other three histograms show the distribution of red, green, and blue in the image; the components that make up each and every pixel in an image. A pure red pixel only has red in it, with no green or blue components; a pure magenta pixel on the other hand is an equal mix of red and blue; and a white pixel is an equal mix of red, green, and blue at their maximum values of 255 (black is a complete absence of red, green, and blue).

The RGB histograms can be used to check that the white balance for a particular scene is set correctly. Take a photo of a neutral gray surface, so that it fills the entire frame (there's a gray card that can be used for this purpose in the cover of this book). If your white balance setting is correct, the red, green, and blue histograms should be identical *(top right)*. If they are not, the white balance is incorrect. If the red histogram is more skewed to the right than the others, the white balance is too warm and should be "cooled" *(center right)*. If it's the blue histogram that's skewed to the right, then the white balance is too cool and so should be "warmed" *(bottom right)*.

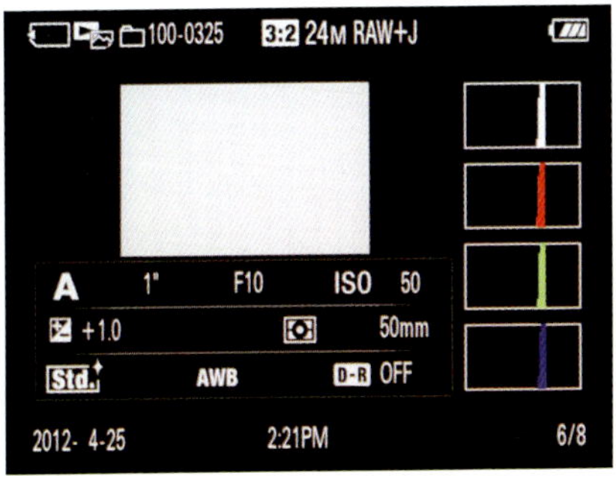

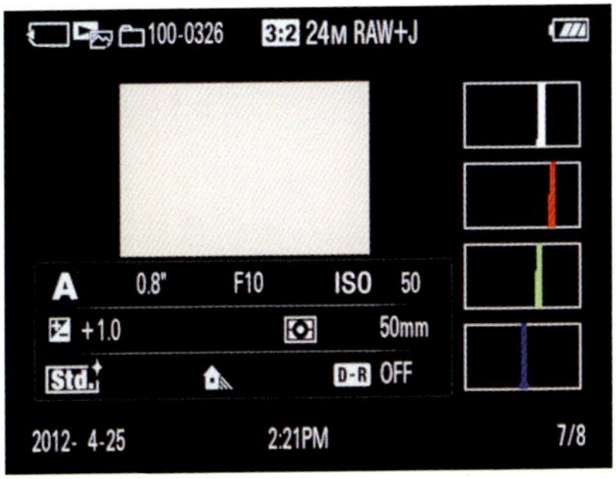

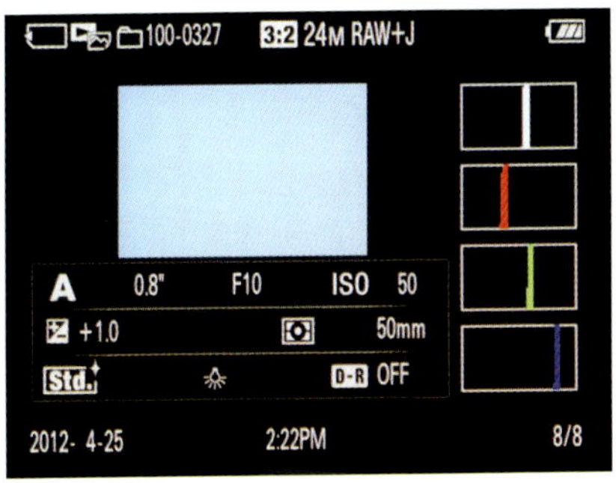

› Flare

Lens flare is caused by non-image-forming light being bounced around the internal optics of a lens before reaching the sensor. The results are unwanted blobs or streaks in the image and occasionally an overall reduction in contrast. Lens flare is most likely to occur when the camera is pointed toward a bright point light source, although it can also be caused when light enters the lens obliquely, even when the light source is just out of shot.

The most common solution to coping with lens flare is to use a lens hood, but this will only cure flare from light entering the lens obliquely: flare will still occur when light is shining directly into the lens. Lens hoods also make life difficult if you want to use a filter holder with your lens as the two items are usually incompatible unless you buy a lens hood built specifically for use with filter holders.

An alternative solution is to mount your A77 on a tripod and shade the lens with your body—making sure that you don't enter the shot at the same time. This is easy to check by swinging the LCD out to a point where you can see it. Keeping your lenses clean will also help to keep flare under control; greasy fingerprints or dust on the lens will increase the risk of flare.

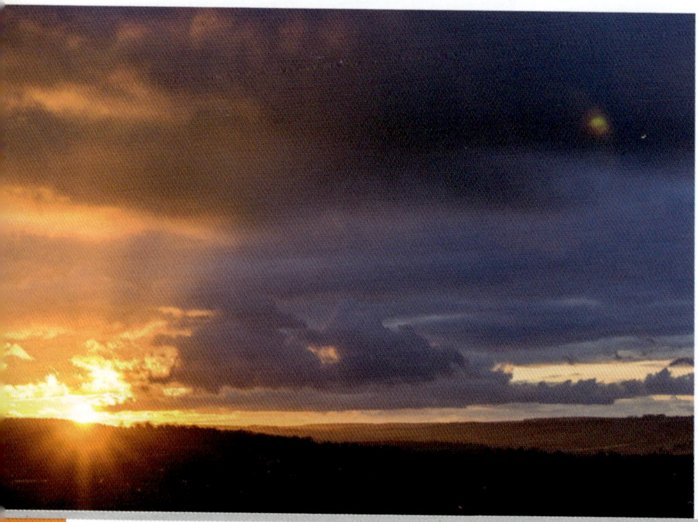

SUNSET «
Direct light from the sun has caused flare in the upper right of this image. In this instance a lens hood would not have helped. The flare is in an area with relatively little detail so in this instance it could conceivably be cloned out during post-production.

› Diffraction and maximizing depth of field

Different lenses have different minimum apertures, and for maximum depth of field, it would be logical to use the minimum setting. However, this isn't a good idea. Lenses don't perform at their best when set to minimum aperture (optically a lens is usually at its peak in the mid-range of apertures), due to an effect known as diffraction. Light is randomly scattered (diffracted) as it strikes the edges of the aperture blades, softening the resulting image. Diffraction becomes more problematic the smaller the lens aperture, so rather counter-intuitively, you may find your images are less sharp when using the minimum aperture than if you'd used a mid-range aperture setting.

Using a wider aperture will of course reduce the available depth of field, but you can optimize the depth of field for a particular aperture by focusing the lens to the hyperfocal distance. When the focus point of a lens is set to the hyperfocal distance, everything from half that distance in front of the focus point to infinity behind it will fall within the depth of field and appear sharp. By focusing precisely, and using the largest aperture that will cover the required depth of field, you will reduce the risk of diffraction. On the next page are tables showing the hyperfocal distance for the 16mm, 24mm, 35mm, and 50mm positions of the A77's standard 16–50mm kit lens.

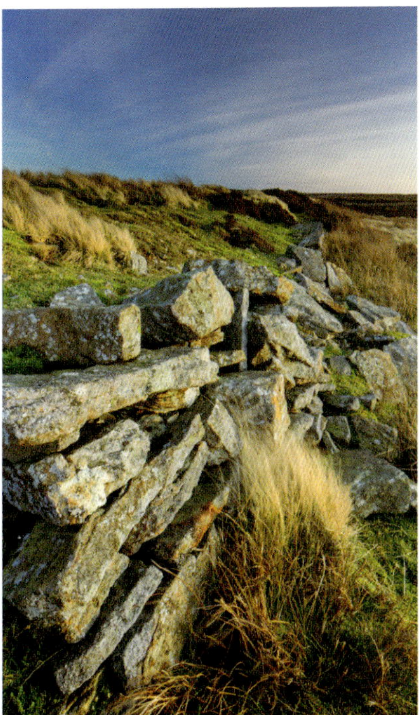

FRONT TO BACK «
Using the hyperfocal distance helps when trying to achieve front-to-back sharpness in an image.

To use the tables, first set the lens to the correct focal length. Once you've done that, set the focus distance to the hyperfocal distance (HD). Finally, set the required aperture. It pays to be slightly conservative so, if in doubt, set the aperture slightly smaller than that specified in the table. Depth of field will stretch from the Near point to Infinity (∞). Note that all distances are in meters.

16mm: Hyperfocal distance

f/2.8		f/4		f/5.6		f/8		f/11		f/16	
Near	HD	Near	HD	Near	HD	Near	HD	Near	HD	Near	HD
2.29	4.57	1.60	3.20	1.14	2.29	0.80	1.60	0.58	1.16	0.40	0.80

24mm: Hyperfocal distance

f/2.8		f/4		f/5.6		f/8		f/11		f/16	
Near	HD	Near	HD	Near	HD	Near	HD	Near	HD	Near	HD
5.14	10.29	3.60	7.20	2.57	5.14	1.80	3.60	1.31	2.62	0.90	1.80

35mm: Hyperfocal distance

f/2.8		f/4		f/5.6		f/8		f/11		f/16	
Near	HD	Near	HD	Near	HD	Near	HD	Near	HD	Near	HD
10.94	21.88	7.66	15.31	5.47	10.94	3.83	7.66	2.78	5.57	1.91	3.83

50mm: Hyperfocal distance

f/2.8		f/4		f/5.6		f/8		f/11		f/16	
Near	HD	Near	HD	Near	HD	Near	HD	Near	HD	Near	HD
22.3	44.60	15.60	31.20	11.16	22.30	7.80	15.60	5.60	11.30	3.91	7.81

› Black and white

The A77 can be set to shoot in black and white, which many diehards would argue is "proper" photography. A good black-and-white photographer sees the world as a series of tones, and the way in which those tones are represented in an image is the art of black-and-white photography.

Creating a black-and-white image means converting the colors in a scene to individual shades of gray. However, it is the reflectivity of an object that determines its gray level, so problems can occur if the scene features objects that are radically different in color, but of similar reflectivity. These objects would be roughly the same shade of gray when converted to black and white, resulting in a rather flat-looking image. In order to separate colors when they are converted to black and white, colored filters must be used. These filters can be physical filters that are fitted to a camera lens, or "electronic" filters applied in-camera or in post-production.

Filters block out colors on the opposite side of a standard color wheel to the filter so a red filter blocks out blue-greens, for example. As a result, using a red filter will cause reds in an image to appear lighter in black and white, while blues and greens will be darkened. This can help separate the tonal values in an image, thereby adding interest. Landscape photographers often use yellow, orange, or red filters to darken blue sky (with red having the greatest effect), while portrait photographers are more likely to use green filters, which help with skin tones. If you're shooting Raw, it's advisable not to use physical filters, although they can be invaluable if you want to give your black-and-white JPEGs extra impact.

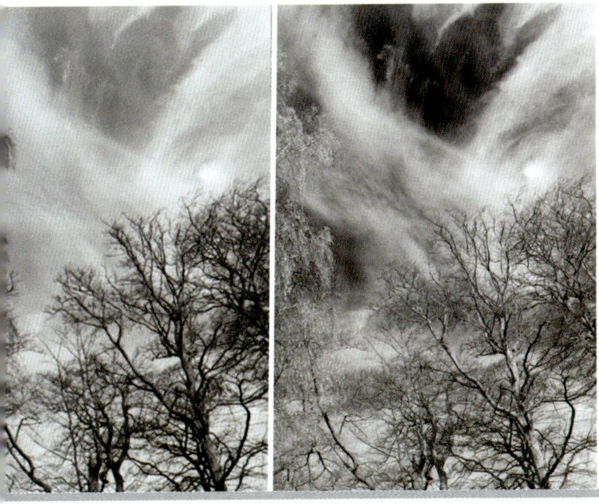

FILTERED «
The image on the far left was created without using filters. The image on the right was created with a red filter, which has deepened the blue of the sky and lightened the yellow leaves of the tree on the left.

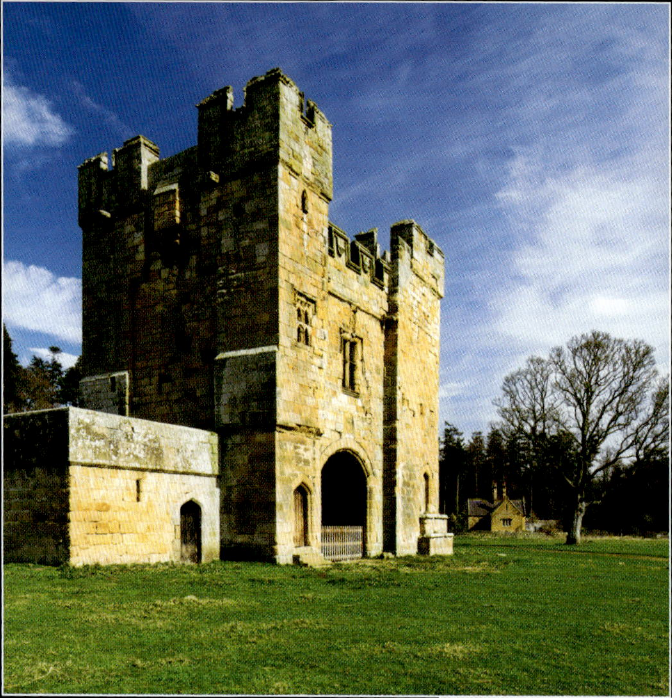

Settings

- *Lens:* 11–18mm (at 15mm)
- *Aperture:* f/11
- *Shutter speed:* 1/125 sec.
- *ISO:* 100

» IN THE MOMENT

A photograph is a record of a particular moment in time. That moment doesn't have to be a brief fraction of a second—it can be seconds, minutes, or even hours. One of the wonders of photography is that it allows you to see the world in a completely different way to how it is normally perceived. This photograph, shot pre-sunrise, required a relatively lengthy exposure that caused the waves to blur, resulting in a less literal interpretation of the scene.

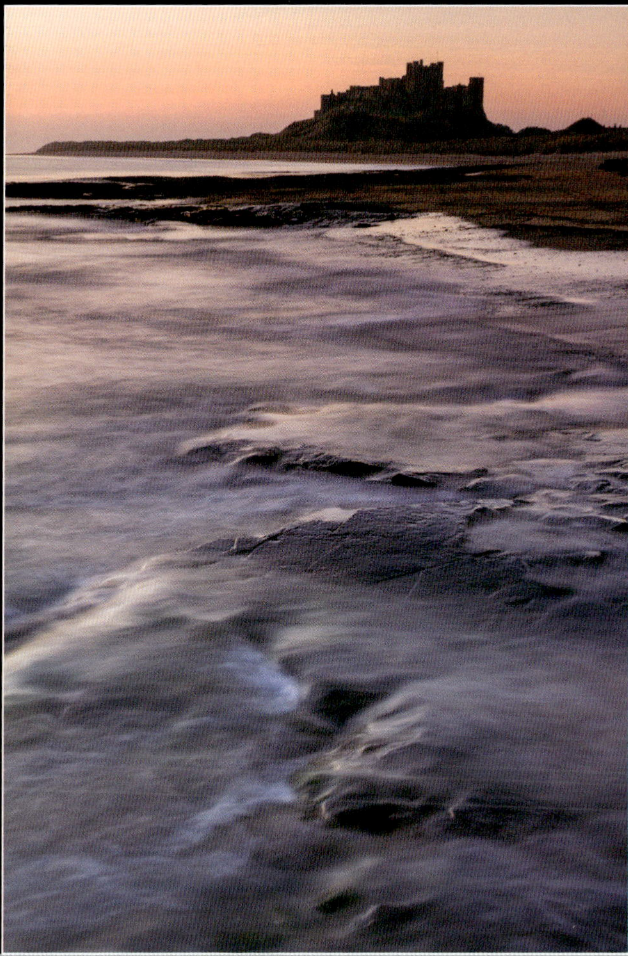

Settings

- *Lens:* 24–70mm (at 32mm)
- *Aperture:* f/16
- *Shutter speed:* 5 sec.
- *ISO:* 100

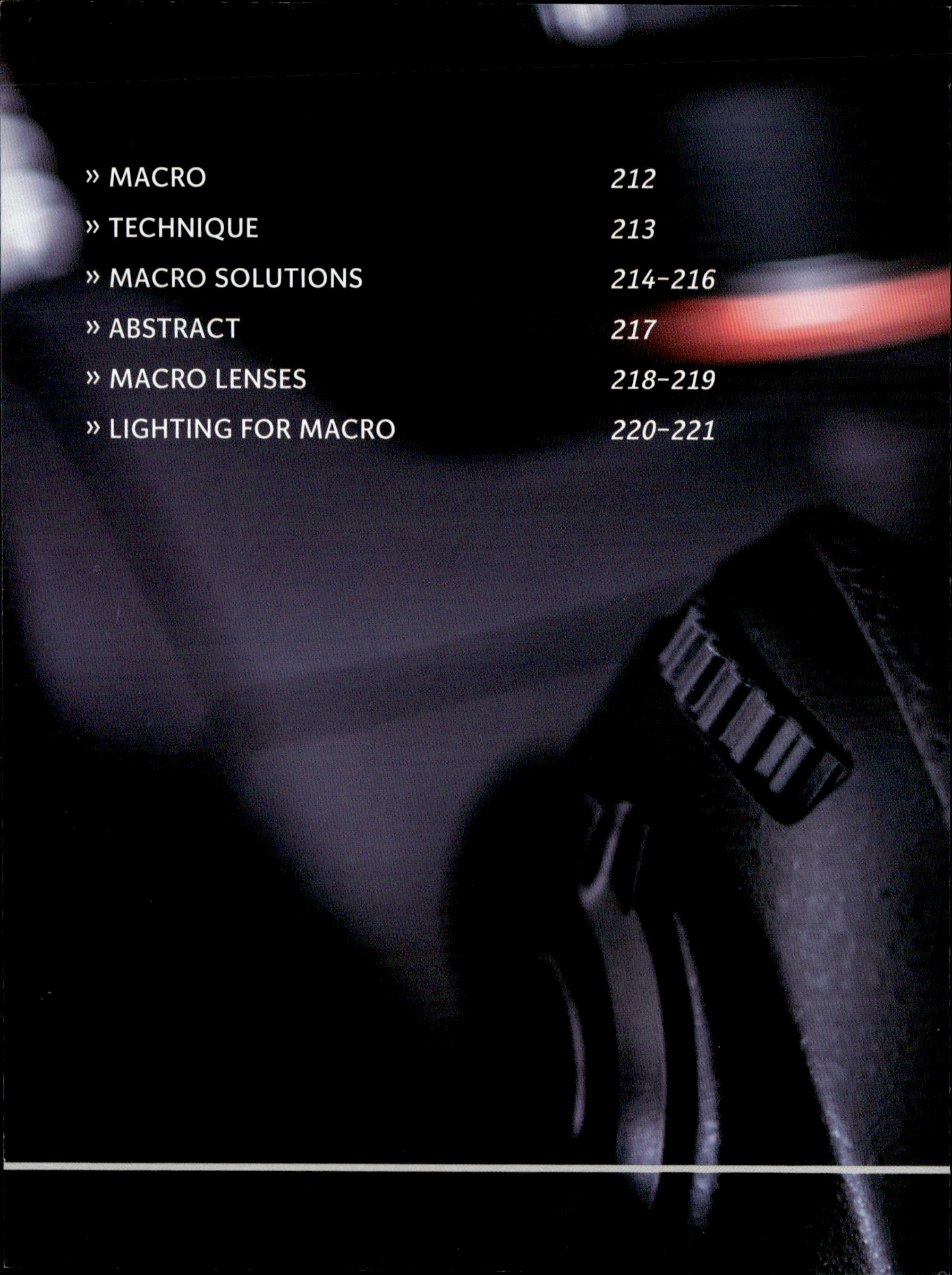

Chapter 8
CLOSE-UP

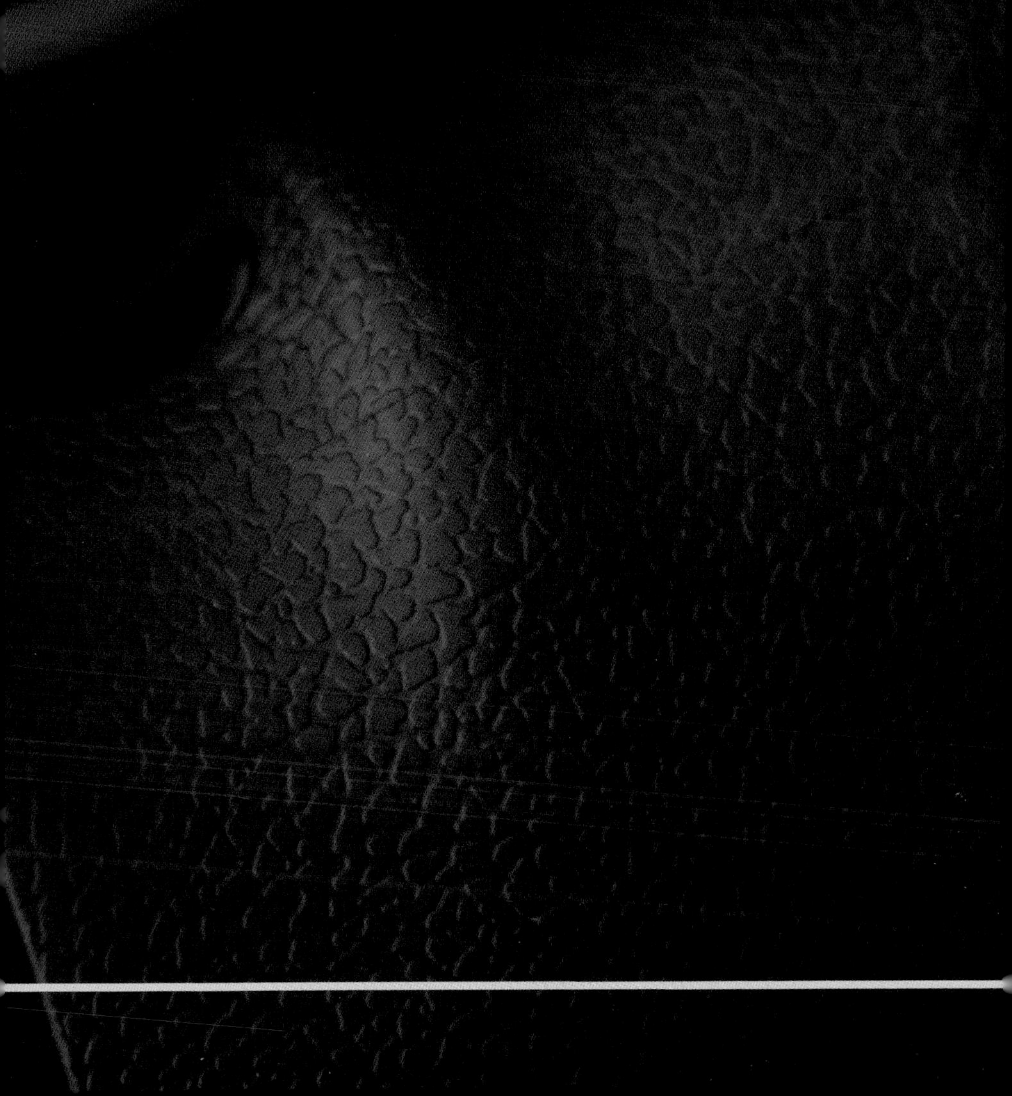

8 CLOSE-UP

Close-up photography is a rewarding genre to explore, and the potential for making pleasing images of the world of the small is almost unlimited.

» MACRO

Strictly speaking, there is a difference between close-up and macro photography. A lens may be able to focus down to a few centimeters (a common feature of digital compact cameras), but this does not necessarily make it a macro lens. To be a true macro, the image projected by the lens onto the sensor must be life-size or larger.

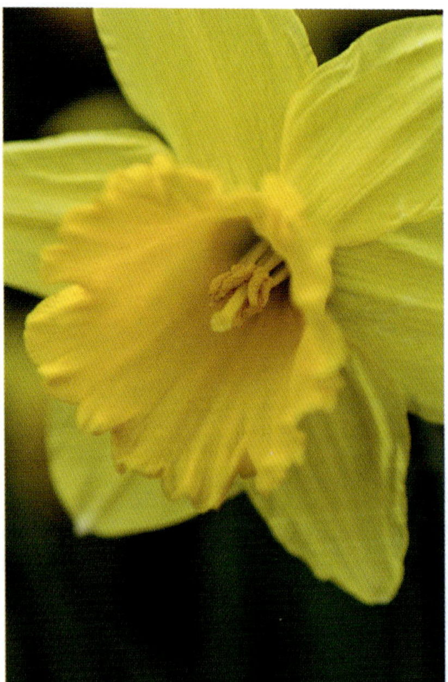

This is referred to as the reproduction or magnification ratio: a life-size image would have a reproduction ratio of 1:1, twice life-size would be 2:1, and so on.

You may see lenses advertised with a "macro" facility that only have a reproduction ratio of 1:2 or even 1:4 (half and quarter life-size respectively). These lenses will allow you to focus closer than a standard lens, but are not true macros. Sony's web site shows the reproduction ratios of currently available Sony and Zeiss lenses.

Note:
Another factor to consider when choosing a macro lens is the working distance. This is the camera-to-subject distance required for a sharp 1:1 or higher image. The working distance of a lens is governed by the focal length: the longer the focal length, the greater the working distance. A longer working distance is useful if your subject is likely to move or be disturbed if you are in close proximity.

CLOSE UP «
This photograph of a spring daffodil was created using a lens capable of close focusing, but it was not a true macro lens.

» TECHNIQUE

One of the challenges of shooting close-up images is the lack of depth of field, even when using small apertures. The closer you focus, the less depth of field you have, and the greater the challenge. Shooting close up therefore requires a disciplined approach in order to maximize what little depth of field there is. This means that accurate focusing is essential, with the focus point placed exactly where you require critical sharpness. If in doubt, shoot multiple images with the focus point shifted between them.

Using a tripod will help enormously as it's much easier to precisely set up a shot when your camera is stable. Another good reason to use a tripod is to avoid camera shake, as even a very slight movement of the camera will lead to unsharp images: SteadyShot is generally less effective when shooting close up. Employing a small aperture setting to gain an increase in depth of field will only exacerbate the problem of movement, as a small aperture will require the use of a longer shutter speed (unless you use a higher ISO with increased noise).

One approach to the problem of a lack of depth of field is to think of it as a positive. Using maximum aperture (and so minimizing depth of field) will help to simplify an image's composition and focus attention on the most important elements of the scene. This will also allow you to use a faster shutter speed, which is useful if your subject is moving.

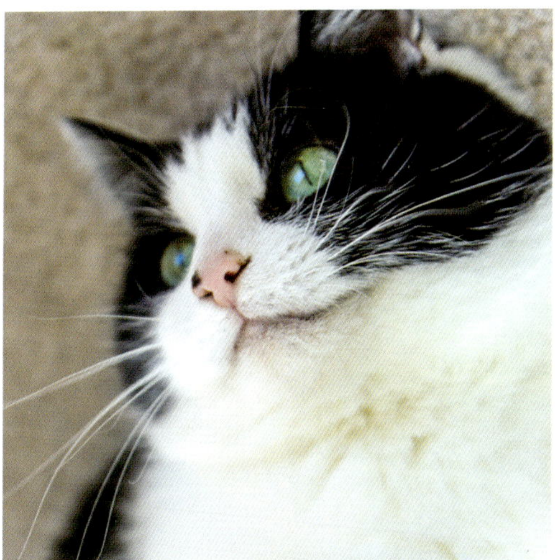

Tip

*Setting [icon] to **Focus Magnifier** on the [icon] 3 menu allows you to check focus more accurately.*

DEPTH OF FIELD «
Shooting at f/2.8, depth of field drops away rapidly from the point of focus (the cat's nose) in this image.

8 » MACRO SOLUTIONS

You don't necessarily have to own a macro lens to shoot close-up images. It's possible to enhance the close focusing capabilities of any lens by the addition of the equipment described on the next few pages. Although this equipment will not give you the image quality of a true macro lens, it will provide a relatively inexpensive entry into the world of close-up and macro photography.

› Close-up attachment lenses

One of the simplest ways to augment a standard lens is to attach a supplementary close-up attachment lens to the filter thread. The close-up attachment lens essentially acts as a magnifying glass for your lens, reducing its minimum focusing distance without interfering with the exposure or focusing systems.

Close-up attachment lenses are most effective when used in conjunction with prime lenses, but they can be used on zoom lenses as well. Sony does not currently produce close-up attachment lenses, but other camera manufacturers, such as Nikon and Canon do—there's no reason why you cannot use them with your Sony lenses.

The strength of close-up attachment lenses is measured in diopters, usually +1, +2, +3, or +4, and the stronger the diopter, the higher the magnification of the lens. Close-up attachment lenses can also be stacked together to increase the magnification further, although this is often at the expense of image quality.

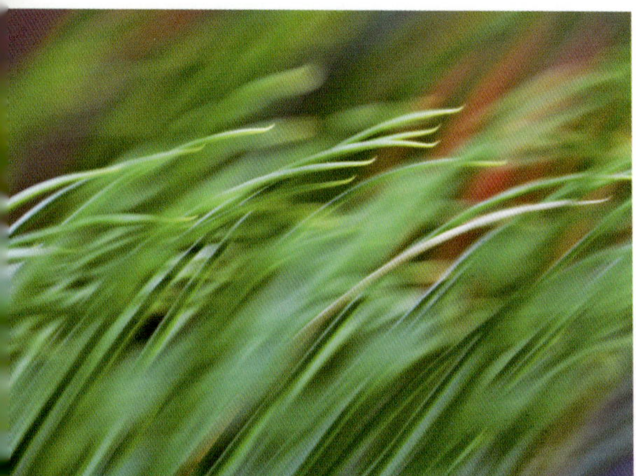

Tip

*Set **Release w/o Lens** to **Enable** on the ⚙ 1 menu so you can fire the shutter if you use an extension tube, bellows, or reversing ring that doesn't have full lens connectivity.*

DECISION TIME «
As depth of field is so small, it's important to decide exactly where to place the focus point when shooting close-ups.

› Extension tubes

Extension tubes (or extension rings) are very simple, hollow metal tubes that fit between a camera and a lens. Extension tubes work by increasing the distance of the lens to the camera body, allowing closer focusing and increasing the magnification of the image projected by the lens onto the sensor.

The big advantage that extension tubes have over close-up attachment lenses is that they contain no glass elements, which means they do not affect image quality. However, because the image projected by the lens is magnified, any flaws the lens may have will be magnified also. Therefore, extension tubes work better with prime lenses than zooms.

Another consequence of magnifying the image is that light is lost in the process. Your A77's exposure meter will compensate for this light loss, but you should still be prepared to set a higher ISO, a longer shutter speed, and/or a wider aperture when extension tubes are used.

Extension tubes typically come in sets of three tubes of different lengths, which can be used individually or combined to obtain the desired magnification. At the time of writing Sony does not produce any extension tubes for its A-mount cameras, but they are readily available from third-party manufacturers such as Kenro.

KENRO EXTENSION TUBES »

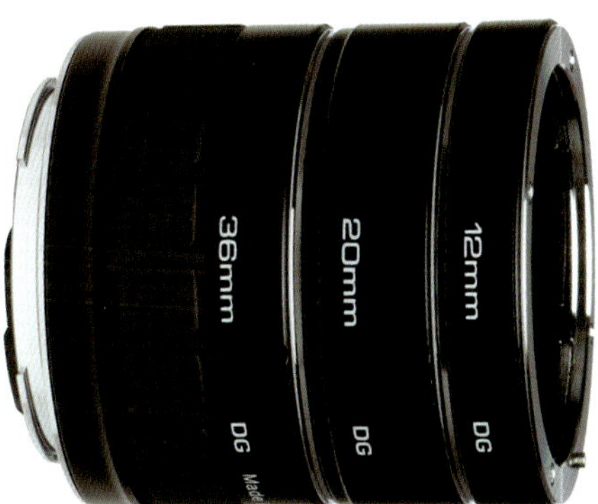

Notes:

Not all extension tubes are equal. The very cheapest do not have a connection between the camera and the lens, so AF and aperture selection will be disabled.

As light is lost when using extension tubes you may find that the efficiency of the A77's AF (if available) is compromised.

Extension tubes are not the same as teleconverters.

› Bellows

Bellows are related to extension tubes, and work on the same principle—the bellows fit between the camera and lens, enabling the lens to focus more closely. However, bellows do not come in set lengths, and instead can be extended or compressed along a guide rail. Once the desired amount of magnification is achieved, the bellows are locked into position. The price of this flexibility is that bellows are far heavier and more cumbersome than extension tubes and are typically confined to use indoors on a tripod. Because they are mechanically more complicated, bellows also tend to be far more expensive than extension tubes.

Novoflex is currently the only company to make bellows that are directly compatible with the Sony A-mount, but there is a wide range of pre-owned bellows available for the M42 lens mount, all of which can be used with the A77 if it is fitted with an M42 adapter.

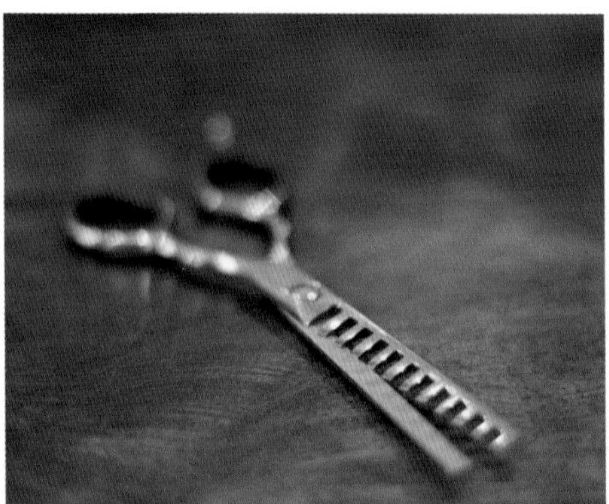

› Reversing ring

Any lens can be turned into a macro lens by reversing it so that the front element of the lens faces into the camera mount. A reversing ring allows you to do this by attaching to the camera's lens mount and providing you with a thread that you can screw the lens' filter thread onto. You need to make sure that you buy a reversing ring with the correct filter thread size for the lens you want to use, but the main benefit of this system is cost—reversing rings are cheap! You can also use a lens from any camera system as long as it has the correct filter thread. The main drawback is that focus and aperture must be set manually.

> ***Note:***
> The M42 lens mount uses a very simple, screw thread fitting. It is a MF system and no electronic information is transmitted between the lens and the camera. To use an M42 bellows with your A77 you would also need to buy an M42 lens, but these are in plentiful supply on auction web sites such as eBay.

TRANSFORMED «
Ordinary household objects take on a new life when shot in close-up.

» ABSTRACT

It's easy to fall into the trap of thinking that photography involves a set of rules that need to be slavishly followed. More fun can be had by experimentation and breaking the rules. This image was part of a series where I deliberately defocused the lens to produce a more painterly, abstract effect.

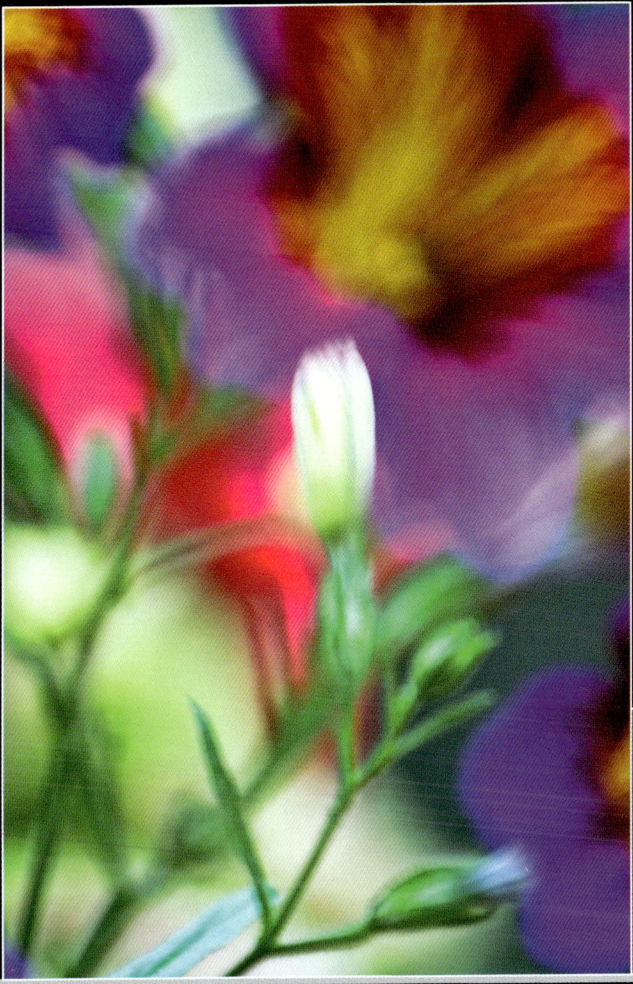

Settings

- *Lens:* 24–70mm (at 192mm)
- *Aperture:* f/4
- *Shutter speed:* 1/80 sec.
- *ISO:* 320

› Sony lenses

A dedicated macro lens is by far the best solution when it comes to ease of use, as you will have both auto exposure and autofocus, and it will also offer the optimum results in terms of final image quality. Sony currently produces three macro lenses for its A-mount, each of which is a prime lens offering "true" 1:1 macro magnification. Although they are sold as macro lenses, they are also perfectly capable of being used as conventional primes for non-macro work.

The least expensive of the trio is the 30mm f/2.8 lens (SAL-30M28), which is a DT lens, and therefore only compatible with APS-C sensor cameras such as the A77. The 30mm focal length is close to the requirements of a "standard" lens, so it's a good choice for a natural perspective when used as a conventional lens. The lens uses the SAM AF system and will focus down to 2cm (0.8in).

Next in price and weight is the 50mm f/2.8 (SAL-50M28). This lens has a few more refinements compared to the 30mm, such as focus hold and the option of a focus limiter (to stop the lens traveling the full distance of its focus range when used as a conventional prime). The minimum focusing distance of 20cm (7.8in), is greater than the 30mm lens, but a greater working distance compensates for this.

The final lens in the range is the 100mm f/2.8 lens (SAL-100M28), which is heavier than both the 30mm and 50mm lenses combined. Features include focus hold and

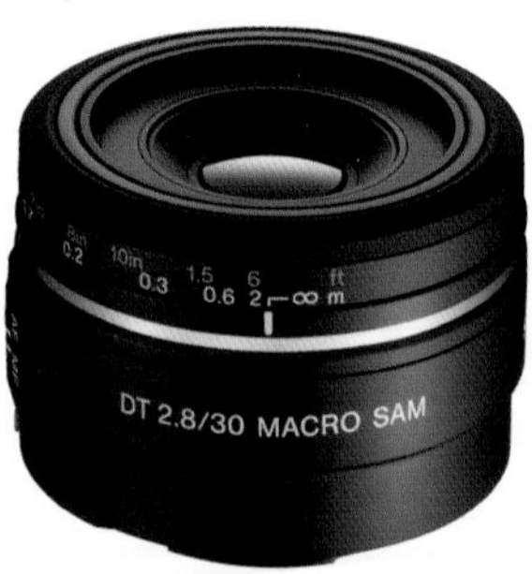

SONY 30MM DT F/2.8 LENS

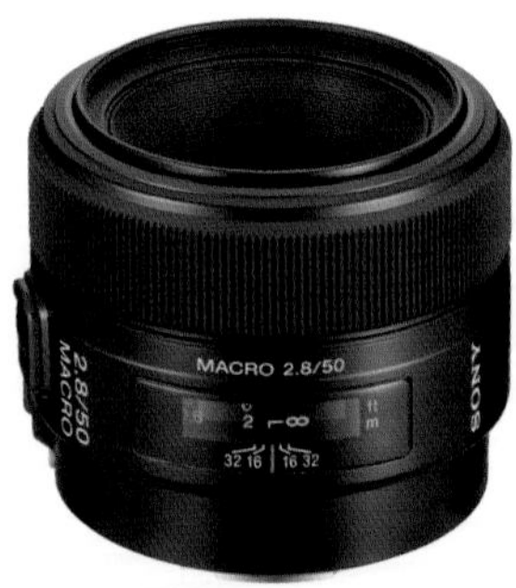

SONY 50MM F/2.8 LENS

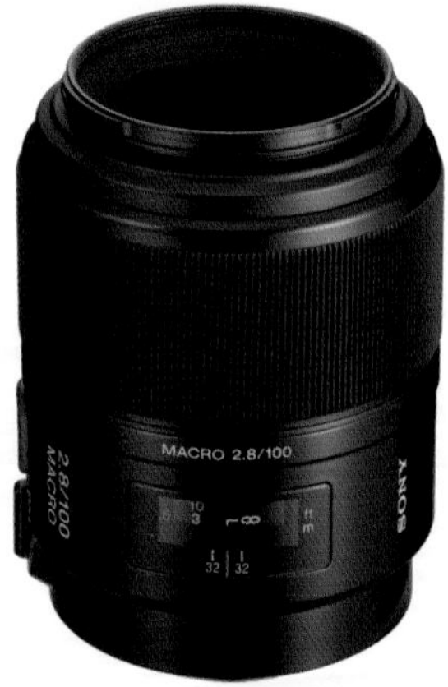

SONY 100MM F/2.8 LENS

internal focusing—which is invaluable if you plan to use filters with this lens—and a minimum focusing distance of 35cm.

› Third-party lenses

Alternatives to Sony's macro lenses are those produced by third-party manufacturers. The grid below shows the current range of lenses produced by Sigma and Tamron.

> ***Note:***
> Some manufacturers give a magnification figure expressed as a decimal. To convert this figure to a magnification ratio divide 1 by the quoted figure. So, if the figure quoted is 0.25x, divide 1 by 0.25 (giving you 4), which tells you the lens has a magnification ratio of 1:4.

SIGMA

Lens	Minimum focus distance (cm)	Magnification ratio	Filter thread size (mm)	Dimension (diameter x length; mm)	Weight (g)
17–70mm f/2.8–4 DC OS HSM	22	1:2.7	72	79 x 88.9	520
50mm f/2.8 EX DG	18	1:1	55	71.4 x 66.5	320
70mm f/2.8 EX DG	25	1:1	62	76 x 95	527
70–300mm f/4–5.6 DG	95	1:2	58	76.6 x 122	545
105mm f/2.8 APO EX DG OS HSM	31	1:1	62	78.3 x 126.4	725

TAMRON

Lens	Minimum focus distance (cm)	Magnification ratio	Filter thread size (mm)	Dimension (diameter x length; mm)	Weight (g)
60mm f/2 Di II LD SP AF	23	1:1	55	73 x 80	390
90mm SP f/2.8 Di	29	1:1	55	71.5 x 97	405
55–200mm f/4–5.6 Di II LD	95	1:3.5	52	71.6 x 83	300
70–300mm f/4–5.6 Di LD	150	1:2	62	76.6 x 116.5	435
180mm f/3.5 SP Di	47	1:1	72	84.8 x 165.7	920

» LIGHTING FOR MACRO

› Artificial lighting

As depth of field is reduced to a minimum in close-up and macro photography the use of small apertures is often necessary, which may mean that you need to employ artificial lighting if you want to maintain a reasonable shutter speed. The built-in flash on your A77 isn't ideal for this purpose, as the lens will cast a shadow over your subject, so Sony instead suggests its HVL-RLAM as the solution to this problem. Although not a flash, it is related to a type of flash known as a ringflash. A ringflash attaches to the front of a lens and provides a soft, even light for macro subjects. The drawback with this type of lighting is that specular highlights on your subject will have a distinct "donut" shape.

› Natural lighting

Using direct sunlight to illuminate macro subjects brings its own problems, the biggest of which is increased contrast. There are several solutions to this. If your subject is relatively small it's possible to use a "light tent," which is a translucent cloth structure that helps to diffuse the light, making it softer. As an added bonus it will also help to shelter your subject from any breeze, reducing the risk of subject movement potentially ruining your shot.

Another solution to the problem is to use a reflector to push light back into the shadow areas of your subject. It's possible to buy commercial reflectors, but often a piece of white card is more than adequate. The final solution is to wait until your subject is naturally in shade. If you shoot this way it's worth checking your A77's white balance, as shade tends to be "cooler" than direct sunlight.

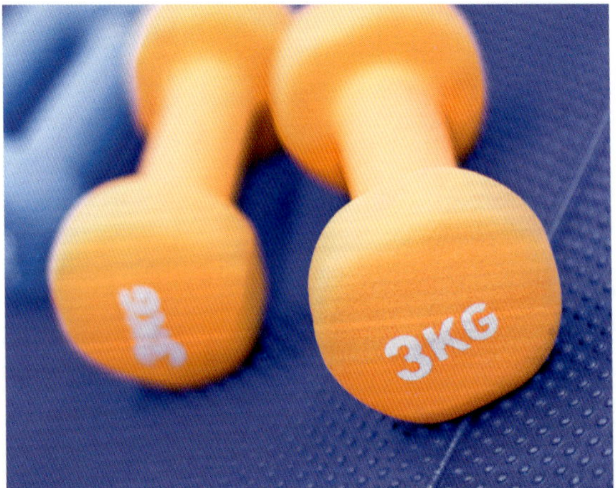

REFLECTED «
I used reflector boards to throw light under these dumbbells, which reduced the heavy shadows caused by the overhead lighting.

› RINGLIGHT (HVL-RLAM)

Sony's HVL-RLAM is an LED ringlight that fits onto your macro lens to provide you with a soft, even, and continuous light. The advantage of this type of light is that the effect on exposure is immediately visible on the screen.

The HVL-RLAM has a choice of two power levels, and there is the option to use the entire ring, or to just illuminate the left or right side. Using the entire ring results in a shadow-free image, whereas illuminating just half of the ring creates shadow and contrast, bringing out detail and texture. When shooting with Sony's 30mm and 50mm macro lenses the optional FA-MA1AM adapter is recommended.

Illumination intensity
150 lux

Effective illumination distance
3.9–19.7in (10–50cm)

Lighting modes
Full; right half only; left half only

Approximate battery life
40 minutes (alkaline batteries)
110 minutes (Ni-MH batteries)

Dimensions (w x h x d)
Control unit: 2⅝ x 3⅛ x 3⅛in (64 x 78 x 79mm)
Ringlight: 5 x 5⅝ x 1in (124 x 141 x 24mm)

Weight
6.4oz (180g) complete, without batteries

Included accessories
Ringlight, 49/55mm adapter ring, soft carry case, accessory shoe adapter, user manual

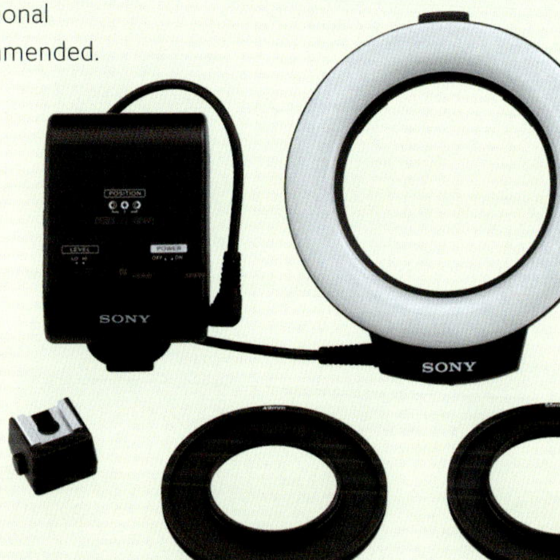

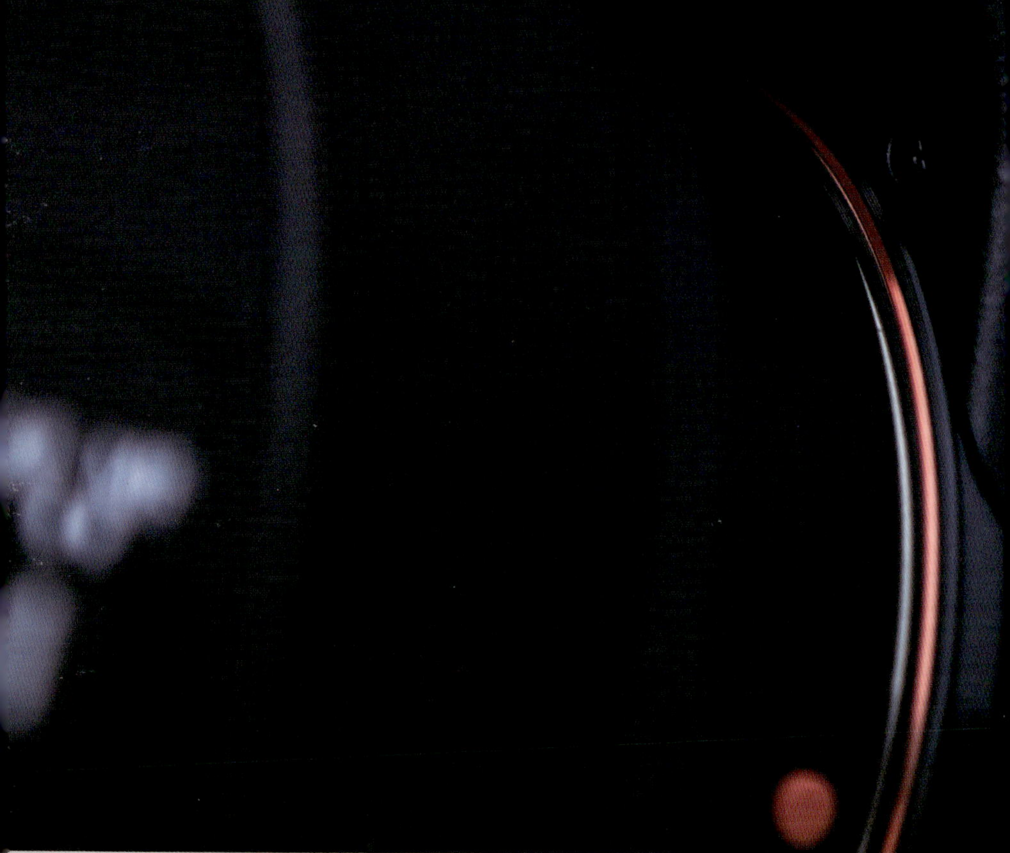

Chapter 9
CONNECTION

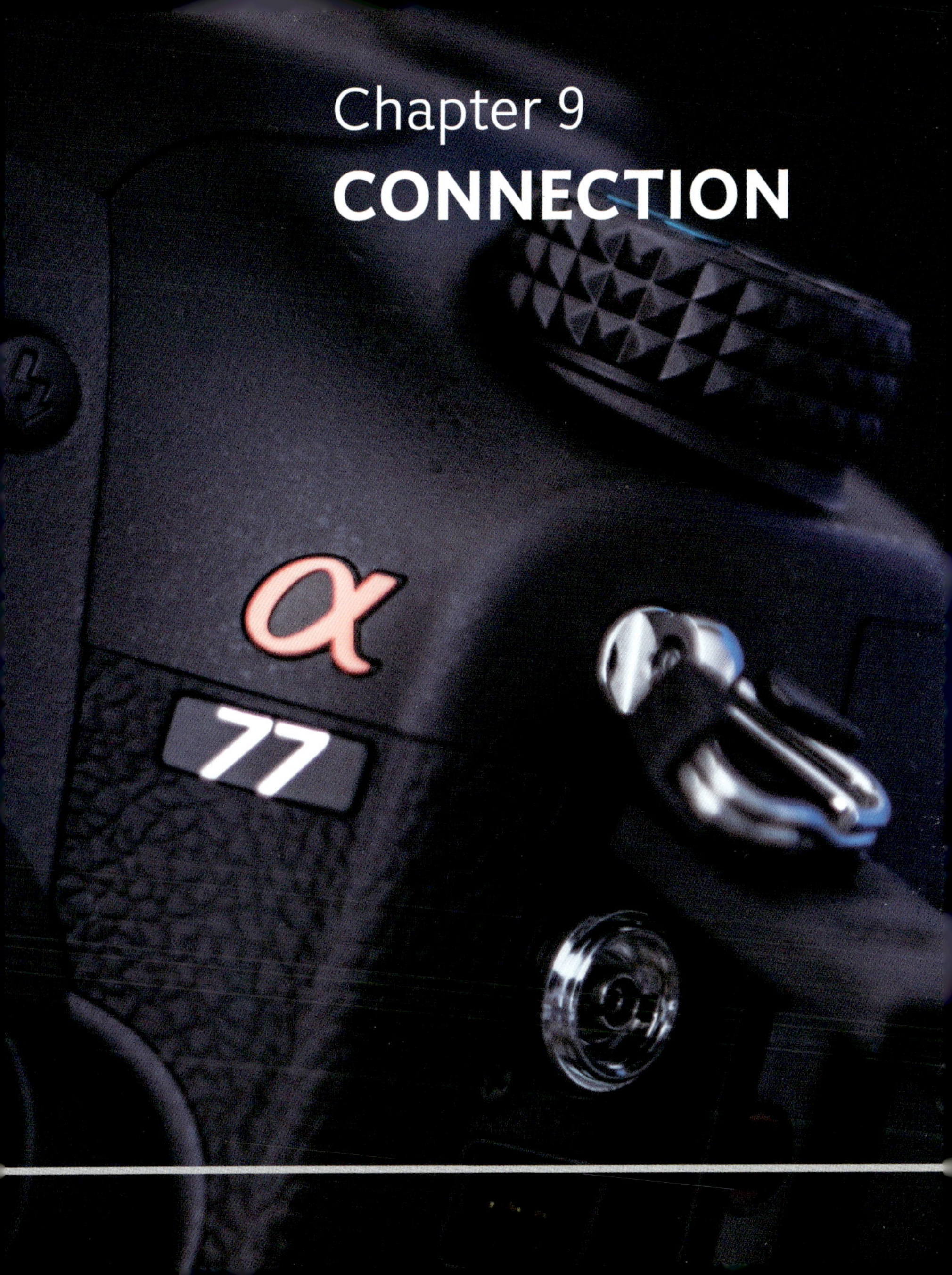

9 CONNECTION

Ultimately you will need to connect your A77 to a computer or printer in order to view, organize, and archive your images as either digital files or as prints.

› Color calibration

Calibrating your computer takes the guesswork out of making prints that match the images that you've taken. The first step is to create a monitor profile, using a hardware color calibrator. A monitor profile is a description of how your monitor displays color and it is stored as an ICC file on your computer. Image-editing software can use this information to correctly display images.

The second step is acquiring an accurate profile for the paper you want to use with your printer. Each type of paper you use should have its own profile, as different papers (and printer) have their own unique qualities when it comes to how colors are reproduced.

For complete accuracy a hardware paper profiler should be used, although the majority of paper manufacturers supply profiles for popular printers, which are free to download.

With an accurate monitor and paper profile your image editing software will be better able to translate the colors seen on screen to those in the final print.

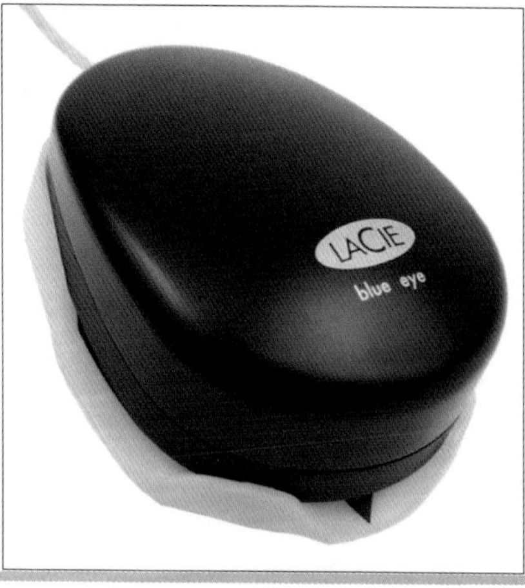

© LaCie

> ***Notes:***
> Printers usually can't print the range of colors that can be seen on a monitor. The more saturated a color, the less likely it can be printed.
>
> On a Windows PC, printer and monitor profiles are found in Windows/System32/Spool/Drivers/Color. On a Mac they are found in Library/ColorSync/Profiles.

LACIE BLUE EYE PRO «
Hardware monitor calibrator.

» CONNECTING TO A COMPUTER

› Installing the software

If you shoot Raw files rather than JPEG you will need suitable software to convert the Raw files to a more universally accepted file format such as TIFF or JPEG. Sony supplies Image Data Converter with the A77 to convert the camera's .ARW Raw files, although other third-party Raw converters such as Adobe Lightroom 4 or Capture One are also available.

Windows software installation

1) Log on as Administrator.

2) Insert the Sony CD-ROM disk into the CD-ROM drive.

3) The software installation screen should appear automatically. If it does not, double click on the CD-ROM icon on My Computer and select *install.exe*.

4) Select both Image Data Converter and PMB and follow the on-screen instructions. Note that you will need to connect your A77 to the PC during the installation process. When installation is complete, you will be prompted to restart your computer.

5) Once your computer has restarted, remove the CD-ROM.

6) The shortcut icons to the installed software will appear on your desktop.

Mac software installation

1) Log on as Administrator.

2) Insert the Sony CD-ROM disk into the CD-ROM drive and double-click on the CD icon when it appears.

3) Double-click on the *IDC_INST*.pkg file in the Mac folder of the CD-ROM.

4) Follow the on-screen instructions to install the software.

5) Once your computer has restarted, remove the CD-ROM.

6) The installed software can now be found in the Applications folder on your Mac's hard drive.

› Sony software

The A77 is supplied with Image Data Converter (Windows and Mac) and Picture Motion Browser (Windows only). It's probably fair to say that these programs aren't as sophisticated as third-party packages such as Adobe Photoshop, but they will allow you to view your images, make minor adjustments, convert your Sony Raw files (Image Data Converter), and then set up a simple database of images (Picture Motion Browser). There is not enough space in this book to provide an in-depth guide to the bundled software, but Sony's online help notes, which are accessible when running the software, are very comprehensive.

> ***Note:***
> You can adjust JPEGs using Image Data Converter, but some correction options will not be available.

Image Data Converter

Sony's .ARW Raw files will need to be converted to a more universally accepted file format for use with other software packages. Image Data Converter will allow you to open .ARW files, apply adjustments to the image and then export the altered file as either a JPEG or TIFF.

Image Data Converter initially uses the image settings applied to the Raw file at the moment of capture, but these settings are not fixed in the same way that they are when you record a JPEG file. Instead, they are the starting point for adjustments.

Image options that can be applied in-camera to JPEGs can also be applied to Raw files using Image Data Converter, which includes Dynamic Range Optimizer and the various Creative Styles such as Landscape and Vivid. Two things that can't be removed in Image Data Converter are chromatic aberration and distortion, although correcting lens vignetting is achieved easily.

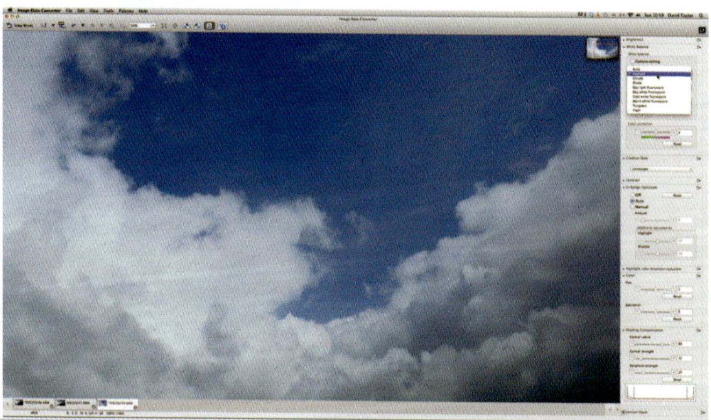

IMAGE DATA CONVERTER «
Sony's Image Data Converter running in Mac OS X.

Picture Motion Browser
This Windows-only software will manage the importing of images for you and add them to a user-friendly database. There are various easy ways to sort and search for images in the database such as the option to apply a rating to them or to tag them with simple keywords. Picture Motion Browser also allows you to apply some very basic image adjustments such as red eye correction.

› Copying files to your computer

There are three ways to copy the images from your A77's memory card: you can physically remove the card and plug it into a card reader attached to your computer; you can connect your camera to your computer using the supplied USB cable; or if you have an Eye-Fi card, you can copy the images to your computer wirelessly.

The A77 complies with the USB 2.0 standard, so if you have a card reader that is USB 3.0 compliant (and your computer is compatible), you will find that using a card reader is quicker than copying direct from the camera. The speed of your Wi-Fi connection will determine whether an Eye-Fi card would be faster still.

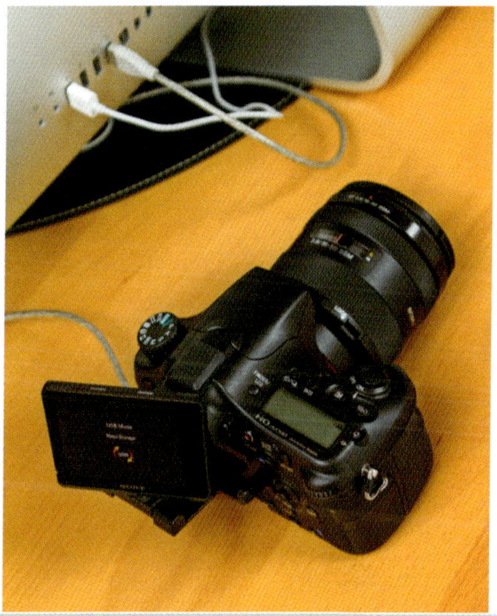

Making the connection directly

1) On the camera set **USB Connection** on the 🔧 2 menu to **Mass Storage** and check that the memory card with the images you want to copy is inserted.

2) Switch the camera off.

3) Connect the USB cable (provided with the camera) to the A77's ⭠⭢ terminal.

4) Connect the other end of the cable to the USB port on the computer.

5) Turn the camera on.

CONNECTING DIRECTLY «
The camera cannot be used when transferring files via USB.

Copying files to your computer: Windows

If the Picture Motion Browser software is installed, this can be used to import your images from the camera, otherwise:

1) When the camera is connected to your computer and switched on, the **Autoplay** wizard will appear.

2) Select **Open folder to view files** and then double-click on the **DCIM** folder (to copy over still images) or **MP_ROOT** folder (for movie files).

3) Double-click on the sub-folder containing the image/movie files.

4) Right-click on the file(s) you want to transfer and select **Copy**.

5) Open the folder you want to copy your images (or movies) to. Right-click inside the folder and select **Paste**.

6) Once the images have been copied, double-click the **Disconnect USB** device icon on the Window's taskbar. Select ⭠ (USB Mass Storage Device) to eject the camera.

7) Switch off the camera and unplug the USB cable.

Copying files to your computer: Mac OS X

1) Double-click on the memory card icon on the desktop.

2) Double-click on the **DCIM** folder to copy still images, or choose the **MP_ROOT** folder to copy movie files.

3) Right-click on the file(s) you want to transfer and select **Copy**.

4) Open the destination folder, right-click, and select **Paste.**

5) Right-click on the memory card icon on the desktop and select **Eject "Card Name"** ("Card Name" being the name assigned to the memory card when it was formatted).

6) Switch off the camera and unplug the USB cable.

› Eye-Fi

Eye-Fi is a company that manufactures or licences the technology to incorporate a Wi-Fi transmitter into an SD memory card. Using a Wi-Fi enabled SD card will allow you to wirelessly transfer images to your computer or file hosting service from your camera. Check the manual that came with the Eye-Fi memory card for initial set up of the card.

Enabling Eye-Fi

1) Press **MENU** and highlight **Eye-Fi Settings** on the 🔧 2 tab and press ●. This menu option is only displayed when an Eye-Fi card is inserted into your A77.

2) Highlight **On** and press ● to activate the Eye-Fi card's wireless capability.

Notes:

File transfer speeds from an Eye-Fi card are dependant on the speed of your wireless connection.

Make sure that the write-protect tab on the Eye-Fi card is set to unlocked.

If you plan to use your A77 on an aircraft or in areas where wireless connections are prohibited, set Eye-Fi Settings to Off.

Switch the Endless Memory Mode on your Eye-Fi card to Off.

You may find the A77's battery will deplete more quickly if Eye-Fi Settings is set constantly to On. If Wi-Fi transmission is not needed, turn this option Off.

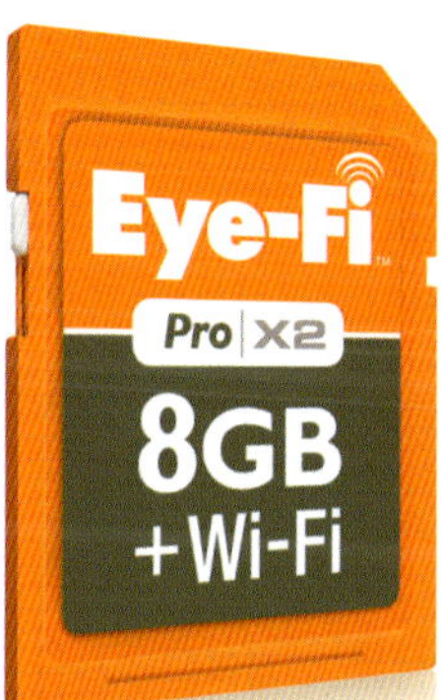

EYE-FI
Eye-Fi cards are available up to 8Gb in size.

Displayed Symbol	Status
	Eye-Fi on standby
	Eye-Fi upload on standby
	Eye-Fi connecting
	Eye-Fi uploading
	Eye-Fi transmission error

9 » THE A77 AND HD TV

Viewing the images from your A77 on an HD TV is a great way to share them with family and friends. The A77 has a built-in slide-show mode that allows you to tailor the show to your own requirements. If you have a compatible HD TV you can use the TV remote to control the display of images, as well as being able to delete them.

Connecting your camera to an HD TV

1) Make sure that the camera and TV are both switched off.

2) Open the HDMI cover on the left side of the camera and insert the HDMI connector into the socket. Connect the other end of the cable to the TV. Refer to your TV's user manual for the location of the HDMI slots.

3) Turn on the TV and set it to the correct channel for HDMI input. The camera will detect the broadcast standard of the TV automatically once it is switched on.

4) Turn the camera on—the first photo should now be displayed. Select the desired photo using ◀/▶. The LCD (and EVF) will remain blank.

> ***Notes:***
> The A77 does not come with the necessary Type C mini-pin HDMI cable to connect it to an HD TV, but these cables can be readily found in most consumer electronics stores.

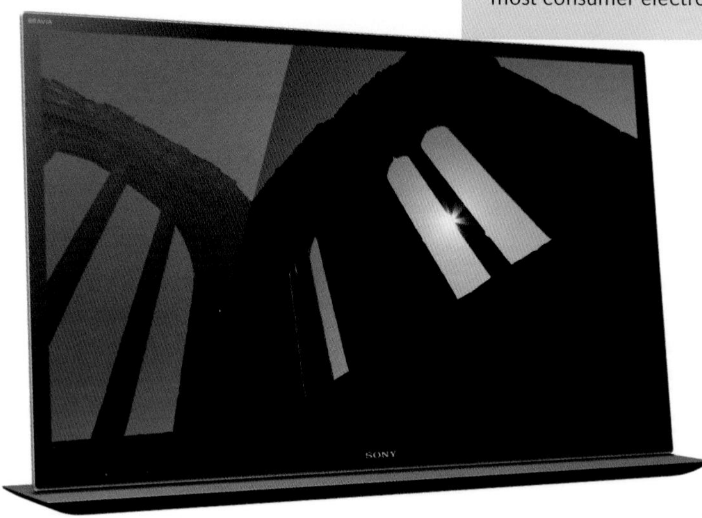

SONY BRAVIA KDL-40HX850 «

› Sony Bravia Sync

If you own a Sony Bravia Sync-compatible TV, the A77 can be controlled using the television's remote control when the camera is connected using an HDMI cable. Non-Sony TVs may occasionally cause the A77 to perform unnecessary operations when operated via the remote control. If this happens set **CTRL FOR HDMI** on Setup 1 menu to **Off**.

Controlling your A77

1) Follow the instructions above to connect the TV and camera.

2) Press the **SYNC MENU** button on the TV remote control.

3) Operate the camera using the control button on the TV remote.

HDMI «
Connection to a TV is through an HDMI standard cable.

Playback options

Slide Show: Play back images using the A77's slide show settings.

Single-image playback: Returns to the single-image screen display.

Image Index: Displays the image index screen.

Delete: Allows the deletion of images from the A77, either one at a time or all at once.

> **Tip**
>
> *Use of the optional AC-PW10AM AC adapter is recommended if your slide show is lengthy. Although the camera will not be harmed should the battery become exhausted, it will cut your slide show short!*

Your A77 can be connected directly to a PictBridge printer via a USB cable, so that images can be printed without using a computer. Which images will be printed is specified using the DPOF settings (see below). Some printers have slots for SD memory cards, which will also allow you to print the images from your A77 without a computer, although neither option will allow Raw files to be printed directly—Raw images need to be converted before they are printed.

Connecting to a printer

1) Check that the camera battery is fully charged before printing, or connect the optional AC-PW10AM AC adapter.

2) Press **MENU** and navigate to 🔧 Setup 2. Set **USB Connection** to **MTP**.

3) Make sure that both the A77 and printer are switched off. Insert the memory card containing the images you want to print into the camera (if it is not already in the camera).

4) Connect the supplied USB cable to the camera's USB terminal.

5) Connect the USB cable to the printer, following the instructions in the manual supplied with the printer.

6) Turn the camera and printer on. The printer should recognize the camera automatically and start printing using the specified DPOF settings.

7) When printing has finished, turn off the A77 and printer, and disconnect the USB cable.

› Digital Print Order Format (DPOF)

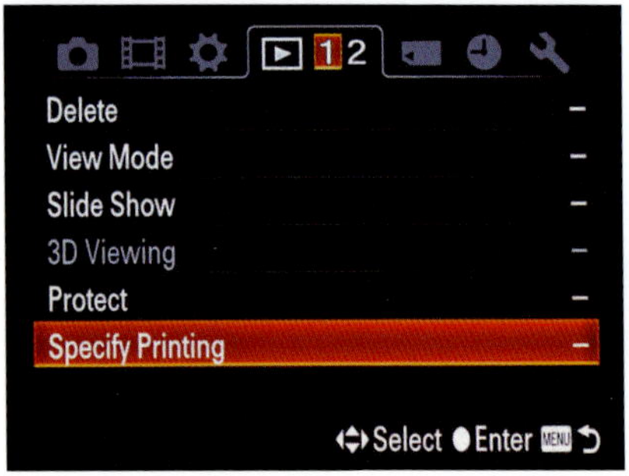

You can use your A77 to specify printing instructions for images that will be printed either by your home printer or by a print store. You can also specify whether the date of printing is overlaid on the printed image. However, DPOF only works with JPEG images and the instructions will be written to the memory card. These instructions stay on the card after printing so you will need to remove them once you have made your prints.

Setting DPOF

1) Press **MENU** and navigate to ▶ Playback 1. Highlight **Specify Printing** and press ●.

2) If **DPOF Setup** is set to **Multiple Img.**, navigate to **Enter** and press ● again.

3) Press ◀/▶ or turn or to navigate through the images on the memory card.

4) Press ● to mark the displayed image for printing. An orange tick symbol will be displayed in a box at the far left of the screen to indicate that the image has been selected. To deselect the image press ● again.

5) Once you've set all the images for printing press **MENU**, highlight **OK**, and press ●.

Cancelling DPOF

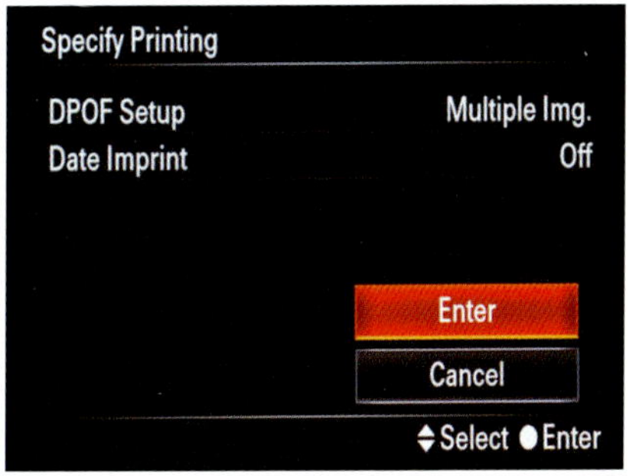

1) Press **MENU** and navigate to ▶ Playback 1. Highlight **Specify Printing** and press ●.

2) Highlight **DPOF Setup** and press ●. Highlight **Cancel All** and press ● again.

3) Highlight **Enter**, press ●, and then press ● with **Enter** highlighted on the **Cancel All?** screen.

Date Imprint

1) Press **MENU** and navigate to ▶ Playback 1. Highlight **Specify Printing** and press ●.

2) Set **Date Imprint** to **On**.

3) Highlight **Enter**, press ●, and follow the instructions from step 3 of *Setting DPOF* above.

> ***Notes:***
>
> Raw files cannot be selected for DPOF. However if you shoot Raw+JPEG you will be able to select and print the JPEG version of the image.
>
> If Date Imprint is selected, the positioning and style of the date information will be determined by the printer. Date Imprint may not work with all printers.

» GLOSSARY

Aberration An imperfection in a photograph, usually caused by the optics of a lens.

AEL ***(automatic exposure lock)*** A camera control that locks in the exposure value, allowing a scene to be recomposed.

Angle of view The area of a scene that a lens takes in, measured in degrees.

Aperture The opening in a camera lens through which light passes to expose the sensor. The relative size of the aperture is denoted by f-stops.

Autofocus (*AF*) A reliable through-the-lens focusing system that allows accurate focus without the user manually turning the lens.

Bracketing Taking a series of identical pictures, changing only the exposure, usually in 1/3-, 1/2-, or 1-stop increments.

Buffer The in-camera memory of a digital camera.

Center-weighted metering A metering pattern that determines the exposure of a photograph by placing importance on the light-meter reading at the center of the frame.

Chromatic aberration The inability of a lens to bring spectrum colors into focus at one point.

Color temperature The color of a light source expressed in degrees Kelvin (K).

Codec A piece of software that is able to interpret and decode a digital file such as Raw.

Compression The process by which digital files are reduced in size.

Contrast The range between the highlight and shadow areas of a photo, or a marked difference in illumination between colors or adjacent areas.

Depth of field (*DOF*) The amount of a photograph that appears acceptably sharp. This is controlled primarily by the aperture: the smaller the aperture, the greater the depth of field.

DPOF Digital Print Order Format.

Diopter Unit expressing the power of a lens.

dpi ***(dots per inch)*** Measure of the resolution of a printer or scanner. The more dots per inch, the higher the resolution.

Dynamic range The ability of the camera's sensor to capture a full range of shadows and highlights.

Dynamic Range Optimizer ***(DRO)*** Method used by Sony to control the contrast of an image in order to avoid or reduce a loss of shadow or highlight detail.

Exposure The amount of light allowed to hit the digital sensor, controlled by aperture, shutter speed, and ISO. Also, the act of taking a photograph, as in "making an exposure."

Extension tubes Hollow spacers that fit between the camera body and lens, typically used for close-up work. The tubes increase the focal length of the lens, and magnify the subject.

Fill-in flash Flash combined with daylight in an exposure. Used with naturally backlit or harshly side-lit or top-lit subjects to prevent silhouettes forming, or to add extra light to the shadow areas of a well-lit scene.

Filter A piece of colored or coated, glass or plastic placed in front of the lens.

Focal length The distance, usually in millimeters, from the optical center point of a lens to its focal point.

fps ***(frames per second)*** A measure of the time needed for a digital camera to process one photograph and be ready to shoot the next.

f-stop Number assigned to a particular lens aperture. Wide apertures are denoted by small numbers (such as f/1.8 and f/2.8), while small apertures are denoted by large numbers (such as f/16 and f/22).

HDMI High Definition Multimedia Interface.

HDR ***(High Dynamic Range)*** A technique that increases the dynamic range of a photograph by merging several shots taken with different exposure settings.

Histogram A graph representing the distribution of tones in a photograph.

Hotshoe An accessory shoe with electrical contacts that allows synchronization between a camera and a flash.

Hotspot A light area with a loss of detail in the highlights. This is a common problem in flash photography.

Incident-light reading Meter reading based on the amount of light falling onto the subject.

Interpolation A method of increasing the file size of a digital photograph by adding pixels, thereby increasing its resolution.

ISO The sensitivity of the digital sensor measured in terms equivalent to the ISO rating of a film.

JPEG ***(Joint Photographic Experts Group)*** JPEG compression can reduce file sizes to about 5% of their original size, but uses a lossy compression system that degrades image quality.

LCD ***(Liquid crystal display)*** The flat screen on a digital camera that allows the user to preview digital photographs.

Macro A term used to describe close focusing and the close-focusing ability of a lens.

Megapixel One million pixels equals one megapixel.

Memory card A removable storage device for digital cameras.

Mirror lock-up A function that allows the reflex mirror of an SLR to be raised and held in the "up" position, before the exposure is made.

Multi-segment metering A metering system whereby light reflected from several subject areas is calculated based on algorithms. Also known as Matrix or Evaluative metering.

Noise Interference visible in a digital image caused by stray electrical signals during exposure.

PictBridge The industry standard for sending information directly from a camera to a printer, without having to connect to a computer.

Pixel Short for "picture element"—the smallest bit of information in a digital photograph.

Predictive AF An AF system that can continuously track a moving subject.

Raw The file format in which the raw data from the sensor is stored without permanent alteration being made.

Red-eye reduction A system that causes the pupils of a subject's eyes to shrink, typically by shining a light prior to taking the flash picture.

Remote release An electronic or cable device used to trigger the camera shutter from a distance to avoid camera shake.

Resolution The number of pixels used to capture or display a photo.

RGB *(red, green, blue)* Computers and other digital devices understand color information as combinations of red, green, and blue.

Rule of thirds A rule of composition that places the key elements of a picture at points along imagined lines that divide the frame into thirds, both vertically and horizontally.

Shutter The mechanism that controls the amount of light reaching the sensor, by opening and closing.

SLR *(single lens reflex)* A type of camera that allows the user to view the scene through the lens, using a reflex mirror.

Soft proofing Using software to mimic onscreen how an image will look once output to another imaging device, typically this will be a printer.

Spot metering A metering pattern that places importance on the intensity of light reflected by a very small portion of the scene.

Teleconvertor A lens that is inserted between the camera body and the main lens, increasing the effective focal length.

Telephoto A lens with a large focal length and a narrow angle of view.

TIFF *(Tagged Image File Format)* A universal file format supported by virtually all relevant software applications. TIFFs are uncompressed digital files.

TTL *(through the lens)* metering A metering system built into the camera that measures light passing through the lens at the time of shooting.

USB *(universal serial bus)* A data transfer standard, used by most cameras when connecting to a computer.

Viewfinder An optical system used for composing, and sometimes for focusing the subject.

White balance A function that allows the correct color balance to be recorded for any given lighting situation.

Wideangle lens A lens with a short focal length and consequently a wide angle of view.

» USEFUL WEB SITES

SONY

Sony US
Home page for the Sony Corporation
www.sony.com

Sony UK
Home page for Sony UK
www.sony.co.uk

Sony User Support
European Technical Support
http://support.sony-europe.com

Sony/Minolta Info
User forum, information, and galleries
www.dyxum.com

GENERAL

Digital Photography Review
Camera and lens review site
www.dpreview.com

Flickr
Photo sharing website with a large user base
www.flickr.com

Luminous Landscape
Photography technique with a bias toward landscape images
www.luminous-landscape.com

Sony Photography Awards
Where to send that potential award-winning photograph you take with your A77!
www.worldphotographyawards.org

David Taylor
Landscape and travel photography
www.davidtaylorphotography.co.uk

EQUIPMENT

Adobe
Photoshop, Photoshop Elements, and Lightroom editing software
www.adobe.com

Apple
Hardware and software manufacturer
www.apple.com/uk

Sigma
Independent Sony-compatible lenses and flash units
www.sigma-imaging-uk.com

Tamron
Independent Sony-compatible lenses
www.tamron.com

Tokina
Independent Sony-compatible lenses
www.tokinalens.com

PHOTOGRAPHY PUBLICATIONS

Photography books & Expanded Camera Guides
www.ammonitepress.com

Black & White Photography magazine
Outdoor Photography magazine
www.thegmcgroup.com

» INDEX

SONY SLT-A77
THE EXPANDED GUIDE
SYMBOLS USED

- Delete
- Playback button
- Exposure compensation
- Flash
- Timer / Drive mode
- Zoom
- SteadyShot
- Battery full
- Battery empty
- Control up
- Control right
- Control down
- Control left
- Setup menu

- White balance / daylight
- White balance / cloudy
- White balance / tungsten
- White balance / fluorescent
- AWB White balance / auto
- WB White balance / flash
- Multi segment metering
- Center-weighted metering
- Spot metering
- USB connection
- Protect / lock
- REAR Rear sync flash
- WL Wireless flash
- SLOW Slow sync flash
- AUTO Auto flash
- No flash
- Flash compensation
- HSS High speed wireless flash
- Focal plane
- White balance / Custom

- Enter
- P Program mode
- A Aperture-priority mode
- S Shutter-priority mode
- M Manual mode
- AUTO Auto mode
- Remote Commander
- Continuous advance
- Self-timer
- Single-shot advance
- Self-timer continuous
- BRK C Bracket: continuous
- Recording menu
- Custom menu
- Control dial
- (lit) Focus locked
- Focus confirmation
- Focus trying
- (flashing) Cannot focus
- White balance / shade

- Camera shake warning
- SteadyShot scale indicator
- Creative Style / Saturation
- Creative Style / Sharpness
- Creative Style / Contrast
- Auto focus wide
- Auto focus spot
- Auto focus local
- Overheating warning
- M.S. Memory stick
- SD SD memory card
- L Image size / large
- M Image size / medium
- S Image size / small
- L 16:9 aspect ratio / large
- M 16:9 aspect ratio / medium
- S 16:9 aspect ratio / small
- D-R OFF Dynamic range off
- DRO AUTO Dynamic range auto
- HDR AUTO HDR auto

HDR	HDR
ON	Face Detection on
OFF	Face Detection off
ON	Smile Shutter on
OF	Smile Sensitivity/off
ON	Smile Sensitivity/normal
ON	Smile Sensitivity/big
S	Speed priority
Hi	Hi-speed drive mode
Lo	Lo-speed drive mode
BRK WB	White balance bracket
✱	AE lock
DRO	D-RangeOptimizer
	Smart teleconverter
MF	Manual focus
	Movie mode
	Control dial rear
	Memory Card
12	Continious priority mode
3D	3D mode

	Eye-Fi connecting
	Eye-Fi uploading
!	Eye-Fi error
1 Std.	Creative Style / Standard
1 Vivid	Creative Style / Vivid
1 Ntrl	Creative Style / Neutral
1 Clear	Creative Style / Clear
1 Deep	Creative Style / Deep
1 Light	Creative Style / Light
1 Port.	Creative Style / Portrait
1 Land.	Creative Style / Landscape
1 Sunset	Creative Style / Sunset
1 Night	Creative Style / Night
1 Autm	Creative Style / Autm
1 B/W	Creative Style / B/W
1 Sepia	Creative Style / Sepia
-1	Fluorescent warm white
0	Fluorescent cool white
+1	Fluorescent day white
+2	Fluorescent daylight

	Sweep panoramic view
SCN	Scene select mode
AUTO +	Auto plus mode
MR	Memory recall
	Flash charging
	Clock
	Multi image mode
	Steadyshot
BRK S	Single bracket mode
BRK DRO	DRO bracket mode
	Portrait mode
	Sports action mode
	Macro mode
	Landscape mode
	Sunset mode
	Night scene mode
	Handheld night mode
	Night Portrait/View mode
	Eye-Fi
	Eye-Fi upload standby

?	Guide button
	Rotate image
OFF	Effect off
Rich BW	Effect rich tone mono
HC BW	Effect High contrast B/W
SftH key	Effect Soft Key/High
!	Warning
ON	Object track on
OFF	Object track off
K	WB Kelvin value
	No GPS signal
	Backlit portrait
	Backlighting
	Spotlight
	Portrait lighting scene
	Low brightness scene
	Tripod night scene
	Baby scene
	Zone AF
	Spot AF